SAGGISTICA 1

Vito Zagarrio

The "Un-Happy Ending"

Vito Zagarrio

The "Un-Happy Ending"

Re-viewing The Cinema of Frank Capra

Bordighera Press

Library of Congress Control Number: 2009904472

All photos herein are from the author's personal archive.

Printed in the United States.

Published by
BORDIGHERA PRESS
John D. Calandra Italian American Institute
25 West 43rd Street, 17th Floor
New York, NY 10036

SAGGISTICA 1
ISBN 978-1-59954-005-4

To Robert Sklar, 1936-2011
Friend and Mentor

Acknowledgments

Robert Sklar, who wrote the foreword, died while this book was in proof. He was riding a bike in Barcelona, where he was attending a conference. He died in action, as he always was. Unfortunately, he will never see this volume in its final print, but he knows it well. The origin of the book is a dissertation defended at NYU in the mid-Nineties, but whose work started in the early Eighties. Bob was my adviser, and he later went on giving me many suggestions to shape the volume into its current shape.

Bob's death is a painful loss for all his students, colleagues, and friends.

It is because of him that I have "my" American Myth. Thanks to my first contact with him I was able to come to the US and establish long-standing relationships between American scholars and Italian institutions. It was not long before I realized how Bob had become a great friend: meeting up with him, his wife Adrienne, and his family became a ritual whenever I was back in NYC.

He was a reference point in terms of culture, ethics, and, of course, film. When he passed away, I cried for him, but at the same time I still feel him alive, and I will always keep his memory alive. This book is my first tribute to a Grand Master and a dear friend.

I want to thank my students Monica Bottini and Alessandra Pepe (for two good dissertations on Capra), my ex students and now colleagues Ofelia Catanea and Christian Uva who helped me in the translating and editing.

I also thank Genine Basinger and the staff of the Wesleyan University's Archives in Middletown, the staff of the Library of Congress and of the Cineteca Nazionale/Centro Sperimentale di Cinematografia in Rome. Bruno Torri and the Mostra Internazionale del Nuovo Cinema/Pesaro Film Festival.

Finally, I thank Anna Camaiti Hostert who suggested to me Bordighera Press and, above all, Anthony Julian Tamburri for his patience in waiting for my work and for his wonderful help.

My affectionate memory goes to some other departed friends who knew my work on Capra: Jay Leyda, William K. Everson, Lino Miccichè. And, of course, Frank Capra, to whom I dedicated many years of my life, and whom I had the honour to meet in La Quinta, in the far winter of 1982.

TABLE OF CONTENTS

FOREWORD

A NEW VIEW OF FRANK CAPRA
by Robert Sklar

Writing in the early 1970s, Warren I. Susman, a historian of United States culture, made one of the first observations that Frank Capra's films offered a vision of life darker than the sentimental optimism that the director's career, at that time, was commonly supposed to represent. In his essay on "The Culture of the Thirties," Susman noted how the heroes of Capra's most popular films of that era – such as *Mr. Deeds Goes to Town*, *Mr. Smith Goes to Washington* and *Meet John Doe* – suffered defeats of a kind familiar to many members of the American middle-classes who had been battered economically, and in self-esteem, by the Great Depression. Capra's protagonists, Susman wrote, experienced "a kind of ritual humiliation of the hero, a humiliation that is often painful and even cruel but from which the hero ultimately emerges with some kind of triumph, even though it be a minor one." This, said the historian keenly interested in issues of social psychology, "provided a special kind of identification for those whose self-image had been less than favourable."

Since that early speculation, no other film scholar in Europe and North America has been as insightful and influential as Vito Zagarrio, in uncovering and analyzing the complexities of a film director too long believed to be one-dimensional. Zagarrio took the lead, moreover, in recovering large parts of Capra's work, the late silent and early sound films made at Columbia between 1928 and 1934, only a small number of which were then in public circulation. At a retrospective and conference sponsored by the Mostra Internationale del Nuovo Cinema at Ancona, in 1988, scholars from Italy and the United States had an opportunity to view some of these films for the first time. In little known but important early films such as *Ladies of Leisure* (1930) and *Forbidden* (1932) they saw clearly a different aspect of Capra than was previously familiar, which Zagarrio in his analysis of these works identifies as a despair deeper and more permanent than the humiliations that the later heroes suffered. Zagarrio's edited catalog of that event, *Accade una notte: Frank Capra (1928-1934) e la Columbia (1934-1945)*, brought into print a viewpoint that has fostered considerable new scholarship on the filmmaker, establishing a fresh perspective on, to quote the title of Leland Poague's 1994 study, "Another Frank Capra." (A further outcome of that 1988 Ancona retrospective and conference was a volume of essays on the director that Zagarrio and I co-edited, *Frank Capra: Authorship and the Studio System.*)

Still, for all the new work on Capra that has been generated over the past several decades, it is an opportune time to have Zagarrio's own extensive treatment, *The "Un-Happy Ending": The Cinema of Frank Capra between American Dream and American Nightmare*, in an English-language edition. Of the twentyone films that Capra directed in the period 1928-1934, only eight are available on DVD in the United States; among the missing titles are the previously mentioned *Ladies of Leisure* and *Forbidden*, as well as other works that figure significantly in Zagarrio's analysis, including *The Way of the Strong* (1928) and *Rain or Shine* (1930). (One may hope that Zagarrio's study might encourage Columbia Pictures to issue an "Early Capra" set on DVD, to include such works as *The Younger Generation* [1929] and several others.)

Zagarrio, however, like Morelli or Sherlock Holmes, looks beyond the established concerns of Capra's interpreters. He illuminates aspects of Capra's works that were, so to speak, hiding in plain sight. "Not invisible but unnoticed," as Holmes says in *A Case of Identity*. Zagarrio reaches back in time before the standard canon of Capra scholarship to dig out neglected works made before the director's Academy Award winning 1934 film It *Happened One Night.* In important early films such as *Ladies of Leisure* (1930) and *Forbidden (1932),* he discovers a despair deeper than humiliation and more permanent than the political machinations in which Smith and Doe found themselves enmeshed. Capra, Zagarrio tells us, articulated the sadness to be found in the innermost transit zone of American culture, where the rigidities of traditional class structures converge with the free-roaming desires that had been liberated by America's democratic myths.

Trained in Italy and the United States, an active teacher, scholar, and filmmaker in both countries, Vito Zagarrio has been in the forefront of fruitful collaboration between Italian and American film scholars over many years, of which I, and many others, have been privileged to benefit. This latest contribution to his lifelong work on Frank Capra brings new luster to his achievements.

INTRODUCTION

A Re-Vision Of Capra's Films

Contemporary Hollywood cinema seems to have developed a strange longing. In *The American President* by Rob Reiner, the journalist Annette Bening, invited to the White House, says: "Here we are, in Frank Capra's kingdom!" After a little while, she meets Michael Douglas, the President, and she falls in love with him, as in a Capra fairy tales.

Steven Frears's *The Accidental Hero,* Peter Weir's *Fearless,* the Coen brothers's *Hudsucker Proxy,* Ivan Reitman's *Dave,* and Bob Zemeckis's *Forrest Gump,* a multiple winner at the 1995 Academy Awards, are all films that somehow evoke a body in the closet—the body of the beloved and detested master of comedy, Frank Capra. Even Zemeckis's *Back to the Future* contains the classical theme of *It's a Wonderful Life,* namely, the nightmare of never being born (or, in the case of *Back to the Future,* the fear of not being born, of not being able to return to the future). Andrew Bergman, who years ago wrote an important book on the Depression years and Capra,[1] directed a sort of Capra remake, *It Could Happen to You.* A clear remake of the new century is *Mr. Deeds* (2002), with Adam Sandler, Wynona Rider, John Turturro, produced by Columbia and New Line (the Old and New Hollywood...).

A few years ago, *Gremlins* by Joe Dante (another member of the Spielberg stable, like Zemeckis) clearly quoted Capra's best-known films (from *It's a Wonderful Life* to *You Can't Take It with You*).

---

[1] Andrew Bergman, *We're in the Money. Depression America and Its Films* (New York: Harper & Row, 1971).

We are witnessing a genuine wave of Caprian reminiscences. In *Accidental Hero* a vagrant, played by Andy Garcia, becomes a media star like Gary Cooper in *Meet John Doe;* the tramp becomes a television star, and the final agreement between Garcia and Hoffman rings true to the bitter analyses of Capra. In *Fearless* Jeff Bridges narrowly eludes death, thanks to his love for his family, and learns to love even his allergy to strawberries, as James Stewart does the petals of his little daughter's flower in *It's a Wonderful Life. The Accidental Hero* and *Fearless,* furthermore, are both "catastrophe" films, because they both begin with an airplane disaster.

In *The Hudsucker Proxy* a "black angel" keeps the protagonist, Tim Robbins, from killing himself on Christmas eve, as in *It's a Wonderful Life;* the Kevin Kline of *Dave* looks like the characters of *State of the Union* and, once again, *John Doe.* Nicholas Cage in *It Could Happen to You* recalls the happy-ending situations of the thirties; and *Forrest Gump* refers back to the naive "accidental heroes" of the New Deal.

The last example (2009) is *17 Again* by Burr Steers, with the teen cult Zac Efron playing the role of a forty-year-old man who is given the miraculous chance to go back tro his seventeen-year-old self and modify his life choices. Here the homage to Capra is explicit: when the protagonist, depressed and frustrated, thinks about committing suicide, and "angel" (i.e., a school janitor) jumps into the water forcing the protagonist to jump in as well in order to save him, just like Clarence does in *It's a Wonderful Life.* The plot also mimics Capra's masterpiece: like George Bailey in the "dream of never being born" sequence, the protagonist lives a "second life" and has the possibility to appreciate his own existence.

Even the brand new films play with Capra. One can find a nice homage to his humour in the new Hollywood comedy in *Sex and the City* (Michael Patrick Douglas, 2010) the protagonist and her husband watch *It Happened One Night* on TV, as an example of the old B/W films he likes (she hates). It is the famous scene in which Claudette Colbert hitchhikes showing her leg. Later in the film, Sarah Jessica Parker, dressed as a Muslim woman, uses the same Colbert's naughty gesture to stop a cab.

Animantion cinema seems to follow the trend: the very recent *Shrek Forever After* (2010, 4ᵗʰ episode in 3D of the Shrek saga, directed by Mike Mitchell and written by Josh Klausner and Darren Lemke), clearly refers to *It's a Wonderful Life*: the villan Rumpelstiltskin tricks an unhappy, mid-life crisis Shrek into allowing himself to be erased from existence and throws him into a dark alternate timeline where Rumpel rules supreme. It is like the nightmare of never being born in Capra's hit, and Rumpel's reign closely recalls the famous Potterville of George's dreamlike experience.

Even the Italian cinema seems to pay homage to the capraesque fairy tales: *The Pursuit of Happiness* by Gabriele Muccino (first Hollywood production for the successfull director of *L'ultimo bacio*), which perhaps unconsciously reproduces Stanley Cavell's title on film comedy, is a clear memory of Capra's Depression films.

What's behind this Caprian revival? Why is Capra pulled like a blanket, left and right, as the need arises?

Perhaps it has something to do with a return to fashion of "populism"—an ambiguous notion that can be grasped from the right and from the left, scorned or historically contextualized. (The "ideology of Populism," as it is reconstructed by Jeffrey Richards, can be traced to Jefferson, James Fenimore Cooper, and Horatio Alger;[2] also, "America's

---

[2] See Jeffrey Richards, "Frank Capra and the Cinema of Populism," in Bill Nichols (ed.), *Movies and Methods* (Berkeley: University of California Press, 1976). See also Jeffrey Richards, *Visions of Yesterday* (London: Routledge & Kegan Paul, 1973); in particular, the chapters, "The Ideology of Populism," 222 and ff., and "Frank Capra: the Classic Populist," 234 and ff. On "populism" see also M. Canovan, "Two Strategies for the Study of Populism," in *Political Studies* 4 (1982), and P. Wiles, "A Syndrome, Not a Doctrine. Some Elementary Theses on Populism," in G. Jonescu and F. Gellner (eds.), *Populism. Its Meanings and National Characteristics* (London: Weidenfeld & Nicholson, 1969).

New Populism" is the title of a March 1995 issue of *Business Week.*[3])
The phenomenon of a generalized "populism," in fact, seems to be making headway throughout the world. Doesn't the tumultuous appearance
of Berlusconi's "Forza Italia Clubs" on the Italian political scene in 1994
recall quite clearly the rise of "John Doe Clubs" in Capra's film?

This book is an attempt at a counter-reading of Frank Capra. The
director's work will be viewed as a record and gauge of American social
conflicts, of collective and personal depressions, and of the contradictions inherent in the "spirit of capitalism" they stereotypically express.

Capra has always been identified as a populist, demagogic, conservative filmmaker. Critics have generally attacked him for being too popular, too naive, or too American to deserve recognition as a major figure
in movie history. His films have long been classified as escapist fantasies
of goodwill portraying a comic, optimistic, sentimental view of American life. Capra, indeed, has often been described as a populist filmmaker
—a man who makes films for and about the "little people" of America,
celebrating the vitality, ingenuity, noble aspirations, strength of character, and sound instincts of the common man.[4] He prescribes small-town
good-neighborliness as an antidote to the greed, evil, and selfishness of
cynical big-city villains. His good-neighbor policy, the taste of "Capra-corn," and the message that happiness comes from little things (and certainly not from money) have defined—but also confined—Capra in terms
of a certain optimistic vision of the New Deal. This has made it easy to
deny him any dignity of "authorship," to place him within the tradition
of "American visions."

My intention is neither to carry on in the "cinéphile" tradition of
Capra's fans, nor to embark upon a pointless dispute over whether or
not Capra is an Author—whether or not he deserves to be included in a

---

3 *Business Week*, 13 March 1995.

4 See, for example, Jeanine Basinger, "America's Love Affair with Frank Capra", *American Film* (March 1982).

politique des auteurs. No judgment of this director can be so schematic. What matters is to consider Capra's films as "texts" capable of revealing new readings that extend beyond the films' apparent ideology. The goal of the book is to cast Capra's films in a new light, pointing out the realistic skepticism coexistent with their fairy-tale optimism, and the pessimism hidden behind the comedy. I hope to demonstrate that Capra must be read in terms of his relationship to social history; and that he can even be turned into a case study, on the basis of which one may suggest a new kind of historical methodology. By reading between the lines, one can find traces unseen on a superficial reading of eerie phenomena that contrast with the apparent reassuring ideology of populism.

Although he is certainly not a transgressive author, one can draw from his films a tragic landscape of America and a pessimistic vision of life that has its roots in immigration, poverty, class struggle, and the contradictions of the American Dream.

A counter-reading of Capra's films reveals symptoms of the pathologies, malaise, and madness of a society of which the director has often felt the pulse. There is a conflicting image of America from the Depression to the postwar period, which Capra offers perhaps *malgré lui,* in spite of himself. Through Capra's eyes one can obtain not so much a photograph, as an X-ray of American society.

Capra's cinema, and even his life, end up acting as litmus paper for twentieth-century America. He finds himself running through the whole not only of American social and political history, but also of the "adventure story of American cinema" (to borrow Jacobs' well-known title).

Perhaps Cinema invented Capra, or perhaps it was the other way around. Perhaps his capacity to meet and, indeed, to anticipate great transformations finds its ideal means of expression in cinema—certainly, from the first comic one-reelers to the self-quoting remakes, from silent film to television, the whole fable of movie-making is there. "Everyman" Capra managed to make the most of it, resisting the major changes.

In Hollywood the former immigrant took revenge on and claimed a role in the world.

Hence the Italo-American director embodies the "fabulous story" of cinema, a story that began with the Lumiere's first screening a few years after Frank's birth, and that therefore links up, like the "chains" of a film, with his life story.

Is Capra an Author? A craftsman? Or a professional movie-maker, an artisan, a filmmaker *de métier*? This is the topic under discussion in the current debate. Certainly, Capra was the last exponent of a legendary idea of cinema, which has vanished today. Cinema will not die—notwithstanding the prophecies of many "grave-diggeres"—but it is surely missing that marvellous traveller to the American Shangri-La.

CHAPTER 1

FRANK CAPRA *Malgré Lui*

ANOTHER CAPRA

When one thinks of an American director with strong links with history, the names that come to mind are Griffith and Ford, or perhaps Hawks and Welles. One rarely thinks of Frank Capra, the maker of light comedies, the creator of films for the middle class that, far from advancing claims to artistic merit, transmit a sugary, respectable view of life known as "Capracorn."[1] This recipe—which called for elements of pathos and often reactionary rhetoric aimed at demonstrating that "*It's a Wonderful Life*" (as his most famous film, of 1946, suggests), or that "happiness has arrived" (as the Italian title of *Mr Deeds Goes to Town*, 1936, claims)—proved to be an almost infallible winner.

Frank Capra has gone down in history as the master of the tearjerker, the director who could coolly and professionally tug at the heartstrings. That tug is repeated every Christmas when one watches *It's a*

---

[1] See the typical approach plied by Richard Schickel in *Frank Capra*, in *The Men Who Made the Movies, Interviews with Frank Capra, George Cukor, Howard Hawks, Alfred Hitchcock, Vincent Minnelli, King Vidor, Raoul Walsh and William Wellman* (New York: Atheneum, 1975). Among the studies on Capra, see Donald Willis, *The Films of Frank Capra* (Metuchen: Scarecrow Press, 1974); R. Glatzer and J. Raeburn, eds., *Frank Capra, The Man and His Films* (Ann Arbor: University of Michigan Press, 1975). Particularly interesting, in this book, is R. Sklar, "The Imagination of Stability: The Depression Films of Frank Capra," pp. 121 and ff. See also Sklar's well-known *Movie-Made America, A Cultural History of American Movies* (New York: Random House, 1975). Reference must be made in this connection to the Mostra internazionale del Nuovo Cinema; cf. V. Zagarrio, ed., *Accadde una notte. Frank Capra (1928-1934) e la Columbia (1934-1945)* (Rome: Di Giacomo, 1988), catalogue published on the occasion of the VIII Rassegna Internazionale Retrospettiva di Ancona, 3-8 December 1988, and the concomitant conference.

Wonderful Life on TV[2]: James Stewart, in a long nightmare, experiences what life would have been like if he had never been born. When he finds the petals of his little girl's flower in his pocket, he realizes that he has returned to the real world. At that moment the audience's deepest chords are touched in some mysterious way, whereas the critic's perspective produces a negative reaction, an unquestionable rejection of the paternalistic, demagogic components in Capra's work.

The current, conventional image thus portrays Capra as a great craftsman who lacks style, lacks that special touch with which Lubitsch and von Sternberg were gifted as a teller of conservative fairy-tales, a reassuring and conciliating "man-on-the-street." Frank Capra can be interpreted in a new way, however: not only in relation to film history and, more generally, to the history of American society, but also as a case study of historiographic methodology. The central idea of this book is that the director of *It's a Wonderful Life*, the greatest constructor of happy endings, in fact represented enormous social contradictions and conflicts that clash with the surface message of his films—even if, perhaps, he was unaware of this fact. By reading his films again, and analyzing some key sequences, one can find "Freudian slips"[3] that reveal very uncomfortable social situations. The director ends up pointing out some of America's social problems in spite of himself. Apparently insignificant narrative segments show a sample of the pathologies, problems, and follies of a country whose state of health was always apparent to Capra. Following the leads provided by these sequences, the critic is legitimized in considering Capra an unreassuring author.

---

2 See, for example, Jeanine Basinger, *The It's a Wonderful Life Book,* in collaboration with the Trustees of the Frank Capra Archives (New York: Alfred A. Knopf, 1986).

3 The notion of the "Freudian slip" is used more broadly here than is customary in psychoanalysis. One might also use the expression "loss of control" to signify the moments when Capra relinquishes control of his ideology in order to build a dramatic climax. See Sebastiano Timpanaro, *The Freudian Slip: Psychoanalysis and Textual Criticism* (London: NLB, 1976).

From this point of view, I feel closer to Michel Cieutat's *Frank Capra*[4] than to Raymond Carney's *American Vision*[5] (although some of the latter's insights are certainly interesting). Carney, by placing Capra within a vast, "deterministic" line of American modernism, of the great tradition of "American transcendental expression," accepts the positive implication of the "American myth" lot, stock, and barrel; whereas Cieutat, while welcoming the obvious presence of that "myth," also points to its contradictions: the pessimism as well as the optimism; the attempted suicides as well as the strength of character; the duality as well as the simplicity of being; the sense of a society in danger, of a family charged with tensions, of individuals brimming with fear, as well as the pursuit of happiness.

My intention is to re-read Capra against the stereotypes, as I tried to do more than twenty years ago, with the first Italian monograph, at several international conferences (one held in Bisacquino, Capra's home town), in the preface to the Italian translation of *The Name above the Title*, and in a book I co-edited with Robert Sklar.[6] In this last book, in fact, I included an essay of mine, "It Is (Not) a Wonderful Life: For a Counter-reading of Frank Capra," in which I severely criticized a book that had been recently published, which still today warrants discussion.

---

[4] Michel Cieutat, *Frank Capra* (Paris: Rivages, 1988).

[5] Raymond Carney, *American Vision, The Films of Frank Capra* (New York and Cambridge: Cambridge University Press, 1986).

[6] Vito Zagarrio, *Frank Capra* (Florence: Il Castoro, 1995); Vito Zagarrio, ed., *Accadde una notte. Frank Capra (1928-1934) e la Columbia (1934-1945)*; Vito Zagarrio, ed., *Studi americani. Modi di produzione a Hollywood dalle origini all'era televisiva* (Venice: Marsilio, 1994), it includes a chapter on Frank Capra; Frank Capra, *Il nome sopra il titolo*, edited by Alberto Rollo, with a preface by Vito Zagarrio (1989; originally published as *The Name above the Title* [New York: McMillan, 1971]). See also, *Frank Capra. Un italiano alla corte di Hollywood*. Rome, Palazzo delle Esposizioni, March 22-29, 1995; *Da Bisacquino a Hollywood. Regia di Frank Capra.* Bisacquino, July 30-August 5, 1997, and within this event there was the conference "Doppio sogno: miti e conflitti americani nel cinema di Frank Capra," organized by Vito Zagarrio; and Robert Sklar and Vito Zagarrio, eds., *Frank Capra. Authorship and the Studio System* (Philadelphia: Temple University Press, 1998).

I refer to the monumental biography by Joseph McBride, whose method is very different from mine, but who nevertheless wrote a seminal work.[7] When his book was published in the early nineties, I was very disappointed and frustrated with the author, mainly for the reasons that follow.

First of all it is a biography, not a work of film analysis, and its arguments reflect the limits of this basic choice. Secondly, it is a contradictory book which denies Capra "authorial" specificity, on one hand, but accepts the "myth" of authorial cinema, on the other. Above all, the systematic personal attack on the director, launched immediately after his death. Emblematic in this sense is the chapter, "The Catastrophe of Success," which gives its title to the entire book. A fine title, by the way, which would go well with my own contention that Capra is a skilful recorder of great and small, micro- or macrocosmic "catastrophes," a sort of seismograph. Unfortunately the "catastrophe" of which McBride speaks is of quite another nature: it is borrowed from Tennessee Williams and is directly tied to Capra's personal history. Capra, according to McBride, suffers a manic depressive crisis typical of the post-success phase: "Capra had schemed and sweated since childhood for the fame that was now his ... but when it came, it left him feeling strangely unworthy" (McBride, 289).

What, according to McBride, is the source of this malaise? Certain psychologists (McBride cites Joan Harvey) speak of an "imposter phenomenon" connected with unresolved Oedipal tensions ("which certainly could apply to Capra, who attributed much of his drive for success to a need to impress his defiantly unimpressed mother"). This is part of the genre of biography. Charles Maland, another biographer of the director, attributes his private insecurities as well as his poetics, to the thirties, to his attendance of the Ecumenical Church, hence to a reli-

---

[7] Joseph McBride, *Frank Capra. The Catastrophe of Success* (New York: Simon & Schuster, 1992).

gious cause. McBride substitutes psychoanalysis for religion: "Becoming famous gave Capra little real satisfaction but only brought out the bitterness and *rage* that was festering below the surface of his combative personality. His first impulse was not to feel grateful towards those who had helped him succeed, but to feel *revengeful*."

According to McBride, Capra was unable not to think that the success of *It Happened One Night* (1934) was some kind of "accident," and, above all, he was unconsciously convinced that he was unworthy of it, that his success was due to others: "In Capra's case, the need to appropriate credit belonging to his writers stemmed from his insecurity about the nature of his own abilities and achievements: like his mother, he was never sure that he deserved all of that money and all of that acclaim just for sitting in a director's chair" (311)."

Whence derives the main thrust of McBride's thesis: Capra is an "impostor," a "angry, vindictive" paranoic who has "appropriated" the work of others. And who are the others? They are the screenwriters, above all his own favorite, Robert Riskin, the true "author," according to McBride, of Capra's cinema. Hence McBride's attempt to overshadow the director's merits: Capra's autobiography, for instance, contains a revealing "error" concerning *Lady for a Day* (1934): "He seemed to think that his four-month stay at MGM working on *Soviet* came after the making of *Lady for a Day,* not before it. Such a significant misplacing of time is hard to accept as a simple memory lapse, and indeed other evidence suggests it may have been a deliberate attempt to obscure the extent of Riskin's contribution to *Lady for a Day*" (312-3).

The fact that Capra makes an error in reconstructing the date of a film conceals a "background intention," an "obsession": to show he is good, at the cost of stealing credit from Riskin. At least one thing is certain: the autobiography is not credible (like most products of the same genre). It must be taken as a "text," not as a reliable "source" for reconstrucing a career, especially that of an "old elephant" of Hollywood at the end of his career. Clearly an aging protagonist reconstructs events as he likes; even events that span the history of the twentieth century, which have to do with the Depression and the New Deal, McCarthyism and Fascism, the Hays Code and the studio system, Hollywood stars and, naturally, his co-workers.

It is also common that an aging protagonist tends to arrogate all the merits of his work to himself, even when, in the case of cinema, the work is a group effort. One need not even engage in psychoanalysis: I happened to meet the Italian director Blasetti before he died, and he claimed he had invented all the techniques of Italian cinema. His daughter, Mara, is still engaged with the task of reassessment and "reappropriation." It is as though a biographer of De Sica were to stand up today and accuse the neorealist director of stealing from Zavattini. Who is the true author, De Sica or Zavattini? In Italy mention has always been made of joint authorship. But if, following McBride's example, one were to opt only for Zavattini (a credible choice: he is the true "author," as well as the "theoretician," of neorealism)[8], would it mean that De Sica is a thief?

"Capra's sense of ethics was more flexible"; the refusal to cite Riskin is the sign of a "cultivated amnesia"; "he embarked on his crusade to deny Riskin his due credit"; "in attempting to prove his case for authorship"[9] The Riskin-Capra dispute is old. It falls within a broader debate on the relations between the director and his troupe. The same argument could be applied to Welles and Gregg Toland; or it could be brought to bear on the relationship between Capra and his trustworthy director of photography, Joseph Walker. The screenwriters are usually angrier with the director; but in the division of labor of the studio system it is

---

[8] Cf., for example, Lino Miccichè (ed.), *De Sica* (Venice: Marsilio, 1991).
[9] Cf. McBride, pp. 292-93.

wrong to call even the "contract director" the author. Recourse must be made to a vast debate on the policy of authorship.

Let us see what McBride has to say about this serious matter: "It was a battle that went beyond simple questions of fairness into complex philosophical issues about the "authorship" of a film, issues that would be lumped together into an acrimonous debate over the *auteur* theory. The debate began in 1954 with the proposal in the French film magazine *Cahiers du Cinéma* by critic (and later director) François Truffaut of "un cinéma des auteurs," which included among its tenets the primary role of the director in determining the thematic content of a film. Truffaut designed *Cahiers'* "politique des auteurs" partially to account for a situation like that of *Lady for a Day,* in which the director is not the screenwriter but still exerts his personality over the material. However, in the translation of the *politique* to American criticism, and even more so in its bastardization by its Hollywood detractors, the distinction between writer-director *auteurs* and nonwriter *auteur* directors largly became lost, and the debate degenerated into hopeless and irresolvable battles between the defenders of the director and the defenders of the writer" (292, 295).

Besides a superficial reconstruction of the *politique des auteurs,* the tone is disheartening for those who have devoted years of honest research to that "hopeless" and "irresolvable" question of "authorship," from Foucault to Sarris, from Wollen to Bordwell.

In the meantime, a new edition of McBride's biography has been published, and I have softened my judgment. McBride is certainly a good scholar, and we share the same passion for Capra's films. Besides, I truly appreciated his presentation at a Capra retrospective in Bologna I will discuss shortly. In this new edition, McBride answers my critique included in the above-mentioned anthology I co-edited with Robert Sklar: "The 1998 'anthology' ... contains the following false and unattributed claim by Zagarrio: 'McBride wanted, in agreement with the

[Capra] family, fore the director to die before publishing the book, which had ben written while Capra was still alive.' In fact, I did not finish editing and revising the manuscript until late January 1992, more than four months after Capra's death, and I made no agreement of any kind with the Capra family, nor any such agreement with anyone else." Indeed, McBride cites a letter from his editor, Bob Bender of Simon & Schuster, who confirms that there was no agreement at all of any kind that would have delayed McBride's 1992 biography until after Capra's death.[10]

McBride is certainly correct, and I apologize to him for the inaccuracy in my previous essay or for any misunderstanding. The problem, however, is another: I am not interested in whether Capra is trustworthy, a liar, or "unreliable," as McBride stated at the Bologna festival. This may very well be true, and this personal characteristic would surely explain Capra's conflicts and the contradictory readings of his films. However, I am interested in a textual analysis of his films qua text and not in a discussion on the reliability of his memories and penchant for recall. *The Name above the Title*, I maintain, is a novel, a Capraesque fairy tale, not a scientific archive of documentation.[11]

I shall now turn to David Bordwell to conclude this discussion of McBride and, in general, of interpretations too closely tied to the ideology of the author (regardless of whether they are friendly or hostile to that ideology). At the beginning of the chapter "Symptomatic Interpretation," in *Making Meaning*, Bordwell provides the example of a father who says to his son: "The grass is so tall I can hardly see the cat walking through it." This simple phrase is heard by a group of scientists,

---

[10] Joseph McBride, *Frank Capra. The Catastrophe of Success* (New York: St. Martin's Griffin, 2000) 658, note. The book cover states: "Contains newly declassified information."

[11] That said, I thank Joseph McBride for a nice personal meeting at the Bologna conference in which we had the opportunity to discuss in person our different positions, and I affirm my high esteem for a scholar who has devoted, as I have also, many years of his intellectual energies to Frank Capra.

who process and analyze it in various ways: some interpret it as a ritual of power, some see in it a bourgeois obsession with property, some find sexual and psychoanalytic symbols (identification of the father with the predator, desire of liberation, fear of castration). In reality, if these observers were to propose their theses to the father, he would vehemently deny them. He has simply observed that the grass is taller. "The social scientists," Bordwell says, "have constructed a set of symptomatic meanings."[12]

This page from Bordwell comes to mind in connection with Capra both when McBride utilizes the director's biography to demolish his authorship, and when more conventional criticism utilizes his autobiography to produce the usual, commonplace portrait of the reactionary populist in love with the Statue of Liberty. Capra is like Bordwell's father, but we scholars are like the social scientists, "willing to grant that an interpreter might understand the author better than he has understood himself" (Bordwell, 72). I intend to analyze Capra *malgré lui* because I may be capable of understanding him better than he understands himself. But in doing so I shall take his films, their internal structures, and their language, as my primary source. The biographical and autobiographical facts will help place the "case study" better in a personal and historic context; but I will concentrate my focus on his "texts," which I shall try to analyze in a new way.

RECENT STUDIES AND RE-READINGS

The need for a revision of Capra's cinema is given confirmation by most recent studies. As a matter of fact, *Another Frank Capra,* is the title

---

12 David Bordwell, *Making Meaning. Inference and Rhetoric in the Interpretation of Cinema* (Cambridge: Harvard University Press, 1989) 71. See in particular Chapter 4, "Symptomatic Interpretation" and the paragraph, "The Contradictory Text."

of a book by Leland Poague[13], a veteran of the films by the Italian American filmmaker, "famed" author of a preceding monograph on him. I will then borrow this nice title, paraphrasing a little the intention of the author himself, to reinforce strongly the need for an "other" reading of Capra: other as in different and alternative, but also as in a deeper sense, given the psychoanalytic nuances of the word. Another Capra also in a mirroring sense, assuming a "double," maybe even indirectly "schizofrenic," of a conflicting alterity, and thus, artistically productive.

The "revision" of his work is visible already in the monograph by Michel Cieutat: in his *Frank Capra[14]*, while welcoming the most obvious presences of the "Myth," he also gets the inner contradictions. Next to the stereotypical optimism, he underlines the implicit pessimism, next to the traditional strength of the character and will, the "attempted suicide," next to the semplicity of good feelings, the duplicity of the being, next to the search for happiness, he unerlines the sense of a society in danger, next to the "christian family," the impression of a familiar unity dense with tensions and fears.

Along the lines of Cieutat, Charles Maland who, after ten years, goes back to studying Capra with a different look and in light of the debate which came in between: "Capra and the Abyss," this is the title of his most recent essay, adjusting the title of his previous book.[15] Where Maland previously traced the influences of a chiristina ecumenism in the work of Capra, he now stresses a dark spot in Capra films: using ex-

---

[13] See L. Poague, *Another Frank Capra* (Cambridge, MA: Cambridge University Press, 1994). See also the useful anthology of interviews with the Hollywood Maestro: L. Poague, *Frank Capra Interviews* (Jackson, MS: University Press of Mississipi, 2004). Poague is the author of a forerunner, if slightly outdated, book on Capra: *The Cinema of Frank Capra. An Approach to Film Comedy* (South Brunswick, NJ: A. S. Barnes, 1975).

[14] M. Cieutat, *Frank Capra*, cit.

[15] C. J. Maland, "Capra and the Abyss: Self-interest versus the Common Good in Depression America," in R. Sklar, V. Zagarrio, cit., 95. As for the previous attempts by Maland, see: *American Visions: The Films of Chaplin, Ford, Capra, and Welles, 1936-1941* (New York: Arno Press, 1977); and *Frank Capra* (Boston: Twayne Publishers, 1980).

pressions like "depth of abyss," "dark scenes," "cultural nightmares"; he writes of *It's a Wonderful Life* as "one of the bleakest films ever made," he focuses his analysis on the attempted suicide of this film as of others by the filmmaker. "Recent work in cultural studies has encouraged us to focus not just on happy endings on films, but also the narrative conflicts that lead up to them (...) I will argue that the despair in his films arose from a tension, widely experienced in American culture and both central to American ideology and crucial in the depression decade, between private interest and pursuit of the common good."[16] McBride's biography also is used to show a dark side in Capra's personality and films, a personal contentiousness that carries over to the more general political strife of America in the early thirties, torn between private and public interest. "The enduring tension in much American middle-class life between capitalism and democracy, self-interest and the common good, is dramatized continually in the films of Frank Capra, and in the moments of abyss outlined here, we witness some of the most disturbing of our collective American nightmares."

The latest opportunity for a re-thinking of Capra's work has been the 2009 edition of the Italian festival "Il cinema ritrovato" (June 27th-July 4th) organized by the Bologna Cinemateque, which focuses on unknown or restored films. One section of this year's event was devoted to the early Capra, which confirms the re-evaluation of the less well known works of the director. The Bologna event, *Mr. Capra Goes to Town* (a paraphrase of one the most famous Capra's movies) was organized and introduced by Joseph McBride, the above-mentioned biographer of Frank Capra.

Among the re-discovered films we find the interesting case of *Fulta Fisher's Boarding House* (1922), a low-budget film taken from a Rudyard Kipling poem (a strange mixture of dark melodrama and literary film),

---

[16] See C. Maland, *Capra and the Abyss*, cit.

certainly not a "light" comedy. But the real discovery is a documentary shot by Capra in 1921: *The Italian Warship Libia*. It is a documentary commissioned by the Italian community in San Francisco to honor the arrival of the Italian Navy ship "Libia" to the Golden Gate port. The film casts new light upon the Italian-American director's identity and the relationship with his roots: as a matter of fact, the film is a great anthropological portrait of the Italian communities in the United States, an important historical document and a significant homage to the Mother Country. Capra shows the boats at sea welcoming the warship, together the large party organized by the "Italia Virtus Club." It is well shot, with a certain directorial touch; it shows the young director at work, Hitchcock like, and it is also a Capraesque "fairy tale": the dream of the Italian Navy, which pre-figures the passage of the "Rex" in Fellini's *Amarcord*.

Speaking of "dreams" and Italian identity, it is worthwhile to look at Francisco Moita Flores and Antonio De Sousa Duarte's book *Frank Capra non era un mafioso*,[17] an odd mixture between novel and historic essay in which the authors imagine the intersecting stories of three Italian-American characters. One is Frank Capra and his story of immigration from Bisacquino to Hollywood, the other one is Vito Cascio Ferro, the famous Mafia boss (the writers imagine him travelling in the same ship that brings Capra to America), and the third is Joe Petrosino, the well-known detective. The opera singer Enrico Caruso also makes a cameo appearance. While the book may not be a masterpiece, it validates Capra's trendiness and how both History and the stories of Italian Americans can be interesting for contemporary readers and spectators.

Another scholar who backtracks after many years is Poague, who, not only "writes another book" on Frank Capra after twenty years, but he also suggests an "other" reading, strenghtened by the vast theoretical

---

[17] Francisco Moita Flores, Antonio De Sousa Duarte, *Frank Capra non era un mafioso. Una storia sul cinema, cosa nostra e l'invenzione dell'american dream*, (Rome: Cavallo di ferro, 2009; Italian translation of *O Sangue da Honra* [Lisbon: Sextante, 2009]).

and methodological debate of these recent, past years. Poague focuses on the analysis of a few films, such as *Meet John Doe* (mostly along the theoretical lines of Nick Browne) or *You Can't Take It with You*, placing Capra's cinema within the context of the complex American theoretical system, from Dudley Andrew to Stanley Cavell, even attempting a "feminist" approach. What really comes forth as a surprise about Poague's book, and delightfully so, is that he adopts a filmological investigation similar to what Bordwell and Thompson have attempted systematically on the classical hollywood cinema; this way his analysis on the directing, the editing, and the construction of certain sequences give back to Capra a statute, legitimising him as a director with his own style and world. I fully agree with Poague method and "other" course (while his first book left some doubts pending), some of his observation match the hypotesis I formulated in all these years of critical production dedicated to Capra.

Capra's "modernity" is today seen through different angles. There are, for instance, the following four readings through which some have analysed his movies: a) the new reading of his *oeuvre* through a more general reflection on his role (that is, for example, the work of the above-mentioned Poague and of Eric Smoodin[18]); b) the textual analysis of some enlightening cases (Smoodin again, Browne, Ray and, among the Italians, Giaime Alonge and Alberto Boschi);[19] c) the attention to the modes of production and to the studio system (Bernard Dick);[20] d) the re-reading of some methodological trends or themes in which we can

---

[18] Eric Smoodin, *Regarding Frank Capra, Audience, Celebrity, and Americam Film Studies, 1930-1960* (Durham-London, Duke University Press, 2004).

[19] A. Boschi, "The Matinee Idol" di Frank Capra," *Cinegrafie* 7. dossier *Trovati nel buio. Lang, Robinson, Murnau, Gance, Capra, Hitch, film muti italiani*, IV (May 1994).
See Smoodin's study on individual films, appearing from time to time on journals: E. Smoodin, "'Compulsory' Viewing for Every Citizen: Mr. Smith and the Rhetoric of Reception," *Cinema Journal*, 35.2 (1996); E. Smoodin, "'This Business in America': Fan Mail, Film Reception and Meet John Doe," *Screen* 372 (Summer 1996).

[20] Bernard F. Dick, *The Merchant Prince of Poverty Row, Harry Cohn of Columbia Pictures* (Lexington: The University Press of Kentucky, 1993).

locate Capra, such as: d1) genre (Cavell, Musser, and, among the Italians, Roberto Campari);[21] d2) gender (Olsin Lent), d3) ethnicity (Bondanella, Lourdeaux and, among the Italians, Giuliana Muscio).[22]

Particularly, the most interesting studies actually come from the analysis of ethnic roots, or from a theory of comedy, or yet again, from unheard of approaches as the attention to the audience and to the vehiculation of the film product, but mostly from the attempts toward an investigation of the film text where evidently Capra has sides yet to be unveiled. There are indeed analyses of individual films, which shed light on Capra's entire oeuvre.

In this light, I would like to consider the position of Robert Ray who, in one of his books on "a certain tendency of Hollywod cinema,"[23] has dedicated one essay to *It's A Wonderful Life*. It is not the "wonderful life" of stereotypical folklore, but actually it is a reading akin to the one I advocate, interested in the "internal contradictions" of Hollywood cinema and to the split between "intent" and "effect" in some notable films of American production: "The split between the intent and effect of the best postwar movies was not new to the American Cinema. In fact, many of Classic Hollywood's most exciting films had manifested the same disjuncture, resulting from their inability of their displacement mechanism to efface completely the anxieties occasioning their surface melodramas" (Ray, 175). This postwar anxiety is not only reflected through contents, but also through the stylistical exceptions to grammar rules;

---

[21] S. Cavell, *Pursuit of Happiness: The Hollywood Comedy of Remarriage* (Boston: Harvard University Press, 1981). R. Campari, *Il discorso amoroso: melodramma e commedia nella Hollywood degli anni d'oro* (Rome: Bulzoni, 1990).

[22] P. Bondanella, *Hollywood Italians. Dagos, Pallokas, Romeos, Wise Guys, and Sopranos* (New York: Continuum, 2004). L. Lourdeaux, *Italian and Irisk Filmmakers in America. Ford, Capra, Coppola and Scorsese* (Philadelphia: Temple University Press, 1990). G. Muscio, *Piccole italie, grandi schermi. Scambi cinematografici tra Italia e Stati Uniti 1895-1945* (Rome: Bulzoni, 2004).

[23] R. B. Ray, *A Certain Tendency of the Hollywod Cinema, 1930-1980* (Princeton, NJ, 1985). On *It's A Wonderful Life* see P. Vecchi, "'La vita è meravigliosa di Frank Capra," *Cineforum* 271 Jan.-Feb 1988).

transgressions which could be detected already in classical cinema (as for example in *Stagecoach* as rightly noted by Ray[24]), but which are accentuated in some postwar films. Ray points to two examples: one is *The Man Who Shot Liberty Valance* by Ford, the other one is, precisely, *It's a Wonderful Life*. Both films show the typical gap of the time between intent and effect and both are striving to sew it up while at the same time dramatizing the increasing incompatibility with the traditional American values. Both films challenge the Hollywood formal conventins: Ford's film by ignoring the formal paradigm already acquired, like the one establishing the best point of view for the spectator; Capra's film by making the "visible style" invisible.

It's a Wonderful Life has a superficial side, the one voluntarily ignoring the huge postwar changesand situates its story in a small midwestern town, but has instead a narrative structure and a mise en scene which question this superficiality, building a much more complicated text. Ray analyses the film from the point of view of its sintax, right from the first sequence, the dramtic preyers of the people to save George, the protagonist, an "un happy" character—Ray writes—as many previous characters in Hollywood, but the first one to be saddened by the very same myth he is chasing: "*It's Wonderful Life*, however, demonstrated that myths that had outlived their basis could in fact become pernicious" (192-93). It is self apparent that the dreams of adventure are causing George to feel frustrated, as he is living in a world which doesn't allow them. The film, "despite its intent," repeatedly demonstrates the incompatibility of Dream, to the point that the protagonist can actually fit into the American "melancholy" noticed by Tocqueville ("Why the Americans Are Often So Restless in the Midst of Their Prosperity?"[25]). Thus, this is an apparenly simple film, however, one which doesn't re-

---

[24] I agree with this kind of analysis: see my "L'orizzonte perduto di Ford" in P. Bertetto (ed.), *Interpretazioni del film* (Venice: Marsilio, 2003).

[25] A. de Tocqueville, *Democracy in America* (Garden City, NY: Anchor, Doubleday, 1969).

concile its tensions and social anxieties; the three oppositions adventure/domesticity, man/community, success/ordinary life, which have often been identified with the polarites of American mythology, don't really work here: "The overt intent of *It'a a Wonderful Life* was to acknowledge George's dilemma and then solve it, to reaffirm the American Dream by showing that conflicts betwen opposed values were illusory (...)But these subtle reconciliations could not entirely resolve the film's basic opposition." We can see how this is really a "new tendency" in the reading of Capra and on the American Dream.

Charles Wolfe too, has dedicated most of its attention to a single Capra text, *Meet John Doe*, to which he devotes an entire volume investigating its various sides, from the socio-historical one to the semiological.[26] It is not by chance that Wolfe has chosen this rather tormented text: "Today the reputation of *Meet John Doe* is that of an ambitious but troubled work, the film in which director Frank Capra's fabled optimism failed him as an adequate guide to topical, political fiction-making." Evidence of the inner troubling is given by the absence of a decisive ending (the famous five endings on which Capra himself has written[27]) to which Wolfe devotes an accurate historical reconstruction.

Among the essays edited in this volume, one needs to mention the famous title by Nick Browne,[28] originally published upon the already mentioned Italian conference on Capra; an essay evidently not yet outdated. In addition to *Meet John Doe*, Browne has devoted an acurate analysis to *Mr. Smith Goes to Washington* too, an essay re-published in

---

[26] C. Wolfe (ed.), *Meet John Doe. Frank Capra, Director* (New Brunswick, NJ: Rutgers University Press, 1989). In addition to the screenplay and the various sources of information on the film, the book offers different analytical positions, through essays, reviews and commentaries, from Lewis Jacobs to Jay Leyda, to Richard Glatzer and Dudley Andrew.

[27] F. Capra, *Five Endings in Search of an Audience*, excerpt from its autobiography published on many journals and books, also in Wolfe, see p. 207.

[28] N. Browne, *"System of Production/System of Representation: Industry Context and Ideological Form"* in Capra's *"Meet John Doe,"* 269, originally published in V. Zagarrio (ed.), *Hollywood in Progress. Itinerari cinema-televisione* (Venice: Marsilio, 1984).

France, too, which puts the film in the context of a larger ideological project, "conceived to preserve the American social ideals, embedding them into the memory of lost times and evoking them in order to save the present."[29] Why is it that in France—reads the introduction to the essay (presumably written by Nöel Burch)—one refers too often and too easily to the myth of a "progressive" Capra, "critical of American society"? Browne, instead, prefers to put off ("being subtler than other commentators") the Capra myth, retaining the old ideological judgment: "Car Capra est, avec Vidor et De Mille, sans doute le plus grand conservateur des 'grandes auteurs' d'Hollywood" (77).

Parallel to the work of Browne is the reading of *Mr. Smith* by Giaime Alonge,[30] according to whom "Capra is completely conscious of his own "organic intellectual" status, and of the role cinema can play in the political battlefield of mass society." Although avoinding the all too easy game of exposing the naïveté and rethoric of Capra's films, Alonge focuses on Mr Smith as a "manifest of Capra's take on society and on American democracy," he puts the film in his cultural-historical context and relates it to the coeval european political imaginary.

If this book's theories are correct, I would be less interested in Browne's and Alonge's ideological positions, but surely their kind of investigation strikes a new type of methodology, one based on textual reading and on a analysis way further from the old interpretaions of Capra. As it is when Alonge analyses the sequence of the tour of Washington's museums, during which the protagonist "is visiting the sacred places of American democracy. In a fast procession, they flash on the screen: the White House, the Congress, the statues of Jefferson, Adams, Hamilton,

---

[29] N. Browne, *Politique de la forme narrative*, in N. Burch (ed), *Revoir Hollywood. La nouvelle critique anglo-américaine* (Tours: Nathan, 1993). Browne's essay was originally published in *Wide Angle* 3.3 (1980).

[30] G. Andrea Alonge, "*Mr. Smith a Washington* ovvero il trionfo della libertà," *Quaderni di cinema* 52 (Oct.-Dec. 1992), subsequently in G. Alonge, *Uno stormo di Stinger. Autori e generi del cinema americano* (Torino: Kaplan, 2004) 29 ff.

the obelisk dedicated to Washington, Arlington, and Lincoln mausoleum." A sequence ending with the star-striped flag blowing in the wind, which Alonge compares to the films of Leni Riefenstahl: the similarities are plain—Alonge says—"the cross-dissolve and the superimpression are two among the most typical elements of the german director's style," who shares with the American filmmaker the similar cultural koynè, the same "new political" language which informs the Thirties and the World War II period. This is where Capra's deep consciousness of himself stems from, he knows very well what is the role of cinema and its power: at one point, while touring, Mr. Smith is distracted by something strange, and he exclaims in a frenzy: "What's that, what's that?!" "Ah, that's a movie theatre," he adds shortly thereafter, less enthusiastically. "For a second, the protagonist misplaces a movie theatre with the temples of American democracy, as if Capra wanted to explicit the spectacular nature of that 'new politics'..." (Alonge, 40; my translation).

Let's now turn to Smoodin and Poague. The former follows a new path, using a very long work of research, mostly derived from the Capra Archives at Wesleyan University, devoting himself to reception studies. As he had done in the previous essays, Smoodin travels through audience reactions, diving into an unprecedented world of emotions coeval to the film's opening: fans' letters, mostly soldiers and prisoners, showing times, film junklets, posters, ehibitors announcements, censor waivers, Capra's statements, advertising, every metafilmic element around Capra's films. This is, as Smoodin himself declares in the introduction to the book, the methodology used in cultural studies, devoted to the audience reception and more interested in all the text risen around the film than in the film itself. Smooding has many collegues: Janet Staiger, Gregory Walzer, Charles Maland, Jackie Stacey, Richard Maltby, Annette Kuhn, Robert Allen, Ben Singer and many more. A kind of "cinema sociology," which, even if distant from my point of view, can be very interesting and full of surprises.

The second author (Poague) focuses on a series of interviews with Capra, which don't really change the traditional vision on the filmmaker —as the author himself admits—but do stand for a revision. Poague standing point is the one already mentioned for *Another Capra*: "Was Capra an idealistic Boy Ranger offfering Capra-corn populism to a nation desperately in need of self-delusion? Or did Capra's own desperation put him in touch with the times to such an extent that his impassioned efforts to pass beyond delusion earned credibility exactly by straining it—to something like the breaking point?."[31] To paraphrase, is Capra a idealistic optimist, offering populist messages, or rather a human being with a strong sense of desperation which puts him in tight relation to its times? My point of view, says Poague, is more aking to the latter than the former, but it is clear that the collected interviews favor the vision of a culturally naive directors who loves fairytales. Poague's observation confirms this schizophrenia between intentions and results, between conscious messages and unconscious drives which determine the conflict, but also the intriguing strength of Capra's cinema.

The opinion on Capra, is changing: see for example the book by Jacqueline Nacache on classical Hollywood cinema, where we find statements like: "his contribution is basically in giving to the gag an epic quality, in the big scenes which require most of the times an anxious crowd [...] Nonetheless it suffices only a tiny bit of anything and these partying crowds change into hostile masses, and the other side of the gag, in Capra is very often a tragic one (see *Forbidden*)."[32]

Studies rise from everywhere in which Capra is protagonist, seen through many angles: on cultural identiy, for instance, and on the question of ethnic belonging as an Italian-American, the most interesting studies are the ones by Lee Lourdeaux and by Giuliana Muscio.

---

[31] L. Poague, *Frank Capra Interviews*, VIII.
[32] J. Nacache, *Le film hollywoodien classique* (Paris: Nathan, 1995) my translation.

The former places Capra in a group of filmmakers of Italian or Irish descendants (Ford, Coppola, Scorsese) and researches the Italian background in his ethnical approach to life and cinema: the family, his pragmatism, the father figure, even the role of the director on set as a Italian style "capofamiglia" are all elements revealing his identity; thus even many of his characters reveal a kind of "Italian vision of America"[33]. The latter studies Capra by "accident" (Muscio explains that her work is on all the people, whether Italian or American, who worked on entertainment before getting to Hollywood) but she devotes an analysis to one of the less known work by Capra, *For the Love of Mike*: the methaphorical story of an orphan adopted by three "fathers" coming from different ethnicities (a Jewish tailor, a German grocer, an Irish street sweeper) and who experiences—autobiographically—an Italian American story. He is sent to study but gambles and loses hard, then he is subdued to being bought (he has to prevent the Yale boat he races in from winning) and in the end has a moment of clarity and reassures his supportive community. The other Capra film Muscio examines is the better known *The Younger Generation*, this one too is set in a non Italian American context (the family is typically Jewish) but it reveals his deep roots: agreeing with Lourdeaux, the representation of the family is typically Italian: "a space of solidarity and loving human relationships [...] an implicitly Italian American family, "assimilated" in the social, even in the sportive spirit." Italo-americano... Muscio underlines the value of the hyphen, the bridge connecting and revealing the strong belonging to the roots; from a certain point on the "Italian Americans" become the "Italian-Americans," they become thus hyphenated with a stronger sense of themselves from the place of their origins.

Strangely, instead, Peter Bondanella does not include Capra in his Hollywood Italians; he deals with him only indirectly, when analysing

---

[33] Cfr. L. Lourdeaux, "Frank Capra and His Italian Vision of America," 130.

the *Sopranos* (Tony Soprano rents *It's a Wonderful Life*—the Mob's favorite film[34]) or when he rightly notices how Capra never considered himslef an Italian but an American, just like Al Capone (12). "When—Muscio seems to agree—in the hyphenated composition the Italian side is weak, it is only natural to move toward the American side."[35]

But there are also other interesting point of views to better relocate Capra, beside his ethnicity and his identity: for instance the gender reading made by Tina Olsin Lent, pointing her analysis mostly on *It Happened One Night*.[36] The journey from Miami to New York of the two potagonists is a route leading the two "fellow travelers" toward each other, in a way that had never been done before in American film and culture as a whole. In the early Thirties—Olsin Lent writes—many popular Hollywood films—and especially *It Happened One Night*—represent the relationship between man and woman in a new and original way, describing their complimentary relation to on another, and their camaraderie, accepting their mutual comfort and sexual attraction (314, 321); Capra's films show an emancipated woman, self-conscious, committed to a "career" (see *Mr. Deeds Goes to Town, Meet John Doe, You Can't Take It With You, Mr. Smith Goes to Washington*). It is as if screwball comedy was actively working on reconciling not only the classes, but the sexes too, once hostile identities (322).

With screwball comedy we are already on the turf of genres, and it is easier here to find studies and opinions. I have already mentioned, and I intend to quote it further more, the work of Stanley Cavell and his

---

[34] Episode "To Save Us All from Satan's Power"; see P. Bondanella, 311

[35] G. Muscio, *Piccole Italie*, 261. The author here puts Capra in relation to another Italian-American, Frank Nugent, who, just like other immigrants, invented a whole new biography to better fit into the new homeland. Capra considered his name to be too "animalier" and he was ashamed of his origins and of his "American shore landing" (148).

[36] T. Olsin Lent, "Romantic Love and Friendship: The Redefinition of Gender Relations in Screwball Comedy," in K. Brunovska Karnick, H. Jenkins (ed.), *Classical Hollywood Comedy* (New York-London: Routledge, Afi Film Readers, 1995).

"comedy of re-marriage."[37] But beside this central work there are other studies, like the ones by Gehring, Musser, or the Italian Campari and Giacovelli.[38] Musser particularly expands on the line of "re-marriage" to other films, from the Thirties and from the previous decade. The position of Cavell, however, is pointed at as the example set for a tentative method of applying philosophical thought to cinema: see, for instance, *Philosophy of Film.*[39]

There are several recent studies that help investigate the Capra mode of production, on Hollywood studios and in particular on his relationship with Columbia: A. Scott Berg, Bernard Dick, Ethan Mordden, and Muscio again.[40] Under this light we can read the references to Capra in the context of the recent historiography on Hollywood industries, like in the studies by Bourget or Laura.[41]

---

[37] S. Cavell, *Pursuit of Happiness.* On Cavell's book I will mention a review by Ira Jaffe: "Stanley Cavell, *Pursuit of Happiness: The Hollywood Comedy of Remarriage,*" *The Journal of the University Film and Video Association* 35.1 (Winter 1983).

[38] W. D. Gehring, *Screwball Comedy: Defining a Film Genre* (Mencie, Indiana: Ball State Monograph, 1983); C. Musser, "Divorce, DeMille and the Comedy of Remarriage," in K. Brunovska Karnick, H. Jenkins (ed.); R. Campari, *Il discorso amoroso* (Rome: Bulzoni, 1990); E. Giacovelli, *La commedia del desiderio, Il linguaggio, i miti, i meccanismo comici, i luoghi comuni, i misteri, i personaggi, la filosofia della commedia sofisticata americana, 1930-1945* (Rome: Gremese, 1991). See also, for a more general debate, S. Neale, *Genre and Hollywood* (London-New York: Routledge, 2000) and R. Altman, *Film/Genre* (London: Bfi, 1999).

[39] T. E. Wartenberg, A. Curan (ed.), *The Philosophy of Film. Introductory Text and Readings* (Malden-Oxford-Carlton: Blackwell, 2005).

[40] A. Scott Berg, *Goldwyn. A Biography* (New York: Ballantine Books, 1989); B. F. Dick (ed.), *Columbia Pictures, Portrait of a Studio* (Lexington: The University Press of Kentucky, 1992); B. F. Dick, *The Merchant of Poverty Row. Harry Cohn of Columbia Pictures* (Lexington: University Press of Kentucky, 1993); E. Mordden Ethan, *The Hollywood Studios, House Style in The Golden Age of the Movies* (New York: Simon & Schuster, 1989 (see also the Spanish edition: *Los Estudios de Hollywood* [Mallorca: Ultramar Editores, 1989]); G. Muscio, *La Casa Bianca e le sette majors. Cinema e mass media negli anni del new deal* (Padova: Il Poligrafo, 1990). Finally let me mention the new edition of a classic: B. Thomas, *King Cohn: the life and times of Harry Cohn* (New York-St. Louis-San Francisco: McGraw-Hill, 1990).

[41] J-L. Bourget, *Hollywood, Années 30. Du Krach à Pearl Harbor* (Renens: Cinq Continents, 1986); E. G. Laura, *Quando Los Angeles si chiamava Hollywood. Cinema americano tra le due guerre* (Rome: Bulzoni, 1996). See also Jill Nelmes, *An Introduction to Film Studies* (New York: Routledge, 1996).

One has to notice two diverging tendencies: the anedoctal and popular publication, or worse, the cinephile-popular[42]; on the other side, books which frame Capra in an ideological context (populism, New Deal and/or Depression, progressism or conservatorism depending on the interpretation, politics and society)[43].

In this perspective, I would like to point out one of the (very few) observations that Gilles Deleuze dedicated to Capra: analysing the notion of "people" he notices how it is precisely in the popular "unanimism" the site of the difference between modern and classical cinema. Unanimism puts into agreement soviet cinema with the American before and after the war: "this time it is not the twists of class struggle and the confrontation of ideologies, but the economic crises, the fight against moral prejudice, profiteers and demagogues, which mark the awareness of a people, at the lowest point of their misfortune as well as at the peak of their hope (the unanimism of King Vidor, Capra, or Ford, the problem runs through the Western as much as through the social drama, both testifying to the existence of a people, in hardships as well as in ways of recovering and rediscovering itself)."[44]

OUTLINES OF METHOD

I am proposing an investigation of Capra, with the aim of conjugating text and context, historical analysis of the social background,

---

[42] See P. F. Boller, Ronald L. Davis, *Hollywood Anecdotes* (New York: Ballatine Books, 1987); S. Cox Stephen, *"It's a Wonderful Life": A Memory Book* (Nashville: Cumberland House, 2001); Jimmy Hawkins, Paul Petersen, *The "It's a Wonderful Life" Trivia Book* (New York: Crown, 1992); See also, among many examples, an Italian book: S. Key, V. Saxe Critton, *Le ricette di "La vita è meravigliosa"* (Torino: Lindau, 1998).

[43] J. Belton, *American Cinema/American Culture* (New York-St. Louis-San Francisco: McGraw Hill, 1994); Brian Neve, *Film and Politics in America. A Social Tradition* (London-New York: Routledge, 1992). Also, the already mentioned W. D. Gehring, *Populism and the Capra Legacy* (Westport-London: Greenwood Press, 1995).

[44] See G. Deleuze, *Cinema 2: The Time-Image* (Minneapolis: University of Minnesota Press, 1989) 216.

evolution of production and ideology, and analysis of the films. One can almost pronounce the words history and story in the same breath.

Those who value Capra tend to place him in one of three traditions: that of an American tradition (as in Raymond Carney's *American Vision*), that of an ancestral ritual of comedy (*The Cinema of Frank Capra* by Leland Poague), or that of religious moralism (*Frank Capra* by Charles Maland). I hope to demonstrate that Capra can be read in terms of his relationship to social history, that his work can be analyzed in accordance with historical method, and that he can actually be considered a case study for a new kind of historical analysis.

I shall also make recourse to that historiography which has used the human sciences to analyze cinema. I am referring above all to Marc Ferro and Pierre Sorlin, who have pointed out new ways of dealing with the medium of cinema and of considering it a fundamental reference for the interpretation of contemporary society.

Geörgy Lukács[45] has suggested that culture is a mirror of the society that produces it, to the extent that it reflects that society's dynamics and contradictions. In this sense cinema, an audio-visual device, can be an excellent mirror of society, a direct or indirect source, to borrow Ferro's terminology.[46] One may view it as the product of a cultural and economic phase or time period; as an archaeological repertory of images, costumes and gestures of a country and of a period in history; or as an archival document revealing the dynamics of a civilization. Lukács's mirror thus becomes the mirror of the *camera obscura*, the diaphragm of a camera that records and preserves documentary and fantastic images of history.

---

[45] Geörgy Lukàcs, *Schriften zur Literatur-Soziologie*. In English see *The Theory of the Novel; a Historico-Philosophical Essay on the Forms of Great Epic Literature* (Cambridge, MA: M.I.T. Press, 1971), and Essay on Realism: Georg Lukacs (Cambridge, MA: M.I.T. Press, 1981).

[46] Marc Ferro, *Cinéma et Histoire* (Italian translation, *Cinema e storia*, [Milan: Feltrinelli, 1980]. English trans: *Cinema and History* [Detroit: Wayne State University Press, 1988]); Marc Ferro, *Analyse de film, analyse de sociétées* (Paris: Classiques Hachette, 1979).

Cinema can also be an agent of history. As a mythmaking device, it can intervene to change history through its propagandizing force or its seductive charm. In this sense the Italian Marxist thinker Antonio Gramsci goes beyond Lukács: art, he says, is always revolutionary. A true work of art is revolutionary to the degree that it changes consciousnesses, betters the public, or stimulates thought and action. This is true of cinema even when the medium's power to provoke change is completely unconscious, as it is for Frank Capra. In any event, "the Capra case" is to be seen in this double sense, as mirror and as agent. Historical investigation alone, however, is not sufficient to reveal this role. The social background must be placed in its proper relation to the filmic product, the historical dynamics in their proper relation to the dynamics of authorship, the context in its proper relation with the text. Only through such an eclectic and trans-methodological effort can a correct and complete analysis be carried out. The area of research so defined may be said to define a square whose corners are four "angles" or "points of view": a) history & ideology; b) the studio system; c) modes of production; d) authorship.

HISTORY AND IDEOLOGY, THE STUDIO SYSTEM,
MODES OF PRODUCTION, AUTHORSHIP

History and Ideology. The synthesis between history and film theory was achieved in Europe a little over a decade ago by Marc Ferro, Pierre Sorlin, and Jean Baudrillard; and in America somewhat later in the books edited by John O'Connor and the initiatives of *Radical History Review*.[47] The twentieth-century historian inevitably encounters cinema and television during his research, writes Pierre Sorlin in his book,

---

47 John O'Connor and Martin Jackson (eds.), *American History / American Film: Interpreting the Hollywood Image* (New York: Ungar, 1979). John O'Connor (ed.), *American History / American Television* (New York: Ungar, 1983). Robert Sklar, "Oh! Althusser!: Historiography and the Rise of Cinema Studies," *Radical History Review*, special issue on film and history, 41, April 1988.

Sociologie du cinéma.[48] And in fact the eighties and nineties were characterized by a massive return to history, as historians overcame their inferiority complexes with respect to younger disciplines (semiology, psychoanalysis, anthropology) and re-appropriated new tools of analysis. Writing in the late 1970s, Jean Baudrillard viewed the return of history in a peculiar way. History is dead, it is a corpse, a fossil, he says: but this is exactly what allows it to become myth and enter the collective imagination. The mass media devour history faster and faster: yesterday's facts become today's history. One saw it happen with Vietnam and with the Gulf War. Baudrillard speaks of a corpse so cumbersome that it becomes a mummy.

But what is this dull and frightening discipline? Why does it call up the ghosts of old ideologies (the Marxism, the Resistance, the Revolution)? Can it be applied as a method, a system of reference? And above all, is it advisable to trouble history for a "little man" like Frank Capra?

History does not necessarily have to describe the great processes of human development, the long-term evolution of the labor movement, Christianity, or capitalism. One may simply describe life in a small village, as LeRoy Ladurie did with Montaillou. Capra's texts and movies may be analyzed in a similar manner to obtain an image that will differ from the conventional one. For history, in Capra's eyes, is on one hand a social scenario, the context in which characters move (as brought to light by Bergman, Roffman, and Purdy). It is the America of the Depression and the New Deal, which Capra's films "reflect," as Lukács would put it. But on the other hand it is reality, including the commonplace reality of daily life, and hence a "document" uncensored by conscious ideologies.

---

[48] Pierre Sorlin, *Sociologie du Cinéma* (Paris: Aubier Montagne, 1977. Italian translation: *Sociologia del cinema,* Milan: Garzanti, 1981). In English see *The Films in History: Restaging the Past* (Totowa, N.J.: Barnes and Noble, 1980); and *European Cinemas, European Societies, 1939-1990* (New York: Routledge, 1991).

The Studio System. With regard to the studio system, the Capra "case" may be played off against more than ten years of archival research and methodological debate. In a survey of analyses of the studio system undertaken in the eighties, Thomas Schatz rightly points to a well-known inquiry by Edward Buscombe as the apex of the most interesting research of the decade.[49] The theme of the text is Columbia Pictures, which Buscombe reconstructs not only with a view to the Studio's financial policy, but also in terms of its ideological merits, the production of meaning, and the Marxian relationship between structure and superstructure. Schatz considers Buscombe's text a true "prophecy" and proceeds down the path that Buscombe marks out (in *Hollywood Genres,* and later in *The Genius of the System*). Other authors of now classic works include Douglas Gomery, who calls for a meticulous historiography reconstructing relations in the production system on the basis of archival data; and the trio of Bordwell, Staiger, and Thompson, who discuss the merits of the complex notion of "production method" in *The Classical Hollywood Cinema.*[50]

Seen in this perspective, Capra offers a unique possibility: his lasting connection with Columbia, his love-hate relationship with the Studio that took him in and made him famous, allows one to study the producer's biography, his artistic output, and the history of the studio that produced this output, with a view to their interrelations. And such an analysis of the tie between one filmmaker and his Studio may allow us to propose a valid method for the rest of the Hollywood system as well. It is one way of establishing a link between history and theory, as is now re-

[49] See Edward Buscombe, "Notes on Columbia Pictures," *Screen,* vol. 16, n. 3, 1975. See also Bob Thomas, *King Cohn* (New York: G.P. Putnam, 1967), and Brian Taves, "Studio Metamorphosis. Columbia's Emergence From Poverty Row," in Robert Sklar and Vito Zagarrio (eds.), *Frank Capra. Authorship and the Studio System,* cit. See also Adriano Aprà (ed.), *Hollywood: lo studio system,* Mostra internazionale del nuovo cinema (Venezia: Marsilio, 1982).
[50] David Bordwell, Janet Staiger, Kristin Thompson, *The Classical Hollywood Cinema, Film & Style & Mode of Production to 1960* (New York: Columbia University Press, 1985).

quired in many parts of the academic world ("'doing history' and 'doing theory,'" writes Schatz, "cannot be regarded as distinct enterprises").

Modes of Production. "A physicist observes the processes of nature where they can be found in their most meaningful form while not being obscured by disturbing influences. Or, where possible, he carries out experiments in situations that assure the unconditioned development of the process. What I must investigate in this volume is the capitalistic mode of production and the corresponding relationships of production and exchange." This is the first time, in *Das Kapital* (preface of the First Edition, 1867), that Marx uses the formula, "mode of production," in reference to capitalism; but he had already used it in the introduction to *Zur Kritik der politischen ökonomie* and in *Grundrisse,* and one finds it also in other texts such as the unpublished chapter VI of *Das Kapital.* "Mode of production" connotes an entire economic system in a given period, analyzed with a view to its complex "relationships of production and exchange," and therefore to the use mechanisms of the goods produced. In Marxist terms the formula can only be applied to macrosystems: capitalistic modes of production, Asian modes of production, etc.

So how can this formula be applied to cinema? Can one reasonably speak of modes of production analyzing not capitalistic society, but the goods/movies produced by artisan/artist Capra for Columbia? Capra's work and his relationship with Columbia can be seen from three points of view. From the first one may study Columbia's economic history, the studio's ties with the world of finance, and the structuring of production in A movies and B movies; one may calculate the cost of Capra's movies and understand his professional course. From the second, Capra may be set in the broader political and social scene (of which Columbia is only a part) ranging from the Depression to the New Deal to the Hays Code; from populism to widespread religious sentiment to the American myth. From the third, one may examine Capra's movies (especially those that are less well-known) before *It Happened One Night* and grasp how they were marked by economic, technological, and ideological influences; by professionalism, power, producers and morals; and how they conveyed or countered the director's artistic aspirations: should Capra be studied only as a pretext for historical or sociological analyses, or may one value him as an author, discover a poetics and a style in his work?

Authorship. "What is an author?" Foucault wrote. "What is a work of art in the age of mechanical reproduction?"—Walter Benjamin wondered. A few years ago, in Italy, something happened that added humorous color to the debate on authorship. The "Modì Hoax" in 1984 involved art critics, public officials, and the mass media. In Leghorn, home of painter Amedeo Modigliani (nicknamed Modì after his visits to Paris), research was begun on a legendary group of unfinished sculptures believed to have been thrown into the river by the dissatisfied artist. One day, much to the press's delight, some of these sculptures were found. The art world was immediately divided: for some, the sculptures were authentic, and finding them was an extraordinary accomplishment; for others they were common forgeries. It was a bitter dispute to which each side brought its own scientific evidence. The two factions expounded their opposing arguments on live television. The celebrated critic Argan defended the authenticity of the sculptures, whereas the equally well-known critic Calvesi denied their legitimacy. What criterion was used by the two opposing critics to form their influential opinions? "What counts," said Argan, "is the critic's 'eye,' a poet's ability to recognize art in spite of whatever photographic evidence there may be." The event ended in its own farcical way: it was discovered that Modì's sculptures had been made by a group of young jokesters with a Black & Decker. They staged a demonstration on live television, re-creating the "heads" in five minutes. It was a bad joke, not art.

This Italian apologue underscores the vagueness of authorship and the increasing difficulty of defining an artistic text. Therefore we can argue with those *auteur* theories that, on the basis of the critic's eye, have confined Frank Capra to an unpleasant purgatory. According to most critics, in fact, Capra was never on a par with Ford or Hawks, and he never had the "Lubitsch touch." But is this really so?

FREUDIAN SLIPS

Allow me to cite a few books by Italian scholars that indirectly support my hypothesis. Umberto Eco, in his volume, *Sei passeggiate nei boschi narrativi* (*Six Walks in the Fictional Woods*),[51] adopts a method similar to that which I have attempted to apply to Capra. Especially in the chapter, "Lo strano caso di via Servandoni" (The Strange Case of Servandoni Street), he ventures upon a police-like investigation that leads to an entirely subjective hypothesis, to an "it could be" reality that is not the only possible truth. Similarly, Sebastiano Timpanaro applies the Freudian slip to literary studies, and Francesco Orlando[52] introduces the scheme of "Freudian negations" into the exegesis of the classic tragedy. With regard to my proposal of a Frank Capra *malgré lui,* the claim could be made that his anxiety to affirm the positive charge of an "American dream" conceals an unconscious desire to portray the American social panorama negatively.

Orlando claims that art emerges despite the author's ideological convictions,[53] citing Racine's *Phedre* as an example. Is it not possible to say the same of Capra?

I shall make a flash-forward to a late film by Capra (who was on the threshold of decline at the time), the famous *It's a Wonderful Life.* Here one finds the classic scenario that made the director's films so suc-

---

[51] Umberto Eco, *Six Walks in the Fictional Woods* (Cambridge, MA: Harvard University Press, 1994). See also his *Sugli specchi ed altri saggi. Il segno, la rappresentazione, l'illusione, l'immagine* (Milan: Bompiani, 1985).

[52] Sebastiano Timpanaro, op. cit.; Francesco Orlando, *Toward a Freudian Theory of Literature: With an Analysis of Racine's Phedre* (Baltimore: Johns Hopkins University Press, 1978).

[53] Racine writes a presentation to his *Phedre* to make clear that the character's ethical values (i.e. the incest) are different from his own values.

cessful: the humble, solitary hero (this time a young, self-made man running a small family business); the small, anonymous town (called Bedford Falls, potentially any town in the Midwest), made the setting for a
fable that is valid for humanity as a whole; the ritual opponent or "bad
guy," this time a heartless, unprincipled moneylender whose sole ideal is
pecuniary; the community of good neighbors, all the ordinary people
who hover between refusal and acceptance, their private lives and interpersonal relationships invariably conditioned by their membership in
the community. After more than twenty years of Capra's filmmaking,
this scenario has been elevated to a style, a repetitive scheme of simple
philosophical ideas raised to the status of an existential ethic. A conflict
between the planned message and the involuntary message comes to a
head, here, perhaps at a conscious level. In fact the film, which met with
production difficulties and was made independently by the director
without assistance from the Hollywood studios, provides the most obvious example of Capra *malgré lui,* the Capra who was subject to extremely significant slips.

In order to highlight his "message," usually linked to an optimistic
happy ending, Capra uses a contrasting "second theme" to emphasize
the first—a theme that also contains contradictions and contrary solutions. In other words, in spite of himself, the director transmits a series
of negative messages that infringe on the more general message, particularly in certain segments of the narrative. These sequences have a role to
play in the final outcome of the story; generally they are the crucial
point in the negative situation, the dramatic climax that precedes and
prepares the way for the happy ending; but they deserve to be read as
independent minifilms. It seems to me that the director loses his ideological control in these fragments and that the images of society and
sediments of civil malaise emerge here as from the collective unconscious, contradicting and negating the sweetened Christian and class-
struggle-free utopias of Capra's films. These are the unconscious clues to

which attention must be addressed, because, as in Freud's analysis of Michelangelo's *Moses*, they can lead to a reversal of current opinion, or at least to a new proposal for an overall interpretation. The "slip" in *It's a Wonderful Life* (and I use this term improperly) is in one special portion of the film: the daydream of George Bailey (James Stewart). In this famous sequence an angel, Clarence, stops the hero of the film, George, from committing suicide by jumping off a bridge, convincing him that life is always worth living by allowing him to experience never having been born. This is a classic device of science fiction and of "counter-history":[54] what would have happened if the Germans had won World War I or the South, the American Civil War? In this didactic nightmare one finds that George's brother would have died, his wife would have been a spinster, Gower the pharmacist would have ended up in prison, but most importantly, the town would have been in the power of the wicked Potter (Lionel Barrymoore) without the actions of the ordinary citizen, George Bailey.

Bedford Falls, the utopian American town, begins to look like a real contemporary city with all its defects and moral degradation—the violent, vulgar bars; the gambling dens; the roads lit up by too many neon lights; the haunts for men only, lured in by flashy promises of girls. The town is now called Pottersville because the evil moneylender has imposed his values on the community in this "other" dimension.[55] It is dominated by violence (the bad cop who shoots to kill, the customers in the bar who beat up George Bailey), by sadness (Gower, the desperate pharmacist who appears as a relic of the Depression), and by solitude (the situations of the lonely wife, Mary, and the prostitute, Violet). This community is more similar to the worst real models of postwar Ameri-

---

[54] See, for example, the Italian novel by Guido Morselli, *Contropassato prossimo. Un'ipotesi retrospettiva* (Milan: Adelphi, 1975).

[55] I use the word "other" also in a psychoanalytic way, after Melanie Klein. Cf. Hanna Segal, *The Work of Hanna Segal: a Kleinian Approach to Clinical Practice* (London: Free Association Books, 1986).

can society than to the village of metaphor and fable. A diabolic, rather than an angelic, trick has transformed the wholesome Bedford Falls of the Golden Age, of good-neighborliness, of loving one's fellow as oneself, into New York, Los Angeles, or Washington.

In the daydreamed fragment Bedford Falls assumes the aspect (and the defects) of a contemporary metropolis, with vulgar and violent bars, excessive neon on the streets, "men-only" clubs with their signs announcing girls, and gambling houses. It is a civilization ruled by the wicked loan shark Potter—a civilization marked by violence (Potter), pain (the desperate pharmacist), and loneliness (the solitary Donna Reed), resembling the real model of American society. The dream reveals actual society. In order to provide a distorted picture of Bedford Falls, Capra introduces the realism of the society in which he lives, unconsciously judging that society and destroying the American myth. And the appalled eye of James Stewart, dilated by a wide-angle shot, suddenly catapulted into a horror film, legitimizes this translation into a parallel dimension.

Even in this fable *par excellence,* this masterpiece of petit-bourgeois agitation and reassurance, one can glimpse a different image of social history. The film is a kind of summation of Capra's dichotomous attitude to history. One part of him presents and reflects the contemporary environment, often intuitively forecasting future developments, while the other part holds up comfortable, optimistic ideological icons. On one hand the director sweetens and doctors the truth in the name of Christian and lay mercy; but on the other he documents and photographs society in a way that is often merciless.

from *It's A Wonderful Life*

CHAPTER 2

THE DARK SIDE OF THE AMERICAN DREAM
THE EARLY CAPRA, 1928-1934

Particularly Capra's early works—the films made from the time he joined Columbia Pictures until he won the Academy Award, from *That Certain Thing* to *It Happened One Night*—cast doubts on the customary evaluation of the director and throw new light on his subsequent works.

I shall proceed synchronically as well as diachronically, reconstructing the director's career in a manner that will be as chronologically correct as possible without neglecting the free logical associations that the various films suggest. The points identified will in this way afford pretexts for an overall rereading of Capra's cinema.

If one scratches the surface of his films, particularly those made between 1928 and 1934, between the end of the silent films and the enforcement of the Movie Industry Production Code by the Production Code Administration, one finds traces of an American history that has not been sweetened, of a dramatic reality that cannot be resolved in a happy ending. Capra's medicine cannot cure the deep-seated ills of the America of those years; on the contrary, it can be a lethal poison, like the "bitter tea" of General Yen, or the mistaken prescription of the pharmacist, Gower, in *It's a Wonderful Life*. One must read apparently unimportant clues, indicative of personal and social conflicts that are often insoluble. Or that can be solved only by a "miracle" or a fairy tale. It is possible to find elements of individual and collective folly that conflict with the apparently reassuring populist ideology.

One discovers a Capra in which the American Dream borders on an American nightmare. All one has to do is cut the ending, which is almost

always possible in Capra's films, to obtain a different reading. It is sufficient to concentrate attention on the sequences constructed by Capra
to obtain a dramatic climax, the catastrophic penultimate situations
necessary to the solution, to the final *deux ex machina,* whether it be the
angel Clarence or the pilot Lefty. These segments can reveal more about
society, history, and the author's dynamics, than all the rest of the film.

This is where the Capracorn, the easy and rather annoying optimism, fails, and a pessimistic view of life emerges in its place.

I propose to analyze the following indicative themes: the unhappy
ending, the obsession with suicide, the coming catastrophe, family conflicts, social conflicts as American nightmares, models and crises of the
System, and off-key frames.

The Unhappy Ending. Let us start with *The Way of the Strong,* made
in 1928. This is an interesting pastiche of categories—comedy, psychological drama, gangster film—a romance with melodramatic overtones
on the theme of Beauty and the Beast. The story is about a gangster who
is ironically known as Pretty Boy because of his monstrous face, covered
with scars and marked by cruelty. Pretty Boy falls in love with a blind
musician, and this inevitably changes the atmosphere of violence and
harshness that permeates his milieu. One of his friends, a young man
who plays the piano in a saloon, also falls in love with the young woman,
and his character likewise improves. There is also a classic tragic case of
mistaken identity, a play on the theme of misunderstanding and doubles: Pretty Boy is ashamed to allow his hideous face to be touched by
the blind girl, so he "borrows" the face of the young pianist. This gives
rise to the tragic comedy of Pretty Boy who, in the end, sacrifices himself
for the sake of love in favor of the more handsome and younger pianist.

This is a many-faceted film, full of psychological conflict; but the
important thing from our point of view is that it has an unhappy ending.
To save the girl and the young man who loves her, the gangster allows
the police to follow him and, when he realizes that all is lost, turns his

gun on himself as a sign of capitulation and expiation. This is the first suicide in Capra's films: others will follow—real, attempted, or imagined. It provides a dramatic finale, in which the bad guy redeems himself when he discovers goodness and love. It is a bitter form of catharsis. No one cares whether the blind girl and the good-looking pianist live happily ever after. Pretty Boy is dead, making payment for his life as an outlaw, without reassuring the viewer.

The Way of the Strong leaves a strange feeling of discomfort. The gangster, now redeemed, turns the gun on himself after having looked at himself for the last time in the rearview mirror of his car (Pretty Boy hates mirrors). This self-destructive gesture conveys a sensation of anxiety and a lack of identity that concern not only the villain, but the whole of contemporary society. As the villain is the real hero of the film, the viewer is forced to identify with him: he involves the viewer by means of his apparent strength, which turns out to be weakness; and by means of the emotional charge of his desperation. Pretty Boy is the monster in every man, in Capra's average man (Harry Langdon was also called "the Boy" in the film, *Long Pants*). A whole society lurks behind that hideous face, behind the suffering, unhappy mask of the bad/good hero. Like King Kong, Pretty Boy combines infantile desires and bestial wickedness, becoming a monster of the American collective unconscious.

Thus *The Way of the Strong* may be taken as a pretext for reconsidering the convention of the happy ending in Capra's works;[1] and for reading his films, or at least some segments of them, as a "mirror" in the sense given by Lukàcs in his theory of the story; following the title of Eco's book (*On Mirrors*);[2] or in the combination of realistic and fairy-

---

[1] One can argue, of course, that what I call the "unhappy ending" of *The Way of the Strong* is only a tool for providing a happy ending. The same observation can be made for *Ladies of Leisure,* a romantic film where a tragic ending would have been illogical. In my opinion, however, the tragic elements that build up to the happy ending constitute "hard evidence" of a possible tragic ending, which calls for a different interpretation of the whole film.

[2] Umberto Eco, *Sugli specchi*, cit.

tale senses given by Pretty Boy (whose relationship with mirrors is reminiscent of that of the witch in Snow White).

THE UN-HAPPY ENDING

The Obsession with Suicide. Pretty Boy's is the first suicide in Capra's films. It will be followed by others, real and symbolic, present like an obsession, a death wish. The first film of 1930, *Ladies of Leisure,* is an interesting example to investigate in this sense. The film tells the story of a painter, the son of a millionaire, who falls in love with a girl from the lower classes, one of Capra's classic screwball themes. Behind the atmosphere of the bourgeois interior and the bohemian life is a sensation of much deeper malaise, of a social distance between the protagonists that cannot be bridged. In fact, one might say that the film contains two endings. The story finishes with the attempted suicide of Barbara Stanwyck, who jumps into the sea from the deck of a ship at the conclusion of her unhappy love affair, and the film does not appear to permit any other type of logical conclusion. But the "official" ending recovers her from the sea and also recovers its optimism, improbably rescuing the heroine and the whole story. The film ends with Kay (Barbara Stanwyck) stretched out on a bed in an infirmary, surrounded by hopeful, reassuring faces; but one has the sensation that this is a tacked-on, falsely reassuring ending, an afterthought. The real ending is not at all happy; the real ending is death.

In addition to the protagonist of *The Way of the Strong,* one of the heroes of *Dirigible* (1929) tries to kill himself, although this is a sacrifice made to save his travelling companions. General Yen kills himself with "bitter tea," like Pretty Boy redeeming with his death the blood he has shed and perhaps also the passion kindled in the breast of the missionary (Barbara Stanwyck again). His suicide disorients the heroine and destroys the rules of the game and the erotic tension, demonstrating that they are historically outdated.

In *Meet John Doe* (1941), according to the versions of the tormented finale, Long John either commits suicide or attempts to do so. His only solution is to jump off a New York skyscraper when the crowd that had acclaimed him suddenly abandons him. George Bailey in *It's a Wonderful Life* also thinks about killing himself, tempted by the icy water of the river. The water into which Kay Arnold throws herself in *Ladies of Leisure* is also icy. Careful analysis of the sequence of the "attempted" suicide supports the hypothesis that the final happy ending is a juxtaposed, false addition. The suicide jump is followed by a black fade-out. Then, with no music, none of the narrative tricks that usually trigger tears, the director fades in to Kay's frozen feet (the chill of death?). Then the camera makes it clear that Kay has been saved, one sees her fiancé, Bill, whispering reassurances, and another fade-out closes the little finale, added perhaps out of conviction, or perhaps as a compromise.

The climax of *American Madness* (1932) is provided by a gun, when the jealousy has broken down the final resistance of the banker, Thomas Dixon, who had managed to survive the loss of his financial assets. Here, too, is a hint of suicide. A tracking shot stops on the gun, suggesting the idea of death and creating suspense. This time it is not a physical suicide, but a moral and private suicide like that of Lulu Smith in *Forbidden* (1932), who kills and commits suicide metaphorically, refusing to accept the confession of the Governor, Grover. Thus she "annihilates" herself in the crowd, in anonymity. She kills herself by silence and oblivion.

That idea of suicide represents the maximum moment of desperation, the peak of a drama that usually finally wends its way toward a happy ending, producing the comforting, moving "Capra effect," as in *It's a Wonderful Life*, is undeniable. Nevertheless the dark Leitmotiv of a renunciation of life is an important clue to the climate of social despair that pemeated the late twenties and the whole of the thirties.[3]

---

3 See the classic work by Andrew Bergman, *We're in the Money. Depression America and Its Films* (New York: Harper & Row, 1971); see also Peter Roffman and Jim Purdy, *The Hollywood Social*

The Coming Catastrophe. There is a feeling of catastrophe,[4] different from that of McBride, in this period that Capra clearly reflects in both his more dramatic films with a social background, and in his lighter, apparently innocuous comedies. Here one needs to go back to Capra's "partnership" with Harry Langdon in *The Strong Man*, an early film in which the private epic of the "little" hero becomes a communal epic, with the protagonist provoking a catastrophic catharsis, a destruction that purifies. In *The Strong Man* Harry Langdon finds himself involved by chance, and for love, in a battle between Good and Evil, between the townspeople debased by alcohol and the temptation of the saloon, and the moralizers led by the heroine's father, the respectable, conventional "good citizen." Langdon acts as a catalyst, and the ideological battle is transformed into a physical battle, into a comic Western brawl in which the ingenuous hero in the unfamiliar role of the "strong man" ends up destroying the saloon. Good triumphs with a catastrophe, and the Walls of Jericho, the name given to the walls of the awful saloon in the film, come tumbling down at the feet of the procession of reformers marching in front of this haunt of perdition. God—or respectability—makes use of the "boy" Langdon to enforce His will.

In this case the catastrophe is positive and prepares the way for the happy ending. But at other times it is less reassuring and leaves behind a sensation of anguish. An example is the thoughtful, ironic finale of *Rain or Shine*, a film taken from a Broadway comedy, which is still full of apprehension. The circus has burned down. The fire has been caused by sparks created by the personal and social conflicts that have emerged in this microcosm. Now that the fire is over, Smiley, the star of the film, lights a cigar with a smouldering piece of rope, surrounded by a desert of

---

Problem Film. Madness, Despair and Politics from the Depression to the Fifties (Bloomington: Indiana University Press, 1981). See again Jeffrey Richards, "Frank Capra and the Cinema of Populism," in Bill Nichols (ed.), *Movies and Methods* (Berkeley: University of California Press, 1976).

[4] The way I use the word "catastrophe" differs greatly from the way Joseph McBride uses it.

destruction. After this, the circus goes on its way as it has done from time immemorial. But Capra shows us that the way is hard, with a shot of a file of elephants marching through rain and mud.

The destruction of the circus in *Rain or Shine* is inevitably associated with the image of another "circus" that burns in a great purifying bonfire: Florence Fallon's tabernacle-tent in *The Miracle Woman*. The part of society shown in *The Miracle Woman* is dominated by an element of the irrational that perverts any attempt at conciliation. The film is about the psychology of the masses, about the grey mob that follows an opinion leader. This time the charismatic figure is a messianic Barbara Stanwyck whose religious mission is exploited for commercial ends, to such an extent that the church ends up by becoming a "circus." But the heroine, Florence, an anguished mixture of good and evil, finally realizes that she has become the victim of a perverse process, rather like John Doe ten years later. The only road to salvation is expiation and sacrifice; in the film's grand finale Florence's diabolical church is destroyed by a purifying fire, together with the ambitious plans of those who were exploiting her.

It is a hallucinated, even macabre, film—a film with no hope and no utopia, even if Florence ends up in the Salvation Army (a much healthier organization) and there is a chance that a blind man will regain his sight. But the blindness of Mary (*The Strong Man*), of Nora (*The Way of the Strong*), and in this film of John (whose impaired corneas constitute an invitation to consider wider intentions of truth) clash with the blindness of the ignorant masses and with the guilty, devilish blindness of the impresario. "It is not a church," Florence shouts to the faithful who have crucified her father, "it's a collection of hypocrites." The masses, therefore, are ignorant and hypocritical, as they are in *American Madness* and *Meet John Doe*, and Florence is the uncertain saint, the forerunner of the ambiguous Christ of *Meet John Doe*.

The films made by Capra in this period are studded with great and small catastrophes. The great catastrophes are the most shocking events, such as the recurrent fires or the equally frequent accidents: the airship destroyed by a storm in *Dirigible*, the accident involving the airplane that competes with the airship in the same film; the similar air accident in *Flight*, the breakdown in *Submarine*. Then there are the small catastrophes, such as the minor accident (highly significant in terms of the plot) in which George Bailey runs his car into a tree on Christmas Eve, just before his "nightmare." The loss of a wallet can be merely a narrative device, as it is in *That Certain Thing*, but loss of a sum to be paid into the bank can provoke an apparently irreversible catastrophe in *It's a Wonderful Life*. These small and great catastrophes can be caused by a letter (*Dirigible, Forbidden*), or by a pile of telegrams (*Mr. Smith Goes to Washington*), or by simple suggestion or mass hysteria.

Family Conflicts. Catastrophe can also be caused by a party, as an emblematic concentration of family and social dynamics. The party in *Lady for a Day* is a catastrophe because no one comes, and so is the party in *Platinum Blonde,* where too many people come, angering the wealthy, unpleasant Jean Harlow. Even the less catastrophic elements of the light comedies and social dramas show signs of a disaster in course. *Platinum Blonde* and *Forbidden* represent the other face of the Depression, in which the drama is more personal and more private, regardless of whether the solution is comic or tragic. These films show the middle class from the inside, the crises of the old values and the decadence of a world riven by class distinctions and social paranoia. On the one hand there is the cold rejection of the upper classes faced with the new demands of the masses and, on the other, the perplexity of the ruling classes faced with private conflicts.

The conflict, both private and public, emerges more clearly in *Forbidden,* the story of the forbidden love of Adolphe Menjou, torn between a successful career and his emotional inclination. The family situations described by Capra are certainly not soothing. With the declared intent of seeking to resolve and heal their contradictions, Capra is forced to display and underline these contradictions. And what can be more conflictual than the stereotype of the bourgeois family, whose apparently happy, calm surface can conceal chasms of incomprehension and alienation?

Especially the films made by Capra in the period, 1928-1934, but also the subsequent ones, from this particular point of view, display numerous indications of this type of family malaise. This evidence is not sufficient to build a case for a Capra who was anti-institutional, an impossible precursor of Cooper, Laing, and Brown on family neurosis; but it can serve as a reflection of contemporary society. One sees a realistic picture of the "respectable" family that conceals deceit and adultery in *Forbidden,* and the neurosis of wealthy families in *Broadway Bill* and in the later and more famous *You Can't Take It with You.* In *Broadway Bill* a stone is thrown at the window of the dining room where the sacred family is gathered together is a liberating sign of revolt. In *You Can't Take It with You* it is quite clear that the sound of a harmonica is not going to solve the class war, and yet one realizes that both the families, rich and poor, create neuroses. A suggestion of shadow always lurks behind these apparently serene surfaces —as, for example, in the potential adultery of the banker's wife in *American Madness.*

Even the basic values of family solidarity, of inherited affections, are put in a position of crisis. These films show conflicts between the generations, from the one lightly sketched in *That Certain Thing* to the more dramatic and serious situation in *The Young Generation.* In the latter, all the problems of the institution of the family seem to be brought to the surface in the person of the ambitious son, Morris, who abandons the ageing patriarch in the name of personal success and in order to make his way in society.

Social Conflicts. This family malaise, this individual and collective neurosis, conceals a much vaster folly. *American Madness*, a film directed by Capra in 1932, is emblematic of a generalized social malaise and is one of the more dramatic representations of the madness of a society in the early thirties. In spite of Capra's good intentions, and notwithstanding his positive heroes, one detects a pessimistic vision of the masses grumbling and prevailing in the background. In *American Madness* and later in *Meet John Doe*, the mass of humanity is not the good neighbor, the trusting people who abound in the more usual Capra film; here it is an anonymous, savage crowd that can be manipulated and deceived.

In Capra's films, a telephone call, a word, a lie, or the name of a horse are enough to unleash a crowd with no powers of judgment, with no moral sense.

In *American Madness* the crowd acts differently, in a perverse spiral, a manoeuvre that is intended to ruin the positive hero, the good financier played by Walter Huston. The sight of someone withdrawing his savings is enough to start a tragic run on the bank. Insistent long shots of frenzied crowds mimic the chaos of the Wall Street financial crash. Naturally, the positive hero, the good financier who lends money on trust, like Bailey in *It's a Wonderful Life*, wins out in the end. But he is shattered by the brutality of the social situation notwithstanding the happy ending.

Another film whose "slips," unconscious moments of denunciation of society, must be analyzed is *Lady for a Day*. In the innocuous, reassuring form of a farcical fable, this film shows some of the "real" people of the Depression; the gangsters, dropouts, outcasts, corrupted politicians, miserable tramps, of whom the star of the pathetic story, the apple-seller Apple Annie, is one. It is a kind of fantasized realism that suggests parallels between the tramps of this film and those of Cesare Zavattini and Vittorio De Sica in *Miracle in Milan*. Certainly, this film, too, has a touch of consolation. You can be rich, if only for a day, if only in terms of affection. However, the hard fact still remains that there is a disquieting background to this fable: poverty, begging, the need for a moment of illusion, to be happy for just one day, in order to confront continuous despair. Cinderella does not, in fact, become a princess: this is the message transmitted. This is the reality conveyed by Capra's films under the more ingenuous, simple message. Without the fairy tale the Cinderella-figures are destined to return to the ranks, as happened to Stew Smith, John Doe, Mr. Deeds, and to Peter Warne in *It Happened One Night*.

Models and Crises of the System. What model of society was Capra displaying behind the conciliatory and "corporative" mask of his ideology (to borrow a term used by the Fascists during these years) in the flashes in the films of this period? To answer this question one has to go back to a minor, ingenuous film that is almost unknown, but is full of social clues, of slips. This film—*That Certain Thing*—in its own way theorizes on the production methods of capitalism and on its possible contradictions.

The certain thing of the title is the secret of the sandwiches made by the heroine, Molly, who becomes a business woman for love. There are many reasons why this film can be considered a historical source, a document of the twenties. The male lead is a classic figure in the cinema of that period, the son of a millionaire. But the interesting feature is that this magnate's son falls in love with a working-class girl, marries her, and is disinherited by his father for doing so. This clash between the classes shows a picture of America that is certainly simplified to the level of a comic strip, but that is also indicative of a certain social climate. This permits the emergence of sketches of the various class protagonists: the trolley-driver, the poor widow, the jealous neighbors, the little dressmaker; the small, crowded, and noisy world of the working classes, in contrast to the sophisticated airs of the dining rooms of the upper classes.

In addition, the film inserts a dominant motif into the classic theme of poor but beautiful against rich but lacking love: the motif of the emergence of the small entrepreneurs, the legitimation of the self-made man. The self-made man is a woman in this particular case, the resourceful Molly, who, quite by chance, realizes that her sandwiches are good, because they are popular with the workers of the company in which the young ex-millionaire is forced to work because he is penniless. Molly decides to start up a business with her homemade sandwiches and succeeds in competing with the shark who owns the A.B.C. food chain, who just happens to be her millionaire father-in-law, and who is taught a lesson by Molly and her husband.

That Certain Thing and Molly's very simple financial formula ("cut the ham thick") can be taken as an emblem of the neocapitalist system. The managerial approach of the neocapitalist entrepreneur is efficient, ready to invest, nonparasitic. Thus, like Capra's more mature work, this symptomatic small film also contains a picture (a mirror, a reflection) of society, as well as a metaphor of the production methods of that society, an analysis of its ethics and its deepest workings. And the contradictions of this system are shown as they really are, in Capra's films.

One may take as an example the classic theme of the little people, the neighbors—a theme that was very dear to Capra. *That Certain Thing* presents a close-up of the neighbors who are "good" but can also be "bad," as happens when Molly returns disappointed after her husband has been disinherited by his father, and the neighbors become aggressive, vindictive monsters. As always, when the surface is scratched, "good" neighbors are capable of tearing each other apart: *homo homini lupus.* And forget about the "little man"! Here, the man-on-the-street is a repulsive trolley driver who courts Molly boorishly. There is even a touch of black humor, for example in one of the earliest sequences, when an intertitle cynically says: "Maggie Kelly always told her husband where to go. One day he did and left her a widow." So much for the ethics of the petit-bourgeois family.

Off-Key Frames. As we see, Capra's films of 1928-1934 can be read in a way that is anything but reassuring. In spite of the director's theoretical and poetic statements, despite his autobiography, against his will, unexpected surges of the collective unconscious emerge—indications of a reality that cannot be explained by the philosophy of Capracorn. One finds a picture of an America in the throes of a radical transformation, in which the new imagery of the masses clashes against the old conflicts of the social situation. Modernism is achieved, but it creates friction with populism; efficiency and dynamism come into conflict with conservation and nostalgia.

In the words of Robert Sklar, Capra is the myth-maker of this hanging America, but sometimes he is also a potential destroyer of the myth, the ironic observer, the hidden accuser. This X-ray picture of American society captures the dynamics of the transformation: the newspapers, the telephones, the radio, the mass media, all bring civilization, but also corruption.

The same is true of the means of transport that travel through the geography of Capra's films: cars, buses, helicopters, trains, submarines, dirigibles—all populated by contradictory personages. The trains carry wagon-loads of tramps; poverty travels on the buses; when the cars stop, the passengers find a world of hunger. *It Happened One Night* contains three extremely significant examples, three sequences that can be taken as emblematic cases of "Freudian slips". In the first, shortly after Peter Warne happily waves at a train at a level crossing, he discovers that dozens of tramps are crammed onto that train—as if to say, the Depression is passing through. The same sensation is produced in *It's a Wonderful Life* when Gower, the pharmacist, goes into Martini's bar in the "nightmare" sequence. With his emaciated look and his grimy clothes, the chill of the Depression seems to enter for a moment.

In the second sequence, a mother faints on the bus where Ellie and Peter meet. She faints from hunger, at the end of her strength. Once again the subject of food comes up—a subtly obsessive factor in Capra's early films, even when it is made less dramatic by a touch of irony. *That Certain Thing* is definitely a film about food, as is *So This Is Love*, where food is a sign of love, but where there is also a desire for prosperity, a wish to satisfy real and symbolic hungers. The film starts with a very amusing sequence in which the hero associates the image of a roast chicken with the face of the woman he loves and, in the finale, the heroine makes sure that the hero wins a boxing match by stuffing his opponent with goodies until he almost explodes. And aren't Apple Annie's good-luck apple and the legendary doughnut of Gable and Colbert similarly symbols?

The third sequence occurs in the motel, when Ellie tries to take a shower, jumping a long line of disheveled women, and discovers a universe anticipating that of *The Grapes of Wrath*. The reality of the Depression is shown, too, in this fleeting image of poverty, a mixture of anguish and exhilaration. And it is even truer because it is given with a few, almost sublime brushstrokes. Attention must be focused on these semi-unconscious messages when one rereads Capra. In this way one will discover that the defender of faith in the American nation, the director who made the "Why We Fight" series for the U.S. Army, can have some surprises in store. As in the case of *Flight*, a war film about a revolution in Nicaragua. There are two small slips in this simplistic, rhetorical film. In one sequence the soldier Lefty tries not to vomit during the flag-raising ceremony; finally he does vomit, in front of the glorious stars and stripes. While it is meant to be funny, the result is desecrating. Another close-up shows the rough but good-hearted officer, Panama, spitting. Starting from this spit and this vomit, one comes to understand that Capracorn can be extremely bitter. And even lethal, like the potion drunk by General Yen.

AMERICAN FAIRY TALES: CINDERELLA WOMEN AND MEN

My search for the "unhappy ending" begins with the fairy-tale structure of Capra's films and its possible reversal. A line in *Lady for a Day* (a film exemplifying the Cinderella plot) is extremely significant in this connection. At the most dramatic moment of the film (the moment I call the "tragic subending"), when Apple Annie's party remains deserted because the police detain Dude's hangers-on, ruining the whole *mise-en-scène* organized for the old mendicant, Dude decides to tell the chief of police the whole truth. He begins by asking, "Do you believe in fairy tales?" His lieutenant echoes him shortly afterward, when the authorities, mayor and governor included, come on the scene: "Ask them if they believe in fairy tales!" An ellipsis follows. Immediately afterward, the triumphal arrival of the authorities at Apple Annie's party demonstrates that fairy tales can indeed come true. But this solution might also be a daydream, an unlikely happy ending intended to smooth over the non-sustainability of the tragic finale (that is, reality), a convention of the Hays Office even before the Code. Or perhaps it is a moment of ironic self-ridicule aimed at the less artless viewer. "I didn't believe in Santa Claus as a kid," Dude's lieutenant confirms when confronted with the happy ending. Whatever the case, *la nave va ...* the ship goes on, to quote a famous metaphorical film by Fellini, another great story-teller.

Far from expressing contempt, the definition "adult fairy tales" is well suited to Capra's films,[5] which establish precise analogies with the themes, structures, and intentions of traditional fairy tales. For example, many fairy tales begin with the death of a parent ("Snow White," "Cinderella" ...), and the feelings of abandonment and anguish in the orphan are not unlike the sense of instability and bewilderment felt by many of Capra's heroes in similar circumstances. In other instances an elderly

---

5 Raymond Carney, op. cit.; chapter, "The Dream and the World," 61.

parent is ready to yield his or her position to the child should the latter prove worthy ("The Three Feathers" by the Brothers Grimm). The life cycle that requires an old king to pass the sceptre to a new king is present as early as the Commedia Nuova,[6] and it is a very old motif in literature, too (Shakespeare's *Hamlet, Macbeth,* or *King Lear*). In *That Certain Thing* or in *Lady for a Day* the myth is recast in a modern mold.

The characters of fairy tales (archetypal figures that represent children's contradictory tendencies and the members of the family circle) are typical as long as their identification can be more precise: every hero implicitly carries all the previously acknowledged connotations of similar characters in other tales. Capra's heroes, too, exemplify this stylistic convention: Deeds, Smith, Doe (as well as many of their precursors) embody the model of the common man: innocent, idealistic, somewhat credulous, perhaps, and sometimes almost annoyingly good; but also strong-willed, imaginative, tenacious, and stubborn. If fairy tales, respecting the polarization that dominates in the child's mind, distinguish the good hero from the evil villain, Capra is certainly closer to reality when he recognizes the complication of human nature, where good and evil coexist with difficulty.

The Manichaean dualism between good and evil poses the problem of ethics and demands the individual's struggle to resolve it. Bruno Bettelheim[7] underscores in this connection that "in fairy tales, as in life, punishment or the fear of punishment is only a limited deterrent for crime. It is not the fact that virtue triumphs in the end which promotes morality, but the fact that the hero appears more attractive for the child." In fairy tales as in Capra's films, then, evil is as present as is virtue; it is not without charm, and it sometimes momentarily manages to

---

[6] Leland A. Poague, *The Cinema of Frank Capra,* cit., Chapter 2, "Capra and the Comic Tradition," 25.

[7] Bruno Bettelheim, *The Children of the Dream* (New York: Macmillan, 1969). I use here the Italian trans: *Il mondo incantato* (Milan, Feltrinelli, 1986) 12.

triumph (hence the tragic subending): nevertheless the reader or the audience always identifies with the hero, suffering the same trials, triumphing with the hero in the happy ending, and hence fortifying his or her own ethic sense and self-confidence. It should be noted that so-called amoral fairy tales (such as the story of Puss 'n Boots, who attains success by deception; or the cycle of the ruthless and cunning Jack) do not aim at consolidating the distinction between the two moral poles, but animate the hope that even the humble can conquer the world. This, as will be seen, is precisely what happens in *That Certain Thing*, where the newlyweds consolidate their financial empire by deceiving A.B. Charles.

Existential dilemmas and ethical problems are always expressed in a simple, concise manner in fairy tales; the simple, linear plots of Capra's early work seem to pursue the same goal. In other words, the director unconsciously grasps the precious cultural and formative value of the fairy tale: "for the child and for the adult who, like Socrates, knows that there is a child even in the wisest of us, fairy tales reveal truths about humanity and ourselves" (Bettelheim, 67). Traditionally the fairy tale, the parable, or the allegory employ purged or deeply stylized forms of expression; in Capra's works, on the contrary, the "passion for the probable" makes the "miracle" appear perfectly ordinary. Even the moral is incorporated in the scenes created.

The Cinderella story directly or indirectly permeates almost all Capra's films: recalling the bitterness and frustration apparent in his autobiography, where his older brothers, who have already found jobs, deride little Frank, one cannot rule out that a form of unconscious revenge helps determine the director's predilection for this tale. Cinderella is a simple, clear story, in which the humble are exalted and true worth is acknowledged. The child learns that, by relying on his own efforts and remaining faithful to his own personality even at the most difficult moments, he can overcome all adversity and transcend a degraded condition. The myth responds in this way to the need for ethnic, personal, and social redemption that the little "dago" unceasingly seeks to work out in his life and in his career (as his obsessive search for recognition by the audience at large as well as by the official cultural establishment, attests). The years Cinderella spends amidst the cinders teach that no one can escape momentary humiliation: the way of salvation comes not from the outside world, but from the ego. This is the best message of hope for an individualist like Capra.

In the director's predilection for this tale, certainly, there are also deeper roots, which tap not only a personal substratum, but the American collective unconscious as well: his success is attributable, as Carney tells us, to the fact that "he was ... making films that explore certain prototypical imaginative situations that are deeply ingrained in the American experience" (Carney, xi). Indeed, Carney places a great deal of emphasis on the fairy tale in order to insert Capra in an idealistic and "transcendental" current of American culture. Notwithstanding the interest of Carney's analysis, however, it is necessary to underscore Capra's adherence to the contemporary historical context and his acute—albeit perhaps unwitting—awareness of the contradictions of society.

THAT CERTAIN THING OF CAPITALISM

The bridge that connects "visionary imagination" with the concrete perception of factual reality is *That Certain Thing*, whose protagonist, Molly, stands midway between the remote, ingenuous Cinderella and the future, cynical "gold diggers" of 1933.[8] *That Certain Thing* clearly shows that Capra knew how to utilize fairy-tale categories, readapting them to contemporary American society, which is revealed to be an extremely hard and real world in which one must struggle to get ahead. The result is a pleasant, agreeable comedy, rich in sketches, in which

---

[8] See the films *Golddiggers* of 1933, 1935, 1937, and the chapter, "Sex and Personal Relations: Women of the Streets, Women of the World," in Bergman, 49.

unreal content (at least in its fairy-tale base) and realistic style are wedded in a highly personal way.

Molly Kelly is a beautiful cigarette-girl. She comes from a poor but honest family: her mother is a widow, her younger brothers are mischievous, her neighborhood is noisy. There is even an obsessive suitor, a bus driver. But Molly has much higher ambitions: she wants to marry a millionaire. And she succeeds, approaching with a strategem (an exchange of wallets) Andy B. Charles, Junior, the son of sandwich king A.B. Charles, founder of the A.B.C. food chain whose lucky formula for making money is "cut the ham thin." The two are married, but the day after the wedding the old capitalist disinherits his son, guilty of having married a fortune hunter. Molly tries to set her husband free, but the young man will not hear of it. He decides to go to work—a new experience, for him, which results in one disaster after another on the job. But Molly has an idea: bringing lunch to her husband one day, she discovers that the workers like her sandwiches more than those of the A.B.C. restaurants. So, the new entrepreneuse invents "lunch boxes" that sell like hotcakes. She soon becomes a dangerous competitor of the A.B.C. chain, and the old capitalist, not knowing that his son is involved in the small company, tries to buy it out. But the son incites his wife to raise the price. In the end they obtain a fortune and demonstrate to the father-in-law (who promptly forgives them) that they are seasoned business people. When the now-tamed old man asks Mary the secret of her sandwiches, she explains her formula: "cut the ham *thick*."

"That certain thing," in addition to being Molly's secret, is also Capra's. The "thick ham" recipe is that of the director's intermediate and mediating style, which here conveys a synthesis of his craft-oriented ideology and his future thematic plans. The opening sequences, in which Viola Dana bathes her younger brothers, come directly from *Our Gang*, a comedy series in which Capra had had a hand as gag writer; indeed, his experience in this field is evident in many of the comic scenes, including the slapstick incidents à la Mack Sennett with which the film is filled (exchanges of wallets, exchanges of hats, kisses behind the butler's back, water pipes broken by mistake, etc.). But the central core is already the situation comedy, with an eye to the mobile social context, that will be typical of the mature Capra. Certainly Ralph Graves embodies, perhaps better than anyone else, the *nimaime*[9] type outlined above: a young, idle millionaire incapable of living normally (his attempts to "work" like a man are comic) is piloted by a woman both in their marriage (she arranges the incident that makes them meet) and in their social comeback (she takes on the man's role and manages the business). As in the more mature Capra, the neighborhood appears in the foreground—a neighborhood that is "good" (the sequence in which Molly announces her wedding with the millionaire looks like some Italian films of the thirties),[10] but can also be "evil."

The narrative structure is that of the romantic comedy that had characterized the films with Langdon, in which emotion and commotion are admirably fused. Nevertheless there is a fundamental difference in the lack of a "comic persona" who becomes the fulcrum of the action, typifying it. The film exemplifies the plot-oriented comedy originating in the classical Commedia Nuova. Its comicality is a heterogeneous blend of old tricks and new discoveries. The opening scene, as mentioned above, carries the mark of *Our Gang*: as Molly bathes her younger brothers the water overflows from the tub and drips to the floor below, where a woman scolds her little dog caught near the puddle. There are also more biting lines, reminiscent of the pungent humor of Sennett. The initial intertitle, it will be recalled, tells that Molly's mother "always

[9] "Nimaime" is a Japanese word used in Japanese theater to define a weak though seductive type of man, as opposed to the "tateyaku" (the strong but solitary, samurai type).

[10] See especially *La segretaria privata* (The Private Secretary), by Goffredo Alessandrini (1931), in which the actress Marisa Merlini sings a very popular song in the middle of the street (Oh, come sono felice..."), in order to tell everyone of her happiness.(The film is based on a German model).

told her husband where to go"; to the bus driver who tells her, "I'm crazy about you," Molly scornfully replies, "Well, when I go crazy too, we'll get married." Last but not least, another caption regarding the young Andy warns that "he loved his father so dearly he was always drinking to his health." The final scene is typical of the comedy of errors, with identities masked and revealed only when the deception is successful. But the main structure remains that of the situation comedy, with precise references to a credible, if amusing, social reality. Capra combines the classical narrative structures of the comedy with a sometimes merciless snapshot of twenties society: on one hand he resorts to the archetypes of the obstacle-parent (a well known Shakespearean device) and of Oedipal liberation; on the other he builds a genuine analysis of the "capitalistic mode of production" around the metaphor of the lunch boxes. This mixture of fairy-tale stereotype and symbolic representation of class conflicts will give rise a few years later to the "screwball comedy".

In *That Certain Thing* the hero and the heroine are worlds apart, both from the economic and from the social viewpoint: one is rich, the other poor (in *Platinum Blonde* and *It Happened One Night* the inversion of roles will not affect the course of the film); one is used to living in luxury and enjoying the family assets, the other is compelled to deal with a thousand difficulties from which she dreams of escaping by marrying a millionaire. Cinderella is a cigarette-girl, and her Prince Charming is not an aristocrat at all, but the son of a capitalist. The third protagonist, the tyrant-father, in keeping with the canons of classical comedy is the old king who wishes to leave his kingdom (the restaurant chain) to his legitimate heir, Andy, on the sole condition the latter demonstrate that he is worthy to receive it. Andy, in short, will not be able simply to exploit his father's hard work, but will have to toil personally in order to merit that which one would think was rightfully his. Initially the young man does not seem very interested in his future: indeed he is the typical spoiled brat, given to alcohol and entertainment. His hasty marriage to Molly appears as a whim, and his father impedes the couple's happiness, convinced that the girl is a social climber. The "good father" symbolically becomes a step-father (Andy is no longer his son), just as in the tale of Cinderella the "good mother" (the real mother) dies, surrendering her place to the step-mother. Had this not happened, had the parent not advanced apparently "cruel" claims, the young man would have lacked a sufficient stimulus to break away from the cosy family nest and seek his own identity elsewhere. To develop to the utmost his own personality he must fight for noble causes (Andy loves Molly and prefers to live with her in poverty rather than to return alone to his father) and work hard (even from a humble material it is possible to draw things of great value if one just knows how). As Bettelheim points out, "Cinderella guides the child from the most serious disappointments ... toward the development of autonomy, activity, and a positive personal identity" (Bettelheim, 265).[11] This is a message that can be put to work by the director to comfort the audience during the dark years of the Depression and to convince it to endure and to work actively and optimistically during the years of the New Deal.

THE END OF THE DREAM

But the optimism crumbles in the more subtle folds of Capra's cinema; even the traditional fairy-tale structure is disseminated with mines ready to explode if one can just find the fuse. In every fairy tale there is a moment of return to reality (in Cinderella it is midnight, when the carriage turns back into a pumpkin), an inverse transformation, a coming to accounts with the real whence one set out. In all the magical transformations worked by imagination there is an intrinsic risk—the risk of losing contact with common reality (understood as the experience of the sensible shared by all people) and of making the fantasies of an

---

[11] See also Christian Viviani, *Frank Capra* (Paris: Editions des Quatre Vents, 1988), chapter 6: "Cendrillon, la presse et la banque;" 41.

alternative reality a refuge to which to escape, in the belief that, once created, they can last forever. Capra knows that dreams die at dawn, and even if they come true for an instant, they cannot last. Thus in his films there is a moment in which the world created by imagination, the world of art or of the fairy tale—in short, the world alternative to the real— seems destined to crumble and overwhelm the protagonists, as solid and attractive as it might have seemed earlier. In *That Certain Thing* this crumbling coincides with the the elderly A.B. Charles's repudiation of Andy after the latter's marriage with the presumed gold digger: the father-son conflict is also a generational conflict; a conflict of classes, ideals, and ideologies.

At first, the young couple seems to yield to the new situation that has been created: reality seems tougher than had been foreseen, resisting every attempt at transformation through the power of imagination on Molly's part. One morning the girl wakes up, literally and figuratively, to discover that her husband has been disinherited by his father: in an instant the world of which she has dreamed, and which had momentarily coincided with the real world, crumbles. Tailors and creditors "dismantle" this fantasy piece by piece, taking away not only the concrete objects that comprise it, but (what is even more painful) also the illusions that surround it. Her rejection of all forms of social convention and family ties, and her search for psychological independence had been the premises for the (re)creation of a new identity; for they had provided the possibility to start all over again, as when one arrives in a new city and invents a new life (Deeds and Smith are two characters whose personality is restructured by others when they move from the country to the city). But Capra reminds us that this new image is fictitious, it is built on a void, so that what makes it possible is also what condemns it to collapse. The dream (which is also the American Dream of socioeconomic escalation) becomes a nightmare: the nightmare of failure, public scandal, and humiliation, in which the American ego is laid bare in all its fragility and insecurity.

Molly returns home passing beneath the eyes of her neighbors as in a trance, as a sleepwalker: and those who had once acclaimed and envied her now are ready to laugh at her humiliation, their faces distorted almost as though to indicate their mental distortion. The "good" neighbors have become aggressive, vindictive monsters.

This is one of the "clue" sequences of which I spoke. This "off-key" sequence, this mini-chapter narrated in the dark tones of tragedy, casts a different light on all the light comedy thus far woven with the thread of the goings-on between Cinderella and her Prince Charming (which will pick up again for the obvious happy ending).

As I said, the "good neighborhood" is suddenly transformed into a nightmare space populated by aweful people (especially the bus driver, Molly's revolting suitor); the reassuring apartment house becomes a theater of shame, a labyrinth of laborious stairs. Even the shooting style changes, turning the commonplace sets of Columbia into an expressionist symbolic architecture full of strong light-shadow contrasts. It is the negative apex of the film, the tragic subending that would correspond better to the climate of the time (the year is 1928: the Wall Street Crash is just around the corner). "Convention" wins out, however, and the Hollywood formula commands a return to optimism, a final respite after anxiety and anguish. But the anxiety and the anguish remain fundamental, both narratively, because they emotionally prepare the effect of the positive resolution, and ideologically, because they leave indelible traces of a social critique.

In *That Certain Thing* the protagonist, finding herself once more in a frustrating situation, again resorts to imagination, but no longer in the escapist form of reverie. Molly carefully observes what is around her, she sees how reality is made, and she sets out to improve her own condition: imagination has become a modern business spirit. The success of her lunch boxes, moreover, is due to a slice of ham cut more thickly—a concrete response to the needs (the hunger) of others. Capra here does not conceive an isolated and misanthropic individual; the little man (or woman) is truly a "social animal," made to live with others and (at least ideally) for others. *That Certain Thing* can thus be divided into two sections: two-thirds of the film are taken up by the dream and by the nightmare, the last third by the capitalistic happy ending. These are two stylistic worlds, two narrative systems, and two versions of life that will often return in Frank Capra's oeuvre.

THE FETISHISM OF GOODS

Raymond Carney insists heavily on Molly's (and hence, Capra's) capacity for imagination and play. For instance (and here I follow Carney's thesis), as I said, the film opens with the sketch of Molly bathing her brothers, making a commonplace activity into a moment of play and thus expressing imaginative energies which, too powerful and rich to remain trapped in the dullness of everyday life, confer meaning even on gestures that would otherwise be devoid of it, transforming them into entertainment. Imaginative activity and play are closely connected from the earliest phases of childhood development, and they must be assessed in a dynamic pespective of maturation of the individual personality in its conscious and unconscious aspects as well as in its social interrelations.

Play in Capra's films is a powerful instrument of maturation and adaptation, an expression of the passage from the isolation of the unconscious to the social fulfillment of the ego. As early as the Langdon films —where the protagonist is represented as a grown-up child—many scenes end in play: witness the bicycle courtship of the vamp Bebe Blair in the early *Long Pants* (1927), where the protagonist succeeds in feeling big and charming. In many scenes of the "Wings Trilogy," Graves and Holt, who are friends and rivals, sublimate in more or less playful physical struggles the competition they experience in their career and in love; Stew Smith, who plays games on the mosaic floor of the Schuyler home, destroys and re-creates the marble-like coldness at his pleasure, making it a unique and personal, rather than a social and oppressive, space. In *You Can't Take It with You*, the members of the Vanderhof family pursue a broad range of fanciful activities (from dance to the accordion) allowing each one to live an existential space of his/her own in the comprehensible chaos of interpersonal relations. Play and fantasy become tools of survival that allow those who use them to overcome the frustrations originating in the gradual assimilation of the rules and regulations of their environment.

Another index of Molly's power of imagination is her capacity for dreaming, understood both as daydreaming and more generally as the desire for a different life. The dream appears in an ambivalent way: it is an effective way of escaping a disappointing and painful reality, but it is also the focal point of the young woman's vital and highly mobile energies.

The romantic dream, the gaze out the window (perhaps to the stars, as in *Ladies of Leisure*), the vision (even the hallucinatory vision of non-existence in *It's a Wonderful Life*) are not to be seen as merely escapist forms, but as special instruments for enriching everyday life: often, however, they are just landing-places after a difficult journey. Molly dreams of "bumping into a millionaire," and this is, literally, what happens to her (as in a fairy tale). By a series of subterfuges, Molly manages to get herself invited to a dance by Andy: it is then that her play capacity takes on a new meaning and becomes skill in acting—that is, in playing a part, literally and metaphorically putting on the clothes of another, borrowed from the character. The young woman does not receive her dress for the ball by magic; she creates it herself, imaginatively combining clothes and accessories obtained from her neighbors. Fantasy is her fairy-godmother. The costume becomes a central element in this play of deceits, as it automatically brings a new identity that is "worn" over an authentic one. This new identity can conceal the wearer (as in *Lady for a Day* or *The Miracle Woman*), or it can seem truer than the true one— or actually the only true one—in a deceptive maneuver of self-persuasion (as in the case of Molly). The choice of the clothing implies the immediate creation of a particular style and identity: in Capra's films, often "we are what we wear," because "costuming is never a neutral event."[12]

When Molly goes down into the courtyard where Andy is waiting for her, "she makes a scene," playing the part of the lady. She has determined to show everyone what she really is, but the effect is the opposite: her gestures and mimicry appear affected and markedly theatrical, and are so low that they seem unnatual (that is, not in conformity with the young woman's true identity). Her performance is clearly a "play within the play." The proof will come in the following scene: Molly does not lose her shoe in a romantic midnight escape, but takes it off because it is too tight. When Molly presents herself to Andy dressed to kill and receives his compliments ("You look marvelous!") she laughs them off with a modest "Oh, it's just a little costume I threw together." Molly is obviously "showing off" to Andy and to the neighborhood: the courtyard becomes a stage, and the windows from which the curious and envious neighbors cast sidelong glances are theater boxes from which the spectators observe the world (the one created precisely by this "theatrical" spectacle).

Carney's observations are certainly pertinent here. Nonetheless, I wonder if once again Capra cannot be read in a much more transgressive manner. For instance, this continuous "camouflaging" of Caprian characters may be seen not so much as playing, but as the incarnation of a "fetish," in the Marxian sense defined in the first chapter of the first book

---

12 Carney, 67. The author puts particular emphasis on the "social performances" in Capra (see "The Pal Is the Thing," 137).

of *Capital*[13]—in the sense, that is, of the "character masks" or roles that social subjects "play" in spite of themselves, reflecting a complex substratum of social contracts and economic laws (goods-money-goods). One is reminded of Renoir's *La régle du jeu* (*jeu* = "play" as well as "game"), in which this interpretation is essential. Reading *That Certain Thing* from this point of view, one finds an extremely interesting metaphor of the capitalist "mode of production" that analyzes its economic and class dynamics and at the same time implicitly contains its critique. An involuntary critique, obviously: Capra's intentions are elsewhere. But it is not the director's intentions that one is bringing to trial here. Molly can become the symbol of the "ethic of capitalism" described by Max Weber and Werner Sombart in their essay on the spirit of Calvinism. Cinderella is no longer an outsider: her spirit of initiative, the fact that she does not grow rich "by marrying money" but through hard work, in the end makes her worthy of a parallel social ascent (achieved by means of her reconciliation with her father-in-law). Molly and Andy deceive the old A.B.C., making him think he is "earning a bundle" (Andy drags the dirty laundry bag before him, feigning that it is full of receipts) and concealing the young woman's true identity from him (A.B.C. goes to her with the intention of acquiring the secret of her sandwiches, without knowing she is his daughter-on-law). For the young people, however, trickery is the only way to prove their own worth and hence the independence gained, so that they can justly be integrated in the established system. Impressed by their commercial skill, the father gives them his blessing, leaving one with the certainty that the two new entrepreneurs will be allowed to enjoy the prerogatives of the dominant class, reconfirming the status quo.

Capra certainly does not aim at major social upheavals. He supports middle-class values (choosing, with rare exceptions, to place his stories

---

[13] Cf. Karl Marx, *Capital. A Critique of Political Economy* (New York: The Modern Library, 1906), chapter 1, vol.1.

in average-to-poor settings), and even when he seems to attack the powerful in a more direct way, he never threatens their authority (the exception is offered by politicians and shysters). At the most, he expresses the wish that they will demonstrate a certain attention, availability, and kindness toward the less fortunate (as in *Lady for a Day*, where even the city authorities—the mayor, the police chief, and the governor—worry about the happiness of a mendicant). Social ascent, surely, but not revolution. The American Dream, but not the destruction of the system. And yet, if one reads Capra in a less commonplace way, even the ideological-political happy ending (and not just that of the plot) is called into question.

It is true that, in *That Certain Thing*, everything falls into place thanks to the "imaginative" mobility of the resilient Molly; and it is true that the old capital of A.B.C. is wedded in the end to the youthful spirit of initiative of neocapitalism. But it is also true that Capra, in spite of himself, brings to light the perverse mechanisms (based on falsehood) of that matrimony. As he has shown the methods of the old system, based on exploitation and speculation, so he reveals the new methods (intelligent, but also sly) based on serialization and the law of the market, aggressive initiative and independence bordering on piracy. Cinderella or gold digger? Inside the lunch boxes of this delicious but ambiguous neocapitalist is an assortment of the fetishes (in both the psychoanalytical and in the Marxian sense) of the Depression. Which explodes in the next fairy tale, *Lady for a Day*.

LADY FOR A DAY AND THE DEPRESSION

Apple Annie is a an elderly vagrant who survives selling apples in Times Square. But Apple Annie has a secret: with her savings she is putting her daughter Louise through a Spanish boarding school. In her correspondence with her daughter (written on the letterhead stationery of a hotel passed to her by the doorman, a friend of Annie's) she has constructed a character: that of Mrs. E. Worthington Manville. The daughter's letters reach her at the hotel, thanks to the good-natured doorman. One fine day she receives a letter in which Louise announces her engagement to the son of a Spanish nobleman and her intention to come to New York to meet Annie before the wedding. Annie feels lost: Louise will discover everything. At this point Annie's friend and patron saint, Dave the Dude, comes on the scene (he protects her partly for superstitious reasons, convinced that her apples bring him luck). Dave is a good gangster, the head of a gang that lives mainly off gambling dens. Together with his woman, Missouri Martin, he organizes the grand *mise-en-scène*: he dresses and makes up the aged mendicant, who miraculously becomes a beautiful old lady, and he transforms his boys and their molls into a crowd of beau-monde savvies. This way Annie is "Lady for a Day." But she lacks a husband. The role will be played by a likeable old rogue who lives on pool games but has a sharp tongue, Judge Blake.

Everything is ready. But with the arrival of Louise, her fiancé, and her father-in-law, Count Romero, things start to go wrong and the misunderstandings multiply. Events precipitate when the police become suspicious of the disappearance of two journalists (Dave has "kidnapped" them so they will not reveal the trick) and haul Dave in. Dave tells the whole story, which from the police station reaches the chief of police, the mayor, and the governor—until everybody, touched, ends up at Apple Annie's party. Everything works out, in the end. Annie has her big day, the daughter goes back for her happy future. From tomorrow on, the old lady will go back to being a vagrant.

"Lady for a Day," writes Donald C. Willis, "is the most perfect film by Capra I have ever seen" (138). Apple Annie manages to give credibility to this world of lovable dropouts, freaks, and outlaws, establishing a delicate balance between poetic realism and fairy tale. The film documents a contradictory America whose conflicts can be solved only "for a day," as in this case, or "for an hour," in Capra's "corny" films. *Lady for a*

Day, which is based on Damon Runyon's *Madame La Gimp,* also conveys Capra's love for metamorphoses. A vagrant is transformed into a lady by a gangster, in order that she might give a dignified welcome to her daughter and the family of her future father-in-law: the whole city participates in the magic, which dissolves, however, in the presence of the newlyweds. On the set it is Capra who with makeup, costumes, and lights transforms the elderly actress (May Robson) into a star with a beauty all her own; moreover he mixes real vagrants (such as Shorty, with whom he could had sold newspapers as a child) with professional actors.

Like Molly, Annie must suddenly live out the dream that thus far had been only a personal reverie; and she must learn to play a new role (the capacity for playing returns) linked to a new costume. The viewer, however, always remains well aware of the precariousness of this pretense: and it is precisely the fragility of the subject in transformation that involves one emotionally, above all toward the end when a thousand contingencies threaten to shatter the illusion. Annie too, in short, discovers the dark side of the dream and has experience of the feelings of humiliation and shame that always remain a familiar threat. This magical metamorphosis, furthermore, not only confuses its spectators (on the set and in the house): Annie herself has trouble recognizing herself in her new guise. An exemplary scene appears in the 1961 remake, *Pocketful of Miracles.* Transformed into Mrs. E. Worthington, the woman looks at herself in the mirror and exclaims, "I don't know who that's in there," and, as though looking for a firm handle in her past, takes up her old basket and mumbles: "Apples?"

If the movement common to *That Certain Thing* and *Lady for a Day* is divided into three parts—dream, nightmare, and reawakening—the nightmare (that is, the threat to the destabilized ego) is certainly the most sincere, meaningful, and cumbersome. It is true of *Lady for a Day* that the historical period in which the film was made counts a great deal: in 1933 the Cinderella myth became also the Jeffersonian dream of an egalitarian society. At the dawning of the New Deal, with the Depression still under way, even the mere illusion of social success and well-being is a motive of hope for viewers who, despite the low credibility of the story, passionately identify with Annie (what is more, she sells apples—a symbol of Depression poverty). Nevertheless, Capra seems to want to underscore that the consolation is short-lived (it can last only a day). The vertical section-view of society is particularly disquieting, and "real" characters (gangsters, politicians, mendicants, fake noblemen) appear on the scene. The indispensable realistic style appears here in the journalistic attention to the reconstruction of a complex and dangerous social milieu.

ELEMENTS OF *MISE EN SCÈNE*

Sometimes Capra's camera is animated by a touch of wisdom, as in a sequence of *Lady for a Day*, when Apple Annie writes a letter to her daughter. After shooting a medium shot of the woman putting on a classical music record, the camera follows her as she moves in the room through a frontal shot, with a cut exactly when she reaches for a bottle of alcohol; now the camera is shooting sideways, while still following the old lady as she moves along the music, in medium shot when she lets got the bottle, dismisses the cat and looks at the picture of her daughter. In the next shot she is framed in long shot, as she leans toward the coffee table again, another cut and she is seated in medium shot. In a point of view of the woman, the spectator is shown Louise's picture. Annie turns the picture toward the camera, takes a sip of the alcohol, turns the picture again and starts writing to her daughter. She stops to make up the name of someone attending the nonexistent ball about which she is writing to the daughter (in this films she looks for a name in some old book, in the remake the book is transformed into Vanity Fair, the mark of the changing times...), takes another sip; then the camera frames a window from the bottom up, from which we have only time to catch a glimpse of a human figure. The next shot shows a sitting woman from the bottom up, looking from downward, sadly, almost at the camera, saying softly over the music: "I am crazy for this music." A shot of a man and a woman sitting in front of a window follows, as well as one of a close up of a young woman with eyeglasses seated next to a banister at the bottom of a stairwell and framed from the upside down and a close up of a man with a sad face and the frozen gaze, framed sideways. The editing returns to Annie who in a monologue reads again the letter she just wrote and ends it by drinking again. Finally a dissolve to black.

It is impossible not to be subdued by this surreal and uncanny sequence which must be read as a tiny, delicious cameo in which a smile gets mixed up with dramatic emotions and in which allucination almost burst on the scene: it comes from the woman looking at the camera and commenting on Annie's music and it comes from the music itself, at one time diegetic and extradiegetic, as it is first herad coming from the record player, but it then becomes the score of the film.

Whose are those faces we see in the sequence? They won't be back throughout the whole story, not even in the remake, they are not Annie's friends, the dispossessed she is acquainted with and who will be close to her to try and make her happy; they simply cease to exist after the moment in which they are listening to Annie's music. The only exit as phantomatic figures, frozen in the Crisis Capra is letting you foresee.

THE BEAST AND THE BEAUTY: *THE WAY OF THE STRONG*

Speaking of gangsters, no discussion of the unhappy ending would be complete without the melodramatic (sub)ending of *The Way of the Strong*. Nora, the beautiful blind violinist, is the only person who is not afraid of "Pretty Boy," who cannot be frightened by the criminal's horrid face. Pretty Boy is moved. He hires Nora in his club, which is suddenly transformed by the sound of her violin. On her arrival, the long beard and rings under the eyes of Dan, the pianist, who abandons alcohol for music and in his turn falls in love with Nora, disappear. But Williams' bootlegger competitor, "Tiger" Louie, kidnaps Nora and blackmails Pretty Boy, obtaining considerable privileges in the clandestine alcohol trade. Pretty Boy and Dan burst into Tiger Louie's headquarters and save the girl, causing a gang war. Amidst the chaos the police arrive and, as the sirens scream, Pretty Boy sacrifices himself: he entrusts Nora to the more worthy Dan and draws the police down his own trail, ending his flight by killing himself to avoid capture.

This is one of Capra's hidden masterpieces, combining melodrama, comedy, fairy tale, film noir, and classical tragedy. I have already dealt with this outstanding "multigenre," made up of transplants and convergences. I might add that with this film Capra tests and refines genres, codes, styles, and languages, to such a degree that it becomes a container of numerous ideas taken up later by Capra himself and by much of Hollywood. An underrated—or unseen—film, *The Way of the Strong* merits a different critical destiny. "Personally I think it is better than a grade B western, but nothing to rave about" (*Exhibitors Herald*, 12 January 1929): Capra himself claims that he had too little experience to manage the story's delicate psychological conflicts successfully. And yet it is a film that, when seen again today, has the fascination of an unfinished puzzle.

The outer structure is that of a gangster film (sudden bursts of machine-gun fire, burning cars, intertitles like "The machine-gun that will stop Pretty Boy has yet to be made"); but it is continuously counterpointed by the tones of the humorous comedy: "Our story"—so the film opens—"begins in a quiet street on an ordinary day" (at that moment, the detail of a wheel braking and a machine-gun shooting immediately create the sense of irony and self-irony that will inspire the film). The intertitles, as in *That Certain Thing*, serve as decisive elements of counterpoint.

The inner structure is that of the melodrama: the impossible love between the horrid gangster, to whom the script devotes a sympathetic psychological portrait (Pretty Boy breaking a mirror because he hates his face), and the beautiful blind street musician, whose destiny it is to fall in love with the handsome young pianist. A melodrama tinged with fable, combining *My Fair Lady* (for two months Pretty Boy goes to hear the blind girl play on the streetcorner, then hires her for his club) and *Beauty and the Beast*. Precisely with the rough delicacy of King Kong, the ogre Pretty Boy measures his ring for Nora on the barrel of his gun.

The infrastructure is a grotesque, bitter comedy à la Cyrano. As in Cyrano (likewise deformed of face and gentle of spirit), and in the classical tragic comedy, one finds the machinery of misunderstandings and situations. For instance Pretty Boy, when Nora wants to "see" his face with her hands, calls the delicate-featured pianist to stand in for him (it will be the beginning of Nora's falling in love with the wrong person).

The joining and disjoining of these three levels (the superstructure, the structure, and the infrastructure) create the dynamic tension of the film, which lives, however, above all on its internal grammar. For the first time, in fact, Capra discovers the camera, fully exploiting the possibilities of motion-picture language, with a mature awareness of on-set editing and of the best use of the various shots; with a richness of detail and a perfection of cutting on movement that are rare for a silent film. In short, a *mélo* that is also a mélange of styles, genres, and syntaxes; a total experimentation of the Hollywood machine carried out with the humility of the "human comedy." But what is perhaps most important is this entrance into the fairy tale of tragedy: the Beast kills himself for the Beauty. Pretty Boy, looking in the rearview mirror for his followers and his face, turns his pistol on himself, like the "villain" doctor in the finale of *Spellbound* by Hitchcock. It is the first suicide "obsession" in Capra's cinema.

from *Lady for A Day*

Chapter 3

Bitter Tea and the "Code"

Notwithstanding its fairy-tale structure, Capra's cinematographic output during the Depression years seems to follow the general trend toward social realism, focusing attention on the everyday environments, characters, situations, and events of contemporary America. Yet in the same year as *American Madness* the director also shot *The Bitter Tea of General Yen*, apparently the most atypical of his films, together with that other exception which is *Lost Horizon*. In *Bitter Tea* Megan Davis arrives in Shanghai to marry the Protestant missionary Bob Strike, but the wedding is interrupted by a series of circumstances. As she is going to the mission, Megan runs into Yen, a Chinese general notorious as a bloodthirsty bandit, whose car runs over her rickshaw driver. Back at the mission she does not find her fiancé, who arrives later and excitedly involves Megan in the rescue of a group of children trapped in an orphanage at Chapei, in the midst of the warring factions. Bob and Megan obtain a safe-conduct pass from General Yen but are soon separated, the woman falling into the hands of Yen.

At this moment a subtle game begins between victim and persecutor. Yen keeps Megan in his summer palace and woos her in a refined manner. Megan is repelled but also attracted by his enigmatic personality, at once subtle and violent. Around Yen are other strange characters: Jones, a Westerner in the service of the Chinese; and Captain Li and Yen's mistress Mah Li, who betray him. When Megan helps Mah Li escape, Yen loses his temper but is unable to kill Megan: he in turn is attracted by her. In the end, just when the woman is ready to yield, Yen drinks a cup of poisoned tea with hieratic calm.

Capra's romances are the object of an analysis by Leland Poague, who, quoting Northop Frye, notes how comedy and romance are part of the same mythic circle—a major literary structure—that moves "from death to rebirth, from decadence to renewal, from winter to spring, and from darkness to light." "Comedy and romance," Poague writes, "are closely connected. They not only share a common mythological heritage, they tend to develop a common ground that emphasizes triumph and renewal" (63). Even in the tragic ending of the film, therefore, one can see a sort of resurrection, a mutation: the redemption and sacrifice of Yen, the elevation of the relationship between Yen and Megan.

Certainly Yen's world is different from the rest of Capra's world. There is room for dreams (as only "the boy" Langdon could have), especially the surrealistic dream of Megan, a nightmare loaded with sexual implications, the oneiric representation of desire. And there develops an atypical story where desire is repressed, as in *Ladies of Leisure* and *Forbidden*, but floods Yen's fantastic residence with vibrations. Yen's "castle," one can say, is the materialization of desire. From this fantastic place beyond reality and the world, gleams of History appear: as at the beginning of the film, when Megan traverses the theater of conflict; or when she watches an execution from a window (a metaphorical window on History from the fortress of fable).

Drawn from the novel of the same name by Grace Zaring Stone, the film turns out to be more a rewrite than an adaptation: the two works are almost independent of one another. In the novel, for instance, Bob and Dr. Strike are two different characters: Strike is a missionary whom Megan admires and a co-protagonist of the story; Bob is her fiancé. In the film the two male heroes are combined to form Bob Strike. Furthermore the novel tells the story from Megan's viewpoint: it is her story, not that of the couple Megan-Yen, as in the film. The novel follows Megan from her childhood, contextualizing the rise of her missionary zeal; in the film this is taken for granted, providing a starting point for the plot. The Megan of the novel is a woman of impulse and enthusiasm: in love with Bob since adolescence, she gladly accepts to marry him and to follow him to China, embracing the cause to which he has devoted himself. Megan chooses to abandon the comfortable life she has known heretofore and to reject the hypocrisy of those around her, even if she does not yet have a clear idea of what awaits her. Her sense of Christian charity, which in the film is genuine, in the novel appears less deeply rooted. Megan in fact sometimes winds up using other characters as tools through which to express herself and fulfill her religious aspirations. As Donald C. Willis points out, in the film the young woman seems to be sincerely interested in Mah-Li's destiny, whereas the Mah-Li of the novel "is just a 'cause' for Megan—women's rights. She [Megan] doesn't just vaguely want to help Mah-Li—she wants to free her from her concubinage" (96). Capra and Edward Paramore[1] effectively avoid investigating the missionary's motivations, emphasizing instead the love story between Megan and Yen. The relationship between the two begins as an impersonal meeting and clashing of two completely different socio-cultural worlds (East and West), but is soon transformed into a love story that at several points challenges the dictates the Hays Code is building up.

During the twenties the Hays Office, in fact, drew up a list of off-limits subjects and risky themes. "The list of no's included, in this order: blasphemy, nudity, illicit drug traffic, sexual perversion, prostitution, sexual relations between whites and blacks (miscegenation), venereal diseases, child-delivery, children's sexual organs, ridicule of the clergy, intentional offense of any nation, race, or creed."[2] It would not be appropriate, here, to go into the details of the Code, to which a broad debate has been devoted for many years. The reader is referred in this connection to the book and conference of the Venice Biennale, *Alle porte di Hays*,[3] and especially to the contributions of the Italian scholar Giulia-

---

[1] Edward Paramore wrote the screenplay, from a novel by Grace Zaring Stone.

[2] Giuliana Muscio, "Riformate Frankenstein! Da Hays al caso Paramount," in V. Zagarrio, ed. *Studi americani*, 33.

[3] Giuliana Muscio, ed. *Prima dei codici 2. Alle porte di Hays / Before the Codes 2. The Gateway to Hays* (Venice: Edizioni Biennale/Fabbri, 1991), published on the occasion of the 48th Venice

na Muscio and the American Lea Jacobs: "Cinema seemed trapped between two irreconcilable images/projections of its own power to be: that of an 'instructive' representation of the world, ethically stable and responding to middle-class ideology (... constituted both by conservative WASPs and by reformers inclined toward a paternalistic vision of the masses ...) and that which emerged from cinema as the melting-pot of popular culture, a synthesis of different spectator experiences (circus, variety, magic lantern, fairs, etc.)."[4]

During the confused years of the Depression, Hollywood was no longer just the gilded world of entertainment; it also became the forge of the myths and ideals that would fill the vacuum left by the collapse of the old Puritan values. The responsibility and power of filmmakers was at a peak. "Hollywood took center stage in the culture and consciousness of the United States.... Not only did the movies amuse and entertain the nation through its most severe economic and social disorder, holding it together by their capacity to create unifying myths and dreams, but movie culture in the 1930s became a dominant culture for many Americans, providing new values and social ideals to replace shattered old traditions."[5]

I have dwelled at length on how Capra was the first more or less consciously to question the archetypal myths of the great American homeland, even when he seemed to want to uphold them unconditionally. A similar ideological movement takes place in *The Bitter Tea of General Yen*, where the dramas contextualized thus far in real worlds are transferred to an unusual, artificial, and exotic environment. In the attempt to win a much longed-for Academy Award, Capra produced a work that in many ways is exemplary of the climate of recurrent mediations that distinguished the "pre-code" American movie industry. In other words, the film tries to satisfy both the director's own needs (the

---

Film Festival. Lea Jacobs, "An American Tragedy: A Comparison of Film and Literary Censorship," in G. Muscio, *Prima dei codici 2*, 145.

[4] Muscio, "Riformate Frankenstein, 34.

[5] Sklar, *Movie-Made America*, 161.

subject and the formal care were to be guarantees of success), and those of the average audience (the main subject is based on one of the "don'ts" of the Hays Office, miscegenation) and the Puritan reformers (the love between Megan and Yen is not fulfilled). Capra's hostility towards any kind of control over his work, though, inevitably led to a refusal of all forms of censorship—even the blandest. "As I am more or less the creator, I must oppose all forms of censorship.... I don't want anyone to tell me what I have to do, what kind of movie I have to make, what subject I have to deal with."[6]

The director, in fact, performed a form of self-censorship dictated more by faithfulness to and respect of certain values than by the necessity to adhere to the bigoted and malleable rules of the movie industry. Honesty and coherence toward oneself and others were constant reference points for Capra. Thus, notwithstanding the economic and artistic fiasco of the film, he could claim with conviction: "I loved the film myself. It had a quality of honesty between these people. This warlord said all the things that needed to be said about miscegenation, about racism. And I felt that this woman had depth enough to understand.... This reformation of this character from a bigot to one who could love anybody—why, this was an honest story to me" (Schickel, 70).

Potentially, the film had good possibilities to succeed: the choice of actors and technicians was an excellent guarantee. Megan is played by Barbara Stanwyck, Yen has the impenetrable countenance of the Swedish actor Nils Asther; Mr. Jones is portrayed by Walter Connolly, a fine Broadway character actor. The technicians are Capra's best and most faithful co-workers. Joseph Walker resorts to short lenses and lateral lighting to create an almost mystical and mysterious atmosphere in which the truly important things are those that are alluded to and not explicitly shown. Stephen Goosson, who also made the grand sets of *American Madness*, built Yen's palace utilizing architectural solutions

---

[6]Jean Debruge and Robert Wagner, "Cinéma et èvolution sociale," *Positif* 317-318 (July-August 1987): 45.

that are both original (the octagonal window in Megan's bedroom or her tester bed) and meaningful (they underscore the difficulties of a fusion between Megan's world and Yen's). Nevertheless *The Bitter Tea of General Yen* failed, perhaps because it did not meet the audience's needs of stability and security. What one sees on the screen is a painful growth process; it calls into question not just Megan, but all that typically Western culture which she represents and with which the audience identifies.

IRRECONCILABLE TENSIONS: SEXUALITY AND RACISM

On one hand the love scenes (always just hinted at) between Megan and Yen are an offense to the somewhat racist tastes of the Anglo-Saxon spectators, who are not at all interested in following the process of maturation and revision to which the woman is subjected. The popular public, on the other hand, finds nothing that can stimulate it: there are no scenes of sex or violence, and the (at least superficially) optimistic and reassuring aspects that usually seem to characterize Capra's oeuvre are likewise missing. Perhaps this time the director misses the target because, in a certain sense, he is more attentive to his own needs than to those of the audience, to which he usually addresses his work. The creator of popular myths proposes a love story too new and disturbing to be understood and appreciated; furthermore he sets it in an artificial and stylized world, far away from the realistic pictures of "everyday life" to which he had accustomed his public. *The Bitter Tea of General Yen* is his first film set not in America, but in a distant, mysterious, exotic country (in China, first in Shanghai and then in Yen's palace), as though the director wished to raise questions without addressing them too directly to the American people. The Homeland and Western culture are brought into play indirectly, in a less conscious and hence, perhaps, less painful manner. Furthermore, the visual construction is generally closer to the refined direction of Sternberg than to the intermediate style characteristic of Capra. The rarefied, soft, sparkling, and subtly sensual atmosphere on which the film hinges re-creates a world that is distant yet disquieting and cumbersome because of the new perspective with which it compels one to regard life, oneself, and others.

Another interesting change is the construction of Yen, the central character. Capra's typical hero is usually a potentially common man who has succeeded in cultivating simple but deeply human virtues yet is not exempt from weaknesses and imperfections. Yen instead has an unattainable heroic stature: his wisdom, cruelty, courage, and nobility of heart make him unequalled—for better and for worse. The noble Mandarin becomes the term of reference with which one's conscience is compelled to collide. His wisdom and power are backed by thousands of years of history; in comparison, the Puritan ideals of America appear extraordinarily young and fragile. The confrontation between these worlds and these ethics carries an unbearable charge of death. Capra seems always to go out of his way to avoid dramatic finales; yet this film finds its conclusion in Yen's suicide (a suicide elsewhere alluded to, contemplated, or attempted, but never really carried out, with the exception, as I said before, of the finale of *The Way of the Strong*). Both the American gangster and the noble Mandarin—apparently worlds apart in terms of culture and status—share an acute sensibility and profound feelings: both are "warlords," men of rapid and courageous decisions, apparently invincible heroes who yield only to the impossibility of realizing their dream of love. A difference, however, appears in the two finales. Williams's suicide is brief, intense, and violent—a rapid gunshot —and is partly determined by his incapacity to accept himself, his ugliness, and the prospect of a life without love. In Yen's case, in contrast, death is a ritual prepared with care and executed with a slowness that underscores the firmness of the decision. Yen kills himself because he believes Megan has offered herself to him only to keep their agreement: and if the loss of power and prestige had not scratched him, the impossibility to fulfill himself and his feelings fully, make the poisoned tea less bitter, for him, than life. His will to die is not dictated by the sudden desperation of a moment, but paradoxically by an acute awareness of the things for which it is truly worthwhile to live.

As Lealand Poague points out, these apparent exceptions create a product that is faithful to a deeper rule of the director—that is, to express the difficulties inherent to every dream (be it of love, success, or social escalation), particularly when this dream is dreamed at the expense of the normative instances of "real" everyday life. Thus *The Bitter Tea of General Yen* can rightly be defined as "the most hardheadedly realistic of all the Capra romances" (Poague, 138). Admittedly the basis of Caprian romances is the innocent-cynical couple that is followed in its maturation and in the conversion of the cynical partner to the perspectives and ideals of the innocent. But the starting points of the lovers have never been so distant and diverse as in this film. So diffferent are they, that it becomes impossible to reconcile them in a traditional happy ending. Megan and Yen are not just individuals portrayed in their specificity, they are also and above all emblems of traditions, cultures, and worlds lying poles apart. Megan is a young Evangelical missionary who soon reveals a mental rigidity, a subtle racism, and an emotional coldness that seem to contrast with her social role.

Over the course of the film Capra treats the racial problem in a very balanced and sensible way, avoiding with equal skill heavy accusations, false sentimentalisms, or an idealized Christianity. For instance, he actually questions the integrity of the missionary drive, ironically showing the distortions in the personality of those who should be the instruments of conversion. The worst examples of racism, in fact, are presented by a missionary couple, the Jacksons. The small, compact missionary community has come together for the wedding of Megan and Bob: while preparing the arrival of the couple, the director deliberately lingers on characters who do not appear elsewhere in the course of the film. The most disquieting figure is Mrs. Jackson, who begins by referring to the wedding as "the slaughter." The quip is more cold-blooded than she had intended it to be: in the initial sequences the viewer had witnessed the real massacre and carnage that the Chinese population is undergoing at just that time. A few minutes later, while helping Megan to dress for the ceremony, the elderly missionary clearly expresses her opinion regarding those to whom, in theory, she should be of spiritual assistance: "They are all tricky, treacherous and immoral. I can't tell one from the other. They're all Chinamen to me." In addition to the evident contempt that filters through these words, that Mrs. Jackson does not acknowledge that uniqueness of the individual that is a focal point of the Christian creed and, more simply, in the personal faith of the director, is particularly grievous.

The speech made by the bishop—in China for fifty years—seems to be more mature and conscious than Mrs. Jackson's chatter. He makes reference to the difficulties that Megan will have to face, as the missionaries in China are only "a lot of persistent ants trying to move a great mountain." Telling of his experience in Mongolia, however, the bishop observes that the interest shown by the bandits in his narrative of the crucifixion of Christ was dictated not by a divine enlightenment, but by the possibility to employ a new kind of torture. The conclusion contains a note of discouragement: "That, my friend, is China." The bishop is aware of the inadequacy of his own efforts in converting the Chinese population to the message of the Gospel but, while he is more sensitive and compassionate than Mrs. Jackson, he too errs in believing the Chinese insufficiently human, thus neglecting many aspects of a civilization that is thousands of years old and, in other respects, surprisingly refined.

Religion is one of the subjects that the censorship said were to be treated with extreme caution. But the director, who had already made *The Miracle Woman*, skillfully managed to overcome this obstacle: observing the Orient from the point of view of Evangelical missionaries, Capra underscored the inadequacy of a judgment imbued with preconceptions and egocentrism.

Bob and Megan are apparently immune to the un-Christian sense of superiority shared by the other missionaries: their faith and convictions seem genuine and deep. Megan symbolizes the old America that is threatened by the Depression. The first thing one learns is that she comes from an old New England family: her personal roots are the European, Puritan roots of the great American homeland. That Capra officially supported the traditional Puritan ideals is known; yet this film harbors a lingering doubt that those ideals, pure as they are, may not be sufficient. America must renew and question itself: it must acknowledge its errors and its shortcomings, its false impulses and its bigoted preconceptions. As a rule, the world of cinema clearly represented the ambivalent tensions that spread among the people at this time: conservative moralism and the desire for new and somewhat sinful stimuli were appeased and satisfied by the system of self-censorship. Capra, however, was not a man of easy compromises; he believed in the necessity of an authentic clarity and a freedom that could be attained only through self-knowledge and self-improvement. Notwithstanding the director's declared intentions, one feels, therefore, that *The Bitter Tea of General Yen* is not so much a film about racism as an invitation to reconsider the most deeply rooted convictions that each individual has—be they religious, ethical, or racial. It is a destabilizing work that questions characters and values, myths and traditions.

In a world already severely tried by the reality of the Depression, Capra did not propose a story respecting the traditional clichés and conveying reassurance and support, but the emblem of a mutation. The film is a continuous metamorphosis—painful and laborious, but necessary in order to arrive at the unforeseeable final equilibrium. It is a stylistic metamorphosis (the initial sequences are of an almost documentary realism that is soon abandoned in favor of an unusual and refined formalism), an ideological metamorphosis (the racism of the missionaries leaves room for a more authentic comprehension of Chinese culture, promoting a new spirit of brotherhood between West and East) and a personal metamorphosis (Megan manages to defeat her racism and to acknowledge the importance of her love for Yen). Nothing is sacred, but what is worse, not all of what is questioned is reconfirmed as valid. In other words, the viewer sets off down a path that may turn out to be more dangerous than he or she thought.

Megan, I was saying, is so attached to her values and ideals as to not accept that they be altered, even when it becomes patently necessary to do so. Her first encounter with Yen, for instance, determines the image she will have of him as a ruthless and cynical man, even if the General lets an acute awareness of the uneasiness and suffering of his people filter through his tough assertions. Yen is just a pragmatic man capable of recognizing the ultimate truth of things without false preconceptions. His very cynicism "is not simply an emotional pose, as is usually the case in Capra, but rather an almost stoical philosophy" (Poague, 138).

The crude reality of the war, the betrayal by Mah-Li and the captain of the guard, as the story is told will create a picture confirming the General's apparently ruthless convictions. Unlike Megan, Yen from the very beginning acknowledges the importance of his feelings and chooses to follow them, although he is aware of the risks involved. The noble Mandarin has an extraordinary ethical sensibility: the ruthless, cruel man is the only one inclined to lay his own life on the line in order to follow his dream of love and to remain faithful to himself. The movement of the film is thus to mitigate Megan's rigid, bigoted zeal as well as Yen's cold cynicism, making love the moderating agent.

One of the dictates of the Hays Office banned interracial relations from the screen: the love between the young missionary and the Chinese general, then, is impossible from the outset and, in a certain sense, is not "concretely" fulfilled. Yet its presence is strong, and its subtle charm is undeniable. As a rule, Capra avoided explicit love scenes: he preferred instead to proceed by hints and allusions, certainly not as a consequence of censorship, but as a form of personal reserve. The director's eroticism is always symbolic, indirect, sublimated, or metaphoric: even in *The Bitter Tea of General Yen* the love between Megan and Yen is imbued with a refined sensuality that continuously oozes from the screen and is at the very basis of Megan's love dilemma.

Separated from Bob during a bombardment, the missionary winds up at Yen's palace and finds herself compelled to deal not only with the General, but also with a culture that she will come truly to know only now. To her mental rigidity corresponds an emotional stiffness and a latent form of sexual frigidity: engaged to a young man whom she has not seen for three years, she is moved not by passion, but by the desire to share the ideals in which he believes. Yen is the opposite of Bob: he not only appears cynical and cruel where the other is generous and compassionate, but he hints at his capacity to love a woman with a passion that the American probably has never known. His sensual side is presented subtly and allusively: his conduct, gestures, and words are always controlled, but numerous clues suggest the potentials of his feelings.

In order to save the orphans, Bob asks Yen for a safe-conduct pass, but the General, after listening to his story, writes in ideograms, "This fool prefers civil war to the loving arms of his bride. General Nobody." The powerful warlord in this short sentence gives perfect expression to an unexpected hierarchy of values: it is clear that he would have privileged the woman he loved. A few shots later Megan and the viewers are allowed to witness the attention that Mah-Li lavishes on her lord: it is not the comradely relationship of Bob and Megan, but a true attitude of submission and total devotion. Yen is in a position of clear superiority and, as one will see later, can even dispose of Mah-Li's life.

Yen's palace also helps point out his love of luxury, refinement, and beauty. The General's home is the manifestation of his soul and his contradictions, and its thousand rooms are the thousand shades of his personality. On one hand there are the large spaces, the sensual softness of the silks, the richness of the furnishings, the refinement of his taste; on the other, the armed guards at every door and the executions of prisoners in the courtyard beneath the window of Megan's room. A prisoner in that palace, the missionary tries to intervene in rhythms and traditions consolidated over the centuries, but her actions are insignificant or even destructive. Megan, who slowly discovers that she is attracted to Yen, is at the center of a sexual and personal, racial and cultural choice, which calls up many taboos deeply rooted in the American collective imagination. The extent of her deepest desires is visualized on the screen in the long sequence of a dream: another rare narrative expedient in the films of Capra, who prefers to maintain strong ties with the real even where he touches the strings of fable.

DREAM AND DEATH

After refusing the General's invitation to dinner once again, Megan falls asleep on the balcony of her room: a fade-out leads immediately into the young woman's nightmare. A grotesque face, pointed ears, protruding teeth, and slicked-down hair create the Hollywood version of the lascivious and dangerous Oriental: nevertheless a superimpression of the General in uniform renders explicit the subconscious connection made by Megan. The vague, distorted shots increase the sense of clearly sexual terror. Pure, physical passion—usually banned from the life of the missionary—is experienced for the first time following the encounter with an Oriental; that is, a man from a distant and unknown world, charming but precisely for this reason to be feared, whose potentials may be uncontrollable.

The demoniacal creature—in a black Chinese costume—leans slowly over its prey and is about to devour it when an unknown masked savior arrives. The lone hero has snow-white Western clothes and defends himself from the Oriental's shifty dagger by flooring him with a right to the jaw. The stereotypes seem perfectly respected: the Oriental is the bad guy who threatens the white virgin, while the cowboy defends her chastity. The clash between the two men not only respects the American collective imagination, it manages also to avoid an explicit scene of sex and violence. According to the Hays Code, evil could be shown only when it was a necessary premise for the triumph of good— and the disturbing but sensual atmosphere of the attempted violence seems to be redeemed in the rescue scene. Surprisingly, however, Capra breaks all the rules. Megan embraces her hero and lifts his mask to discover ... the face of Yen (this time human and without distortions): instead of rejecting him, as she does in reality, Megan, languid, smiling, and yielding, pulls him to her, and the two slip arm-in-arm onto the bed. The background of the image begins to spin dizzyingly, making it impossible to see more but also evoking the overwhelming rapture of love.

Even while avoiding showing the sequel of the dream, Capra at this point has made Megan's deepest thoughts and feelings clear. Equally evident are the contradictions implicit in the young woman's desire—a slave to her own prejudices, she can love Yen only by separating his Western gallantry from his Oriental barbarity. The missionary's error, in fact, is to associate the positive qualities with the West and the negative ones with the East; instead "there's no 'Western' gallantry that can be easily separated from Yen's 'Oriental' callousness, because Yen's real sensitivity and civility are a matter of his Easternness" (Poague, 143-4). Megan—and with her the viewer—must learn that good is never completely on one side, and that it is not a prerogative of Western civilization which, without a plausible reason, believes itself to be the repository of truth. The General is not a slave to prejudice and indeed ironizes on the racial difference that separates him from Megan. He has a self-control that is unequalled by any other character: to the insults of Megan, who calls him "yellow swine," he responds with an elegant bow: "you'll always find me your most humble servant." His world view is pragmatic and disenchanted, but for just this reason it is the most balanced and wisest. In the sequence that follows Megan's dream, the General and the girl together admire the beauty of the garden and the splendor of the moon. Yen tries to make the missionary understand the richness of Oriental culture, of its poetry, its music, its painting. The discourse is suffused with a subtle sensuality, and the celebration of refined pleasures ends with an affirmation loaded with allusions: "There has never been a people more purely artists, and therefore more purely lovers than the Chinese." The capacity to create beauty artificially, both in a cultural experience and in an architectural realization (such as the Palace garden) is associated with a greater aesthetic and emotional sensitivity and with a particularly rich and varied inner world.

The ideal connection of sensuality and sexuality to an artificial atmosphere is a fairly recurrent stylistic device in pre-Code cinema, thanks to the distancing effect it succeeds in producing while allowing pregnant allusions: in Capra's work, instead, the use of landscapes and falsely natural backgrounds has richer connotations. In *The Bitter Tea of General Yen* Capra faces for the first time the aesthetic experience of a refined, formal style. The set design, lighting, and costumes are particularly refined and well done; the construction shooting privileges long shots with a surprising iconographic effect, because they aim at portraying not only the character, but the entire world in which he moves. The result of this original stylistic stamp is not uniform, and if certain sequences are pure poetry (Yen's suicide is memorable, for instance), others are prosaic (i.e., the long sequence of the card game).

    Bitter Tea, at any rate, is never reduced to an empty aesthetic perfection, because its own artificiality subtends a very profound argument: "Yen and Megan are typical Capra characters, ovecoming romantic barriers and finding personal fulfillment in the emotional integrity of love freely given, but the physical world has no place for their kind of emotional honesty. There is no Mandrake Falls to retreat to, and the only way Yen can preserve their love is to take it beyond the physical universe, into the providential realm of artifice and immortality" (Poague, 152). The careful construction of the images, the refined exotic setting, the splendor unfolded in Yen's palace are utilized to create the impression of an unusually cruel world, where the hard reality of war and betrayal keep the lovers from crowning their dream of love. Yen's universe does not allow the intervention of divine providence or of a higher justice: that which in other films was present as a threat—suicide—here is completely realized. Yen's death is more epic than that of Pretty Boy. In that tragic finale the anti-hero yields to a destiny that is stronger to his will: although he sacrifices all he possesses—even his life—he discovers that he is unable to make his hopes come true. Yen instead dies by choice: he is perfectly in tune to the ruthless and fascinating world in which he moves, and with which he is deeply familiar. His suicide reconfirms the love he feels for Megan: if on one hand his death impedes the union with the white missionary, on the other hand it makes that love stronger than if it had actually been consummated.

Yen triumphs in death because he is finally able to complete the process of maturation that has begun in Megan. The missionary only now understands that it is not her ideals in themselves that are wrong, but the obsessive desire to carry them out indiscriminately, without taking account of circumstances and of people: in this sense *The Bitter Tea of General Yen* is a great romance. But it is also a "clue" to the non-reformable and "non reconcilable" (to borrow Straub's title) world of Capra's cinema. Not coincidentally, the moment his cinema is set free from the conventions of the classical comedy, the tragic finale explodes, reaching its highest expression in the suicide of the hero, the death of the protagonist (because General Yen, like Pretty Boy in *The Way of the Strong*, is the true protagonist of the story).

Two sequences, especially (two "off-key" sequences), cast new light on the film and on the rest of Capra's production: Megan's dream and Yen's death. The General's suicide calls to mind, by means of obvious associations, the many attempted, imagined, or successfully executed suicides in Capra's films: Dixon's suicide attempt in *American Madness* (the hand that reaches for the gun at the moment of deepest desperation); the suicide attempt of Senator Paine in *Mr. Smith Goes to Washington* (here too there is a false happy ending in the unhappy ending, as the logical conclusion of the plot is the villain's real suicide); the pondered suicide of *Meet John Doe* (which in one of the five versions of the film becomes real); the dreamed suicide of Bailey in *It's a Wonderful Life*; the "moral" suicide of Lulu Smith in the bitter (certainly unhappy) ending of *Forbidden*; the real suicide, with which I shall deal shortly, of Kay Arnold in *Ladies of Leisure* (following which she is fished up physically—from the sea—and metaphorically—from the script—by the forced artificial conclusion).

But Megan's dream is also disquieting: it recalls Bailey's famous nightmare in *It's a Wonderful Life*. In this case too, the camera technique and the staging change (especially noteworthy is the use of deforming wide-angle lenses). In *It's a Wonderful Life* a surrealistic world suddenly opens up in the midst of Capra's "intermediate" directing style. Here in

Bitter Tea an expressionistic shadow extends over the Sternberg-like sweetened surface. The dream necessitates a different reading of Capra's later work, too, not only because of the author's "visionary" quality, somewhat overemphasized by Carney, but because of the anxiety, the psychoanalytic tension (or more precisely, psycho-social: it is determined by a collective unconscious) that creates and seriously undermines the fragile architectures of the fable, its reassuring optimism, and its "Polyanna" aesthetic.

As the dream paves the way for the nightmare, so the American Dream is about to change into an American Nightmare (like Megan's, run through with sexual tremors and erotic repressions), bringing the sense of catastrophe out of the personal and collective unconscious and making it conscious.

from *Forbidden*

Chapter 4

The Coming Catastrophe

Materials Are Symbolic Catastrophes

There's a background of impending catastrophe that stands behind Capra's films and Hollywood cinema in general during the thirties. The catastrophe is to be understood also in an etymological sense, as a great change, a sudden swerving and upsetting of consciences, ideologies, and values. Catastrophe in Capra's films takes place on the material level (as in the "Wings" Trilogy or *Rain or Shine*), on the individual level (the various fallen women) and on the collective or mass level (from *American Madness* to *It's a Wonderful Life*, the films based on the idea of a bankruptcy that is as ethical as it is financial). This is the context of American society and of the Studio system between 1928 and 1934; and it seems to coincide with the more typical "social" and "realistic" output of Warner Bros. "Hollywood moviemakers perpetrated one of the most remarkable challenges to traditional values in the history of mass commercial entertainment. The movies called into question sexual propriety, social decorum, and the institutions of law and order."[1] The films about fallen women also treat of the Depression, in terms less of socio-economic problems than of ethical concerns, notwithstanding the clear references to the social context. Here the happy ending is possible only by resorting to artificial and improbable narrative expedients; and this in turn points out how difficult it is to stick to the old values, given the harshness of the new times.

The middle-class woman, who learned to appreciate luxury and adventure after the industrial revolution, with the advent of the Depression completely lost her newly acquired economic independence and found

---

[1] Sklar, *Movie-Made America*, 175.

herself relegated to the margins of society. She often tried to struggle to overcome her difficulties, but she discovered herself to be a "slave not merely of individual men but of a male society, with no options for individual action or genuine freedom" (Bergman, 50). The collapse of the morality of the individual is tightly bound up with social change: in a world regulated by the tough rules of supply and demand, women soon discover that the only thing they have to sell is their body; and "the films supplement the image of the ... individual ... [as] an innocent victim entrapped by a broken-down society with few options open to him or her" (25). The fallen woman appears on the screen as an unwed mother, as the mistress of a married man, or as a prostitute. Her moral decline in any case must be rationalized as a last resource, and it is never a positive or successful experience as much as it is a tragic degradation that is its own severe punishment. Female sexuality is a fascinating but dangerous new element for Capra, and the fallen women cycle subtends a serious paradox. In the society afflicted by the Depression, a woman's body often becomes her only negotiable merchandise and sin her only means of survival, a state of affairs that provokes the condemnation of respectable Puritan society. The sinful women live torn by the remorse and unhappiness deriving from the seriousness of their faults, so that traditional values can be implicitly upheld and reconfirmed.

As Andrew Bergman recalls, "women were left with a choice which was no choice at all: find an abiding love or perish. Movie heroines were in a really untenable position: the opportunities for sexual expression, identity, and a sense of individual potential were closed off" (54-5). Initially the heroine resolves her economic predicament by falling into sin (it is what Florence Fallon, too, would do in *The Miracle Woman*), but later on, repenting thanks to the man she loves, she will be able to erase that sin. Traditional ethical values are reaffirmed in an unstable and precarious manner notwithstanding the original intentions. The films, in fact, often end with an unplausible message: that love is more important than wealth, and at any rate can easily be achieved within the established system. Capra embraces this narrative scheme only in part: at the end of his films the two lovers may be united and happy (as occurs in *Ladies of Leisure* and *The Miracle Woman*), yet the viewer is left to wonder what their concrete destiny in everyday life will be.

Ladies of Leisure, The Miracle Woman, and *Forbidden,* all three interpreted by Barbara Stanwyck, take up certain stylistic devices of the fallen women cycle but contain an unusual element: that mixture of sincere admiration and fear with which Capra often approached the mysterious female universe. His heroines are apparently cynical young women who can redeem (and regenerate) themselves only thanks to the love of a man pure of heart. "In effect this, as a life-enhancing force and symbol of the future of the country, symbolized in a highly pertinent way the uncertainties the director had himself just gone through" (Michel Cieutat, 37). The innocent/cynic couples embody opposite and complementary principles: fertility and sterility, life and death, natural and artificial, personal and impersonal. However they are already non-Manichaean heroes, characters who embody both good and evil and who precede the numerous "imperfect protagonists" of the more mature films (Deeds, Smith, Doe, and Bailey are idealists with moments of more or less serious weakness). Thus the innocent, sometimes, can prove to be cynical and the cynic can rediscover his or her lost innocence. The moral path of *The Miracle Woman* can actually be summed up in a movement from innocent to cynic to innocent. Repentance and "conversion" are fundamental experiences because they give the sinner the right to a second chance: for Capra everyone must have the possiblility to improve himself and his own living conditions, even if in reality this is a difficult task. Lea Jacobs[2] points out that the theme of redemption is so meaningful in Capra's oeuvre that it becomes part of his "authoriality" even if one adds the requests of the Hays Office to the director's genuine interest.

---

[2]Lea Jacobs, "Capra and the code," paper for the Ancona conference: "Accadde una notte: la Columbia e Frank Capra, 1928-1934," organized on the occasion of the International Film Retrospective, December 1989.

LADIES OF LEISURE, OR THE FALLEN WOMEN

Jerry Strong, the son of a wealthy contractor, prefers art to business and devotes himself to painting in a New York attic. His girlfriend, Claire, organizes a party in the studio, which ends in an orgy. Jerry, nauseated, goes for a spin in the car. He meets Kay Arnold, who also has left a party and is somehow different from the superficial girls to whom Jerry is accustomed. The young painter hires her as a model for a painting on which he is working, called *Hope*. The long sittings bring out Kay's true character, which is quite different from that of the *femme fatale* which she would like to project. Meanwhile, the love stories grow more complicated: Kay rejects Bill, Jerry's friend, who courts her assiduously and then, disillusioned, consoles himself with Kay's friend; and she also refuses Jerry's advances, thinking that love with a millionaire's son is impracticable. So, she embarks for Cuba with Bill, finally accepting his advances. But she can't deal with this situation, either: in her desperation she jumps overboard. When she awakes Jerry is by her bedside.

Sacrifice and difference. It seems like the dress rehearsal for *Forbidden*, a film of a couple of years later. Here, too, Barbara Stanwyck sacrifices herself and renounces love because of the class difference of which she is conscious. Here, too, the family is a monolithic institution that makes those who attempt to break the rules and mar its compactness and continuity feel guilty. In this case the transgression is not the more scabrous adultery, but the mixing of social conditions that had been a theme of *That Certain Thing*. As in the earlier comedy, this dramatic love story contains the surly and intolerant millionaire father-in-law and the parallel description of diverse social environments (the furnished room shared by Kay and her friend as opposed to Jerry's house): it thus contains the typical Capra motif of the opposition of social states and values (money vs. love, power vs. happiness, etc.). But there is more— hence the similarity of tone with the later film—namely, the sense of the "forbidden," the tangibility of repressed desire. Exemplary in this connection is the long sequence in which Kay passes the night at Jerry's home, for whom she has accepted to model: a long series of details (the closeup of the handle of the door that Kay wishes would open, Kay biting the blanket, a play of reflections through the window panes) and an extenuation of the film's pace, charge the atmosphere with a subtle eroticism. This is certainly not the facile and intermediate Capra; it is the more refined and vaguely perverse director of *Bitter Tea,* conditioned perhaps by the falsely ingenuous presence of Stanwyck, who tinges with pessimism and cynicism a theatrical piece (the film also begins on a Broadway location) suspended between social comedy and psychological drama.

The film resorts to certain stereotypes of the twenties: Jerry's father is the gruff millionaire father-in-law of *That Certain Thing,* whereas Jerry—wealthy, young, and estranged (his discomfort in the world of the leisure class is clear from the very beginning)—is an all-too-familiar character in thirties popular iconography. As in *That Certain Thing* and *Platinum Blonde,* the comic obstacle is a rigidly structured family; and the transgression will lie precisely in the attempt to unite different and irreconcilable social groups (upper class and lower class). In this romantic drama Capra avoids connecting the possible economic troubles to Kay's profession, as if the broader social context were removed the moment the two lovers meet. Kay and Jerry live a private dimension suspended between heaven and earth (most of the scenes are shot in the painter's attic): friends and relatives may make occasional appearances, but they are unable to establish convincing and profound relations with the two protagonists.

The true narrative invention of *Ladies of Leisure* consists in the particular characterization of the two lovers and in the choice of the main theme: "a cynical heroine converted to hopeful idealism by a vulnerable yet idealistic hero" (Maland, 53). Jerry—created by the screenwriter Jo Swerling—reproposes Langdon's naïvité, adding a new idealism: he is the first of Capra's heroes visibly out of place in the world to which he belongs by right. In his person dreams, aspirations, and reality seem to collide. Refusing to work with his father, the young man chooses art: he wants to express the inexpressible (Hope) and to transfer to the canvas the spiritual. Whereas Stew Smith, in *Platinum Blonde*, is obviously gifted with an imaginative mobility combined with shrewdness, Jerry seems to dream dreams that cannot come true in any way—on the canvas, or in life. Incapable of establishing responsible, fruitful, and creative relations with people, he frequently repudiates others, taking his distance. "Jerry's capacity not only socially to turn his back on society ... but ... to leave it imaginatively behind ... is to establish imaginative limits to its power, to recognize the artificiality and arbitrariness of its roles, structures, and institutions" (Carney, 159). The meditative moments are visually characterized by movements that isolate the hero (he leaves the party and goes out on the balcony) or by gazes directed toward the boundless horizon or a starry sky (that is, an unlimited space).

Jerry is an individualistic hero; his dream is not to transform society, but to abandon his environment and escape to Arizona. The purity of his aspirations is joined with a bitterly critical and disillusioned attitude toward the world of the leisure class: the city of the Depression is a hothouse of corruption and malaise. The salvation from the moral plague seems to be escape to a distant world, a mythical Arcadia that will allow the individual to regenerate. The fortuitous encounter with Kay and the slow blossoming of love produce a two-fold change, however. Jerry in fact is now able to give a face to Hope, implicitly addressing an appeal to the apathetic and disheartened and thus reestablishing a contact with them. But the movement will be slow and difficult, also because, at the outset, Kay is the kind of woman who seems to be least suited to reflecting and embodying the spirituality that Jerry seeks.

The two lovers meet by chance after they have left a party for different reasons; but the differences that separate them are clear from the beginning. The romantic knight ready to rescue the damsel in distress with a gallant "Can I do something for you?" clashes with the disinterested response of the woman-of-the-world: "Yes. Do you have a cigarette?" Kay behaves in a free and easy way (climbing into the car she lets a shoulder strap of her dress slip, commenting, "a little embarrassing"); but while she sleeps on Jerry's shoulder the painter sees in her the incarnation of that spirit which he has long been trying to visualize. In a country lane, in a natural (and hence "fertile," Poague would say) setting, a primitive illumination takes place, a moment of truth and revelation: but the return to the city will coincide with the return of falsehood and the resumption of "social masks" (the reference is again to Marx). During the long sittings, Jerry tries to rediscover that dreamy and pure expression, but Kay seems to have gone back to being the cynical and disinterested girl of before, the social climber who has long given up her dreams in order to satisfy more concrete needs. Each time Kay resists the attempt to change, placing the accent instead on her physicality, sensuality, and seductiveness.

The film repeatedly underscores Stanwyck's beauty while she undresses to take a bath or go to bed, or as she shows her legs while crossing them. The viewer thus ends up feeling that she is much more real, much more woman than Jerry, who attempts to "dematerialize" her in an abstract allegory, would have her be. Nevertheless, the voyeuristic tendency toward Kay is always restrained: backlighting, high-tone illumination, and close-ups with a diffuse light and filters, accord her a halo of luminous spirituality, making her marvelous and ethereal. The confusion regarding her identity in the end is perceived by the heroine herself, who is no longer certain which role reflects her more faithfully: party girl or model of Hope. Furthermore even the role of model is not devoid of ambiguity: for her it is a new possibility to seduce, whereas Jerry, who wants to see her true face, paradoxically imposes a mask on her during the sittings. Accustomed to struggling to survive and to counting on her own charm, Kay gradually relinquishes her *femme fatale* poses to leave room for those pure, deep feelings that dwell behind the mask of cynicism and irony. Her redemption as a woman and as a human being is possible only because she has the courage to abandon all calculated defenses, yielding to love, which will heal her of her sins.

One evening Kay dreamily listens to the description that Jerry gives of Arizona, where "even the stars seem closer. You can almost reach up and grasp the big dipper by the handle." The painter presents to her as concrete—albeit in the imaginary and idealized description—an alternative world, a mythic and happy homeland, an America where it is not necessary to struggle with the difficulties of survival. The girl ends up believing in that dream, making it her own; the next day, proposing the longed-for escape, she will exclaim: "You can paint. I can work. We don't need money." Thus Kay metaphorically becomes a symbol of the embittered, disillusioned, cynical, and desperate America of the Depression, which Capra attempts to cure precisely by restoring hope and optimism.

After posing all night long, in the morning Kay fixes breakfast for Jerry: the picture is that of a tranquil middle-class interior; the woman moves awkwardly in her new role as housewife, but appears happy next to the man she loves. And yet this solution is too simple: something, in effect, is wrong. After professing years of calculated, rational control of her emotions (separating sex from love), Kay now discovers a new fragility connected with the overwhelming intensity of her feelings (looking at Jerry she breaks out crying), in addition to the fear that her love will not be returned. Believing her romantic dream to be unrealizable, Kay gives up on Jerry and runs away with Bill—a likeable dandy, but all things considered mediocre in his faults. Bergman acutely observes that in the films of the fallen women cycle the journey toward the warm climates of the South is a recurrent metaphor of the moral fall of the protagonist, almost a symbolic descent into hell: "What is significant is how accurately it demonstrates the really iron-clad moralism of the fallen women pictures. The heavy symbolism of deflowered women sweating off their sins in fetid tropics gave away Hollywood's assumptions about sin and its price" (Bergman, 54).

Kay at this point has lost her chameleon capacities, and the sincerity of her feelings rules out every kind of pose (thus far her specialty). Finally gaining a true identity, giving in to her own nature, seem to condemn her: after gazing at the stars Kay attempts to take her own life by jumping overboard. This subending is particularly bitter: in fact, she who symbolizes hope carries out the act which is the very negation of hope, leaving the viewer with a sharp sense of discomfort. Furthermore the camera lingers with an unusual insistence on Stanwyck's frozen feet, slowly tracking up her whole body to her face: Capra not only seems to want to exasperate suspense, but also to make his happy ending less liberatory and easy. What one sees on the screen is no longer the charming and lively girl of the beginning, but a pale, immobile body apparently devoid of signs of life.

Once purified, Kay will be saved to be rejoined to Jerry. The sinner has expiated her faults, and the new baptism (water and fire are meaningful elements in Capra's semantics) apparently gives her the right to a regenerated, redeemed, and happy life. In the last scene, Jerry comforts her with an affectionate "there's nothing to worry about." Nonetheless the problems of the two lovers are just beginning, as it has already been revealed (during the course of this film and in earlier films such as *Platinum Blonde*) that survival in contemporary society is anything but simple once one steps outside conventional roles. What is more, the fusion of the classes continues to be unproposable (nothing suggests that Jerry's father will lovingly welcome the couple). Thus is delineated Capra's ambivalent ethic, "which consists at once in launching an accusation against the world of respectability and in having but one goal: to be part of it."[3]

INDIVIDUAL AND MASS CATASTROPHES: *THE MIRACLE WOMAN*

The moral redemption of an initially cynical heroine thanks to the love of a man and a finale of subtle uneasiness about the destiny of the "happily" united couple also characterize *The Miracle Woman*, where "Capra and Stanwyck feel the need to root their female protagonist more firmly in the surrounding social context" (C. Viviani and Y. Tobin, 21). It is the story of Florence "Faith" Fallon. The daughter of a Protestant minister, the young woman lays the responsibility for the death of her father on the community of the faithful, who forced him to relinquish his position because of his age and who troubled him by never managing to

---

[3]C. Viviani and Y. Tobin, "Capra et Barbara Stanwyck: eclat et èclatement du mèlo," in *Positif* 317-8 (July-August 1987): 21.

understand his message. Playing on these feelings, Hornsby, an entrepreneur from the big city, convinces Florence to capitalize on her rhetorical gifts and religious knowledge by organizing a mystic center. Florence, mingling business and the Bible, accepts. Hornsby becomes her manager. Florence's new "church" is always full, and the ceremony is staged as a circus act (Florence arrives in a lion cage and launches her mystical message with the charm of a barker).

One day Florence meets John Carson, a blind aviator dissuaded from his intentions of suicide by one of Florence's radio speeches. The encounter makes her understand the power that her imposture has placed in her hands. Florence falls in love with John, but Hornsby does not accept the fact and threatens to unmask Florence. The woman understands that if she does not accept the deal Hornsby proposes (to go to Monte Carlo, pretending to go to the Holy Land) her whole castle will collapse, including her plans for revenge. She decides to beat Hornsby to the draw, and in a dramatic session reveals her sham to the faithful. Her manager tries to stop her, causing a short-circuit that bursts into a fire. Hornsby dies. Florence and John escape toward a happier and truer life.

Religion as spectacle, the church as circus. A hallucinatory and even macabre film, without hope and without a utopia, even if all apparently ends well: Florence winds up in the Salvation Army and there is a possibility that the blind pilot will recover his eyesight. But the blindness of Mary (*The Strong Man*), Nora (*The Way of the Strong*), and here of John—a blindness of the cornea that invites one to think of wider perceptions of truth—clash with the blindness of the ignorant mob and with the guilty and demoniacal blindness of the entrepreneur. "This is not a church," Florence cries to the faithful guilty of having crucified her father, "it is a meeting of hypocrites." The masses are ignorant and hypocritical, as in *American Madness* and *Meet John Doe*. *Against* and not only *for* them, the *marabout* of the day rises up; Florence in this case is the ambiguous saint who anticipates the ambiguous Christ of John Doe.

What is the nature of Capra's relationship with religion? Charles J. Maland underscores its importance.[4] Religion is undoubtably a major issue for Capra, from the cross on the snows of *Dirigible* to the angel of *It's a Wonderful Life*. But his is a popular religion: his moralism and his craving for messages, his ethic of the common people and his naïve faith, count more than any particular dogma. Capra received a Catholic education, and he frequented the Christian Science Church in the mid-thirties. The director's religious sense, therefore, is a hybrid of Catholicism, Protestantism, and personal convictions, summed up in the declaration that "we can all worship in the ecumenical church called Humanism" (Maland, 92). His is not the cold and impersonal religion of the theologists, but a mixture of brotherly love, human warmth, faith, optimism, and idealism. For Capra, the Sermon on the Mount includes all the truly important human and ethical values. In short, his is a "popular religiousness."

Although the profession of pastor was relatively unusual for a woman, in this film, too, the eye of the camera is focused on a contemporary phenomenon, namely, the burgeoning of self-styled Protestant preachers: one can thus speak of critical realism. Yet this is not just the transposition of a fact of chronicle: Capra seems also to want to denounce an America on the skid, disoriented and confused, blind and dull-minded, ready to follow anyone who appears sufficiently self-assured. "Barbara Stanwyck is a character tormented by contradictions,... who symbolically represents an America bound up in the false values of the past (here, her father) and of the present (her impresario) and who ends up breaking these bonds to find happiness in balance" (Viviani and Tobin, 22). After the death of the father, Florence is happy to accept the proposal of the unscrupulous impresario. Left to herself, the heroine survives by selling not her body, but her image and her thorough knowledge of the Bible: she cynically denies Evangelistic ideals and devotes herself to mere exploitation, becoming the *vedette* of a one-woman show.

---

[4]Charles Maland, *Frank Capra*, 64 and Chapter 4, "The Ecumenical Church of Humanism," 89.

Stanwyck proved to be the perfect actress for bringing to the screen a strong and disenchanted woman capable of making her way in a world of false appearances and vile threats, where the crowd foreshadows the ignorant and hypocritical masses of *American Madness* or *Meet John Doe*. Proud and independent, animated above all by the desire to avenge her father, with Hornsby's support Florence becomes an unprincipled opportunist: in a world in which traditional religious and ethical values are shaken to the root, cynicism and shrewdness become the only means of survival. Even a precious gift such as faith becomes merchandise. Religion thus offers an opportunity for grand staging of a colossal turnover. The Temple of Faith in reality is a temple of falsehood, halfway between a circus and a Hollywood Studio, populated by false cripples ready to fake a miracle at the right moment.

Certainly the result of the film makes one's blood run cold, so numerous and so strong are the signs of fire (real and symbolic) and of the uncontrollability of mass society and the culture of entertainment. "We are professionals, not amateurs," says the impresario as the spotlights of the church come on, the band plays, and the lions enter as though awaiting new martyrs. Notwithstanding the apparently reassuring finale, *The Miracle Woman* is an extremely bitter film. Capra in fact presents a society where there is very little room for honest people and the innocent have no guardian angel: if they wish to survive they must resort to the help of a cynical and corrupt shyster to act as their protector. "A criminal society demands that you be criminal, that you must victimize or be victimized" (Roffman and Purdy, 33). Much of the meaning of the film is given precisely by the fact that the viewer is well aware of the sham under way, as he is constantly reminded of the strident contrast between reality and appearance.

THE SPECTACLE OF CATASTROPHE

Spectacle is often an essential element of Capra's films, in addition to being the only reference to the world of show business to which the director belongs. There is never direct reference to film people in his pictures, despite their acute concern for the outside world. Nevertheless they deal with the representation of the world of entertainment: *The Matinee Idol* revolves around a company of strolling players; *Rain or Shine* is tied to the story of a circus in which "the show must go on ... rain or shine." At other times, the world itself or a part of it becomes spectacle (I recall a scene in *Dirigible*, in which the maneuvers of the aerostat are defined by the colonel as "a good show").

Florence's success is that of a Hollywood star, and her temple is not just the circus ring where the lions await the new martyr, but also the majestic set of many thirties musicals: "it is a place created exclusively to generate and sustain glittering, gaudy, crowd-pleasing Hollywood effects" (Carney, 365). The director, however, always tries to avoid the danger of gratuitousness: his stage remains the real world, and the characters must be equally credible. Nevertheless a dilemma that permeates the film, remaining unsolved throughout, is the degree to which Florence believes in the sham she helps create, and the degree to which she is just a puppet to whom a skillful ventriloquist gives voice and movement. The film, moreover, contains a real puppet, Al, a "friend" of John who is always present when the two lovers meet.

Here, for the first time, Capra explores the threats to the individual in mass society. *The Miracle Woman* "is dominated by an irrational component that overwhelms every conciliatory effort of society," and shows a "gray crowd following an opinion leader." Florence Fallon is presented as a character created by the media, who lives in a world "in which there are no realities outside of media events, advertising splashes, public relations blitzes and image-building appearances. Personalities have been replaced by 'personalities'" (Carney, 347). The preacher-lady lives a public life that is a farce orchestrated by Hornsby; but she also has a private life—the romantic scenes with John—in which she goes back to being herself. And this opening will deliver her from the danger of exploitation.

Capra fears mass society precisely because he fears the depersonalization of the individual: "I wanted to put the accent on the person who seemed most important to me, that is to say, the individual, and how one tried to make it conform to death, in the sense wanted by big business, government, advertising, big industry, big 'sex,' big music, and everything that tried to diminish it more and more" (Debruge and Wagner, 42). Radio speeches, a carefully organized advertising campaign, and a sumptuous *mise-en-scène* are the tools that allow Hornsby to manipulate a credulous and hypocritical audience. The message is clear: when people quit thinking, they inevitably cease to exist as autonomous individuals and become a tool of the cunning and the powerful. As Maland writes, "*The Miracle Woman* is notable largely because the conflicts it raises are those which would be repeated and refined in later Capra films." (Maland, 57). The threats to freedom of expression, however, will become increasingly less personal and more institutional in the following films (think of *Mr. Deeds Goes to Town, Mr. Smith Goes to Washington,* and *Meet John Doe*). And if the common man originally is proposed as one who could change the system (or at least assumes the personal commitment to do so), in the end he runs the risk of seeing his identity collapse in a solitary and unequal struggle (as in *It's a Wonderful Life*).

In *The Miracle Woman* the consequences are still contained, because the threat to the individual can be led back to a single villain, Hornsby, whereas *Meet John Doe*, for instance, clearly foreshadows collective catastrophes of enormous importance (this is the period of the fascist dictatorships). Hornsby is one of the numerous cynical, corrupt, and greedy big-city bad guys created by Riskin. He presents himself to Florence as an outsider with respect to the social order: "I have no chains at all, no profession, no town, no particular belief, and no limit." He is not the innocent, carefree tramp of the films with Langdon; he is the fruit of the Depression, ready to assess everything in strictly economic terms. Thus "religion is great if you can sell it, no good if you have to give it away." Capra allows no illusions: in the America of the thirties faith is a marketable commodity, a consumer good just like so many others. In a traditionally Puritan country, the Calvinistic motto, "work and earn" has become a cynical "swindle and earn." A way to salvation, nevertheless, is still available in the inner resources that are not lacking to those who remain individuals: resources that can be utilized only with the aid of another person. John Carson will make the young woman understand the power of her pretence and will slowly provoke change of mind in her. John's blindness is linked to a more highly developed capacity to see beyond appearances: the depth of his gaze is precluded to the fanatic and hypocritical crowd. Meeting John, Florence finally establishes a personal relationship that permits her to escape a world where everything that is individual is substituted by impersonal relations and functions, and even technology becomes repressive the moment it is expressive. Refusing to be blackmailed by her manager, Florence decides to reveal the fraud to her faithful herself, but a short circuit provokes a fire that destroys the temple. In this catastrophe fire is at once regenerative and destructive (as also in *Rain or Shine*). Its effects on the individual and on the masses are profoundly different: for the lovers, the fire represents a purifying catharsis; for the crowd, it is a "Nemesis." The romantic love between Florence and John becomes their salvation, but only with difficulty will be able to defeat the cynicism, blindness, indifference, and spiritual aridity of the crowd: in the end, the audience goes away impressed more by the lack of hope and the hallucinatory tone of the major sequences than by the Battle Hymn of the Republic of the finale.

SOCIAL MASKS: *FORBIDDEN*

The peaks of melodrama, however, are reached by Capra in *Forbidden*, which faithfully conforms to the stylistic line of the fallen women cycle beginning with the motivation of the moral fall. If Kay and Florence are presented as controlled and calculating women who rediscover their innocence thanks to the love of an idealistic and dreamy man, the protagonist of *Forbidden*, an unwed mother and lover of a married man, will find her redemption in an autonomous manner, and only in the last sequence of the film.

Lulu Smith, a small-town librarian, decides one day to allow herself a Cuban vacation. On the steamer for Havana she meets Bob Grover, a district attorney, and falls in love with him. When they return to New York, however, Bob confesses that he is married, with a handicapped wife he cannot abandon. She leaves him, but discovers she is pregnant. The two become lovers. While his wife is in Vienna, Grover invites Lulu, who is now working as an archivist in a newspaper, to live with him. But politics interferes with their love: Grover's career is shaping up, and the reporters are trying to get something on him. The story of the child, particularly, would be a catastrophic discovery for public opinion. So, when a journalist who works for the same paper, Al Holland, surprises Lulu in a park with Grover and the child, the woman pretends to be the babysitter. She continues to play the part when Grover's wife returns, too, but in the end she can no longer bear to see her child in the arms of another mother and returns to the paper—to write a lonely hearts column. A long time afterward, Grover is running for governor but would like to run away with Lulu. To keep him from ruining his career Lulu sacrifices herself again and marries Al Holland. Grover is elected governor, but Lulu's new husband discovers the affair and threatens to reveal everything. The desperate Lulu kills him to destroy the evidence of the child's birth. When she gets out of prison, Lulu goes to see Grover, who is dying. Now the governor wants to redeem himself and decides to make his secret love and the identity of the mother of his child public: he writes a letter that demonstrates Lulu's silent heroism, rehabilitating and indemnifying her. But Lulu makes the extreme sacrifice. When Grover breathes his last breath, she tears up the letter that would clear her but sully Grover, and sadly sets out down the crowded street.

Here one really feels the "Capra touch": in the consciousness of the cinematic medium, and even in the hints of authorship. Walker's photography is put on display, in filters on the close-ups and in soft glimmers that intensify the emotion, and the camera is unusually "exhibited." Three sequences especially come to mind. Lulu accepts the compromise and becomes her child's governess and babysitter: the camera frames the two "legal" spouses embracing, then quickly and violently pans toward Lulu, on the stairs. Lulu has just killed her husband; a "dramatic" tracking shot ends with a close close-up of the woman trembling next to the fireplace while the police arrive; there follows a slow pan from the woman to the door and back again, to suggest the conclusion of the incident. Lulu and Grover on a bench; a long sequential shot shows the two lovers together, then the man alone, the woman returning, and the two embracing in the rain.

Again, there are the newspapers: the newspaper where Lulu works as archivist and the newspaper cuttings that constitute her diary and her memory of the happy days. The newspaper as a fetish, as a slice of life, an object of longing. And as an antagonist: her evil husband is a reporter. One last observation in the sacrifical and sanctificatory direction outlined above: the anonymous pseudonym that Lulu gives as the mother of Grover's child is Jane Doe, like her homonymous messianic colleague, John Doe.

In the year in which the consequences of the Depression became more acute, Capra seems to have modified his heroine, giving her new power and an even more radical spirit of independence and of sacrifice. *Forbidden* opens with a series of cross-fades that re-create the sense of spring: the earth is regenerated and life is renewed. Lulu Smith, the stern-looking librarian, metaphorically participates in a tradition of archaic rites and, suddenly, decides to quit her job and set out on a romantic cruise to Havana, in search of a place where no one knows her. At different moments, Kay, Florence, and Lulu share an acute dissatisfaction with their roles and their "social masks" (party girl, preacher, "spinster" librarian) and try to invent another role or to change into someone else, united also by their penchant for acting. But whereas for the former two the metamorphosis is successful after an initial catastrophe, in *Forbidden* it becomes the cause of an even greater catastrophe. The cool, sound, precise woman that the viewer has briefly met in the initial lines of her colleagues, on the staircase of the ship appears completely transformed: her clothes, makeup, and above all Walker's lighting make

Stanwyck very attractive. Nevertheless, Lulu seems incapable of finding a partner.

One night, however, she finds a drunken man stretched out on her bed; she wakes him, and he excuses himself explaining that he has mistaken the cabins: the number on the door, in fact, has been turned upside down. The two immediately become friends and henceforth jokingly call each other "Sixty-Six" and "Ninety-Nine." The confusing of the numbers is not just the pretext for a pleasant gag; it becomes a *memento* of the fact that the entire relationship between the two lovers arises from an error and from the fault of both. In fact neither inquires about the background of the other, and the numerical nickname tends to safeguard this depersonalization. "Both will play at not being themselves, or at being more than themselves. They call each other by the room number of the boat where they met, and Capra shows them to us, in unreal lights, horseback riding side by side, out of the world and out of time."[5] They alone can recognize each other using this special code, which, however, paradoxically, ends up making them unknown: for Capra no one exists if not in an adequate context of social and interpersonal relations.

The days in Havana (once again an exotic place becomes synonymous with downfall and perdition) soon end: Lulu starts work in the editorial offices of the *Daily Record,* and Bob sets out on his political career. At this point the trouble begins. In the beginning of the film Capra seems to adhere perfectly to the conventions of the melodrama: he skillfully doses climaxes, passing from smiles to melancholy and back again; he uses dialogue of a simplicity that is never banal. His careful direction, split between realism and formalism, and Stanwyck's intense acting, produce a sensitive representation of the society of the day, although the film was judged by the director himself to be "a soggy, 99.44% pure soap opera" (Capra, 134).

On Halloween Bob arrives at Lulu's house with a mask: each has decided to give a new turn to their relationship by revealing the truth to the

---

[5]Bernhard Cohn, "1930-1933. Un general, une blond, un banquier, des clowns, des explorateurs," *Positif* 133 (December 1971): 40.

other. But there is a communication problem. "It is always more or less a matter of masks, roles and theatrical scenes that can betray us or hide us, even as they express us" (Poague, 180). Here the sequence of the masks is extremely pointed. Is it Swerling's merit? Capra's invention? A sign of the double reading *malgré eux*? Certainly, the scene would seem to confirm the fetishistic signal (in the double, psychoanalytic and Marxian implication) of the *charakter masque*. A clue to bear in mind when rereading Capra.

The two protagonists play in a triple sense: they "act out" a funny pantomime of love; they "act in" the carnival of Halloween, and they "take on" social roles. She poses as the perfect housewife; he makes a bouquet of flowers appear as if by magic. As often happens in Capra's pictures, the emotionally more intense moments (like the love scenes) are realized with a sort of modesty: the characters' deep feelings are revealed in an oblique, indirect way, through words and gestures that apparently have nothing to do with them. "Catastrophe," however, once again hangs over the destiny of the heroes: Bob is married and cannot leave his wife, who was crippled in an accident he caused. Henceforth the film's light tone is definitively abandoned: during the course of events the two lovers will break up and come back together again (they will also have a child, Roberta), but their time together is illegitimate and devoid of the carefree joy of the days in Havana. One of the two must face a personal dilemma: drama in Capra is in fact always a question of choices. Bob must choose between true love and his marriage and career; Lulu between an honest life without love or sin in the shadow of the man she loves. Nevertheless the moral fiber of the two is profoundly different. Bob chooses his career; and even if he will officially adopt Roberta, he seems too cowardly truly to merit happiness. His moral weakness condemns him. Lulu, instead, although she finds herself in an ethically blameworthy position, wins the viewer's heart with her purity and with the immensity and the gratuitous nature of her love. The empathy toward the heroine, in any case, does not succeed in being total, because it is clear that she denies her own needs and desires to live a out a romanticism that is fatal to her.

The character of Lulu, therefore, is particularly complex. She does not sin out of naïvité or superficiality (as was in the nineteenth-century tradition of the *feuilleton*): she is wise enough to acknowledge her own faults and responsibilities, refusing the "seduced and abandoned" role. She is a strong and determined woman, with a "heroism" of her own in choosing sin and accepting the unpleasant role it involves. She will accuse Bob of being "poison" for her ("You are poison for me, poison ..."), but her feelings have an unarrestable force: as she advises in her broken-hearts column, "If you love him and he loves you, what else matters?" Even the decision to let her daughter be adopted by Bob will be made in the name of abnegation; the album in which she pastes the newspaper clippings regarding Roberta offers eloquent testimony of her love for her. For love of Bob Lulu marries Al Holland (one of Capra's more tenacious and amoral newshawks), and then kills him when he threatens scandal; to save Bob's memory, in the end, she destroys the testament in which she is acknowledged as a relation and with which she would inherit half of his assets.

Self-sacrifice, the main element of the melodrama, is a gesture that touches on self-destruction, and that Capra implicitly opposes to the hypocrisy, electoral careerism, and journalistic sensationalism of the male leads. In her final gesture, then, the heroine finds the strength to rebel against a society based on success and money, realizing also that moral redemption which becomes the justification and legitimization of her earlier sin (and by the way saving the whole film from censorship). After Bob's death, Lulu silently leaves the building and goes down into the street: the camera follows her in a long shot, while she mixes with the crowd, returning to an anonymous life but to the light of the sun. This is a very important narrative solution, because Lulu is a character that contains *in nuce* the strong, courageous woman of the New Deal: an efficient and somewhat cynical woman, whose bittersweet smile dissolves in a disarming tenderness.

Far even physically from the other actresses of the time, Stanwyck owed her popularity to her spontaneous but captivating acting, her natural tics, and her peculiar traits. "The mixture she embodied of the instinctive and the hyperprofessional made her the actress par excellence for Capra" (Viviani and Tobin, 20). Vulnerable and tough at the same time, like all the protagonists of the popular culture of the Depression, she has a life-impulse and an irrepressible energy which, in the following films, will make her also a symbol of the hopes of recovery connected with Roosevelt. With her, in fact, Capra began to delineate a female figure that he would propose again later on. His heroines will develop an acute sense of independence and the capacity to survive by their own efforts, without having to resort to the support of a man. On the contrary, often they will help their partners in trouble, thus revealing the tender and passionate aspect concealed behind the *façade* of self-sufficiency: "They could also be very kind to the men in whom they took interest, become their support, becoming stronger than their men and inciting them to act" (Debruge and Wagner, 44).

In the three films I have just analyzed, Capra shows that he has developed an acute awareness of collective problems, of the difficulties connected with the physical and mental survival of the individual, and of the dangers of a society that is at once falsely moralistic and blind toward those who are truly guilty: hope, faith, and love seem to have disappeared from 1930s America. The happy ending appears more than ever as a forced and unsubstantial solution; for a severe sense of threat accompanies the viewer even after the final scenes: the psychological, physical, or moral catastrophes are so grave that it is almost impossible for the director to repair the damage they cause.

A CYNICAL AND CORRUPTED WORLD: THE POWER OF THE PRESS

There is one film of the early Capra's production which is more difficult to insert in our scheme: as matter of fact, *The Power of the Press* (sort of "detective story," like *The Donovan Affair*) seems more conventional and structured on a more traditional "happy ending." Neverheless, like *Forbidden* is another film emphasizing the dark side of the Amercan society, based (confirming Bergman's analysis) on cinical journalists and corrupted politicians.

The Power of the Press is one of those titles among Capra's films considered impossible to find and now, instead, made available at the Washington Library of Congress[6]. Here the happy ending is more traditional, but nonetheless it is very interesting to watch the description (as in *American Madness*) of the social corruption involving the press and the politics and contributing to a non-reassuring setting of America on the verge of Depression. A Columbia film of 1928, produced, as usual by Harry "King" Cohn, the movie seems atypical even in its cast and credit: the cinematographer is not Joseph Walker, with whom Capra has worked since *Say It with Sables* and who will be his first collaborator from Submarine on; the male lead is given to the renowned Douglas Fairbanks Jr., who won't be part of Capra's filmography ever again. Fairbanks stars in the role of Clem Rogers, a reporter (once again!) involved in a shady story of homicide and corruption: he finds out that the beautiful Jane, daughter of prospective major Atwill, was in the company of District Attorney when he was murdered. It is a first page scoop, leading to Jane's apprehension. But the story is not so simple. Jane maintains she's innocent, and while out on bail, she manages to convince Clem that someone else has shot the D.A. And that's how it is, of course. Working together as amateur detectives, Clem and Jane find out that Blake, the political adversary of her father, is responsible for the murder. Clem has his scoop again, only this time he manages to save the innocent and marry her.

It is then a detective story with deep undertones of comedy, and it fits perfectly the category of vulture reporters so well described by Andrew Bergman. It is a pityless world, in which reporters are ready to slaughter each other—metaphorically speaking—for a piece, and in which po-

---

[6]Library of Congress, reference number F24306.

liticians are ready to slaughter each other—this time for real—to gain power.

What is really surprising is Capra's maturity who, as he already showed in *The Matinee Idol* and in *The Way of the Strong*, has a very clear idea of *mise en scéne* and of camera movements'rethoric, apart from a natural talent in directing actors.

For instance, even in the first shots: the opening title is superimposed on the rotary press, immediately clarifying the "genre"; a long side track shows the space of the editorial room, a triple cross dissolve with left and right fast pans. Here we find the fisrt characters (the envious journalist who despises Clem, the old guy who pulls his paper to make him go faster) and the gags (trips and other slapstick comedy ideas). Clem aspires to become a writer, and even though his signature articles are only about the weather, he doesn't renounce to literary profusion: "Clear skies. Think what that means to the birds and flowers. Think what it means to the farmer that hardy son of toil upon whose shoulders the wealth of nations rests. Think of the mothers and children in the parks and fields and bubbling brooks. Sunshine and health and happiness to all is what I promise today." His boss of course censors all his jinventions and Clem complains: "No surprise you paper is so stupid, you make great reporters like me write on the weather and obituaries!" Then he is at it again: "There is a classic for you. Change a word and you ruin it." Of course his boss deletes everything once again. Then, all of a sudden, the chance of a lifetime: Clem has to report on the murder of the district attorney.

Following the rules, the director seems to experiment with new narrative solutions: for instance, an establishing shot of the editorial office in which the reporters vanish with a simple but effective trick; or also a singular shot in which Clem is shown in close up talking on the phone while the space behind him is in deep focus; or even a shot inside an elevator developing in a gag sequence (clem goes up only to go back down as he has forgotten the address he is supposed to go to).

The tone is the one typical of comedy, there is even the classical mix up theme: in this case it is a piece of paper with the word "Press" stamped on it which the editor puts on Clem's hat and which Clems swaps with someone else (the clumsy reporter first collides with a girl, then with a man). Comedy prevails on any scene regarding the editorial offices of the newspaper: later in the story, for instance, after he obtained his scoop, he puffs smoke in his two adversaries' faces, demands a typewriter with his name on, compete on who can chew faster and so on. He even buffs smoke into Jane's kind face, who is accusing him of ruining her reputation:

> J: If I were a man, I'd punch your nose.
>
> C: We newspaper men must print the news, no matter who it hurts.
>
> J: And just to create a sensation, to sell your filthy paper, you disgrace an innocent family.

This passage from the dialogue is a testimony of Capra's opinion on the press jackals. Shortly before, Clem has just stated that the paper is as "lovely as the undertakers" and a photographer has aggressively taken a snapshot, producing a smoke very similar to the one produced by a shotgun. And shortly after, Clem himself will state much emphatically "I just ruined one candidate, now I'll ruin another..." casting a sinister shadow on the society of that time. When Clem, seduced and convinced by Jane, gets fired, the two opposing reporters are showing their satisfaction and he kicks the most odious of the two right into his bottom.

Soon enough though, the tone moves from the comedy to the detective story: the spectatore, follows Clems investigation through his eeys and, most interestingly, a times through the eyes of the murderer (who we will find out is a hired killer paid by Blake). An intense series of flashbacks, for instance, are constructed on the principle of voyeurism. At first we se the crime scene through a reconstruction made by Jane—thus through her eyes. In a second flashback the spectator is introduced inside the same location through the point of view of the killer (and absolutely voyeuristic is the detail of the peephole and of the hand opening the door, followed by the extreme close up of the henchman nodding). Later on we see Clem hismelf spying on the murderer (Van) speaking with his boss, Blake. In a third flashback, the spectator is present at the agony of the D.A., through the point of view of someone we later learn is Jane (a new piece of information clearing Jane's position as the D.A. Hands her a folder with a classified information which will help "her father be elected"). Clem starts tailing the culprit and he spies him while he is in the company of Blake; later on, through a peephole, very similar to the one we have previously seen, Clem is spied on by the killer, who says: "Maybe that reporter wasn't so drunk...."

Clem, in order to frame Blake, has pretended to be drunk, along with all the appropriate gags (a slapstick with a waiter, doubles and fake roles—she sings a cabaret song, he does the "Happy Al", and so on). And again the tone seems to oscillate between comedy and detection, Fairbanks is at his peak, playing his best comedic acts, and giving us intense close ups. Clem in close up sees Van with a bootlegger just before playing drunk; and in close up, when you can see that Van is finally framed, he winks at the camera: "That's a Great Story!".

It is a only superficially simple film. And while it's true that it may fall into its happy ending way too easily (a news—of course on the paper—reports: "Van and Blake brought to justice ... Jane Atwill soon to become the wife of this reporter") and that it is naïve in its murder plot reconstruction, it is also true that it contains a mix of genres (comedy, detective story and romance), an intresting structure of flashbacks, and a not at all dull set of gazes and points of view. And it is also an important film when it comes to its sociological and ideological stance (portraying a professional world—the newspaper—and a class—the upper bourgeoisie to which Jane belongs) and it is worth a serious analysis of its *mise en scéne*. To the first area belongs an interesting segment (when Clem obtains his first scoop and gains first page) which has an almost documentary quality: the director shows the spectator how you build up a paper, how to make up and unmake the first page, how the rotary works, the matrix, the press and so on. To the second area belong the camera movements and the rethorics of the narration: the matches on axis, the trackings and the horizontal pans, the alternate editing, and the non linear structure of the narrative, with its abundant use of the point of view shot. Among the many moments in which the directorial talent emerges, we can remember a match on axis from an establishing shot to a medium close up, during the tripping gag in the editorial room; another match on axis from establishing shot to medium shot takes place when John Atwill, Jane's father arrives; a fast tracking reveals Jane hidden behind a door on the crime scene; a point of view shot of Clem on Jane running away; Van's point of view and a tracking shot from left to right at first following him, then preceding him through the hallway; a preceding tracking on Van in the park; the shot from inside a telephone booth which reminds of the one inside the elevator at the beginning of the film; the detail of Van's feet menacingly entering; the match on axis from long shot to medium shot on Van holding a gun; the "theatrical" establishing shot with a match from medium shot to long shot when the murderer is apprehended and he his cuffed; the triple match on axis on the D.A. dying, on the first murder flashback. And then all the upper class setting, well-decorated, in the same flashback, or some female characters, as the wicked Marie Weston, or the rather shady lonely hearts column writer Connie Haven who, dressed with jacket and tie, is watching Jane closely, suggesting a homosexual propension.

All these elements are, to draw a conclusion, adding substance to new reflections on Capra's cinema.

CATASTROPHES IN A MICROCOSM. *RAIN OR SHINE*

We are in the circus world. Smiley Johnson is an impresario who, for love of Mary, tries to make a fortune of her father's circus. But Mary is in love with Bud, a young man of a good family who has joined the circus to indulge his taste for adventure. Bud wants his father to help the circus financially, and for this purpose organizes a dinner in his family's home. But Smiley's ridiculous behavior ruins everything, and all possibility of doing business vanishes. Mary fires Smiley and chooses Dalton, the director of the circus, to be her impresario. But Dalton and Foltz, the lion-tamer, conspire against Mary and her father, inciting the workers of the circus, who go on strike. The moment is critical: if the show does not go on, it will be the end of the circus. But Smiley arrives and saves everyone: he organizes a one-man show, a solitary but extraordinary performance, which wins the support of Bud and his friends. The circus people split into two camps; the good and the evil come into conflict. Even the audience of the circus becomes tumultuous. The tent goes up in flames and all ends in a gigantic fire, from which Bud manages to save Mary. Over the ashes of the circus, Smiley abandons all ambitions of love and ironizes about destiny and life.

A surrealistic film that sums up various historical tones of the comic: the commedia dell'arte of the strolling players, the slapstick comedy of Sennett and of Langdon, the melancholic comedy of Chaplin, the lunar "acrobatics" of Harpo Marx. An entirely spoken film, a feast of sound that avoids theatrical staging and, indeed, shows a mature sense of the space of the set and of the movement of the camera. But the film's key lies, once again, in a comicality that is at once catastrophic and critical (the final fire of the circus leaves the artists, under what is left of the tent, perplexed). And there is also an anti-middle-class vein, a call for the values of naïvité (the circus) as opposed to those of the worldly drawing room and its respectable habitués. Smiley is the transgressive hero who upsets the conventions of right-thinking people but who also intervenes, in a paternalistic and "corporative" way, to end the strike of the circus workers (a small crowd, ignorant and manipulable as always). The microcosm of the circus is the test-tube trial of larger apocolypses. The latter are apocalypses of matter, like the purifying fire that destroys the circus, or like the other fire of *The Miracle Woman*; but they are also apocalypses of the heart. Even the acrobats are swept away by the chaotic typhoon that overwhelms everything and everyone. The very last scenes of the film, as the "last fires" are extinguished, is a mixture of bitter smiles, clenched-teeth comedy, and hints at the impossibility of being happy.[7] The unhappy ending, therefore, crops up like a monster from the unconscious. This happens in all the films, even the simplest and "corniest"—the ones, that seem to support the image of the director as a reassuring and optimistic mythmaker.

CATASTROPHE, RACE AND THE SHOW: *THE MATINEE IDOL*

Recently found and restored films by Capra are contributing also to add further elements of reflection. For instance, the spectacle of catastrophe and the sense of impossibility of a positive reconciliation, are further confirmed by the (relatively recent) founding of a "lost" film: *The Matinee Idol*.[8] The main actress is Bessie Love, who will become the star of *Broadway Melody* the following year, a famous sound film by MGM (and the French title is appropriately *Bessie à Broadway*).

It is the story of an actor who is a great success at Broadway for his role as a black singer (a plain reference to Al Jolson's *The Jazz Singer*); one day with his agent, he crosses ways with a smalltown acting company, filled with naïve amateurs, and directed by the strong-minded Ginger Bolivar (Bessie Love). The actor (Don Wilson) gets hired by Ginger for a rendition of a civil war drama. He has to sub for one of the company's actor, while he hasn't revealed his real identity. The drama is so badly performed and directed that it becomes hilarious to the agent who is by chance seeing the performance. A chance for an involuntarily comic situation, a little like *The Producers*, by Mel Brooks. The agent wants to repeat the comical effect in Broadway and he invites Ginger and her company to his theatre. Here Don will be forced into the typical double role with masquerade, as in the also typical comedy of misunder-

---

[7]"*Rain or Shine* gives mixed political signals, probably because of the clash of Capra's fundamentally conservative attitudes with more liberal ideas that were in the air at the time" (McBride, 220).

[8]The film, shot in 1928, was rescued by the Cinématheque Française and today it is also available at the Cineteca in Bologna (it was first screened at one of the Festivals of "Cinema Ritrovato"). See Boschi Alberto, "The Matinée Idol" di Frank Capra, in *Cinegrafie* 7, dossier *Trovati nel buio. Lang, Robinson, Murnau, Gance, Capra, Hitch e film muti italiani*, anno IV, maggio 1994.

standings: on one side he is acting as the black singer, on the other he is an actor of the amateur acting company.

Naturally, in the end there disaster will take place: the drama staged by Ginger's company will end amogn general laughs and Don's identity and two-timing scheme will be revealed, giving way to Ginger's heartbreak.

It is precisely in these moments of dramatic clima, one has to look for the true nature of Capra's cinema. In the usual tragic sub-ending, Ginger pays a visit to her father, desperate, conscious of her catastrophic result of her *pièce*: her world has been thrown apart, she has become conscious not only of her delusions, but also of how much people lack pietas, how the world can be mean and cynical, exploiting her without any regret. And, under the pouring rain, Ginger meets Don, who tries to console her; but the rain dissolves his black make up revealing his true face: a highly dramatic scene, of chilling pathos.

Of course, a happy ending will ensue briefly. But it will sound fake, even though there will be the detail of Ginger's torn pantyhose, while she is kissing Don, passing through a highly metaphorical curtain of the company's theatre.

Again the drama serves the comic resolution. It is a fact, though, that even in these "green" and secondary films, Capra sometimes "melts the make up" (as with Don's make up, melted by the rain) to America, revealing an interesting portrait of his homeland. An America to which Capra has often ruined the maquillage, the superficial covering, giving way to the deeper wrinkles, less easy to hide, the most dramatic cracks; an America to whom the fimlamaker has always checked the pulse, to to whom has given his most powerful images.

from *It Happened One Night*

CHAPTER 5

NARRATIVE STRUCTURE OF THE "CATASTROPHE"

OFF-KEY FRAMES: THE EXAMPLE OF THE "WINGS" TRILOGY

After the success of Capra's first "quickies," Cohn engaged the director to make *Submarine*, the first film with which Columbia attempted to break into the world of major productions (the budget was $250,000). Irvin Willat, an expert in underwater photography, began the shooting, but the producer was not satisfied with the results. Overcoming the initial opposition of actor Jack Holt and the skepticism with which he was met by much of the troupe, Capra managed to make a highly successful film that led to the reutilization of the Capra-Graves-Holt trio in two more productions with similar plots, *Flight* and *Dirigible*. These three pictures form an ideal trilogy that testifies to Capra's capacity to invent "serial products," both in the creation of a character (like the civic hero of *Deeds, Smith, Doe,* and the following films), and in the construction of a current in which the same actors and even the same narrative movements are used again and again.

Submarine. Jack Dorgan, a Marine officer and expert diver, falls in love with Bessie, a ballroom entraîneuse, and marries her. Shortly afterward he is sent to the Pacific to work on the recovery of a wreck. Meanwhile Bob Mason, a handsome young officer and close friend of Jack's, meets Bessie in the same Oakland ballroom where Bessie and Jack had met. The girl flirts with Bob and does not tell him she is married. And so the inevitable happens: when Jack returns he discovers Bob and Bessie in each other's arms and blames his best friend. He contemplates his revenge, and he has the possibility to carry it out when Bob's submarine gets stuck on the bottom, trapping the entire crew in certain, slow agony. Jack is the only diver capable of reaching the submarine, but his pride has been wounded and his vision is too clouded by jealousy to act.

In the end, however, after much suspense, Bessie confesses that it was she who hooked Bob, and Jack, suddenly realizing the truth, leaps to the rescue. He puts on his diving suit and lowers himself into the sea depths to save Bob and the whole crew. He succeeds, adventurously. The two friends are reconciled in the end, in spite of Bessie and all the women of this world.

The construction of the "strong" character continues (Jerry Strong, *The Way of the Strong, The Strong Man...*). Here the "strong man", tough but weak, macho but feminine, is embodied in Jack Holt. It is he who, in a diving suit, descends into the abysses, almost to guide the modern viewer in a journey into the depths of the popular American imagination. There is a historical case in Italian cinema that constitutes a direct parallel to this film, placed halfway between realism and sketch: *Uomini sul fondo* (1941) by Francesco De Robertis.

Flight. Lefty Phelps joins the Marine Air Corps. He has an inglorious past: in a crucial Harvard-Yale football game, entering the field from the bench he managed to carry the ball into his own end zone, handing the victory to his adversaries. In the Marines Lefty meets Panama Williams, a good-natured instructor who, though he is aware of Lefty's error (he was present at the famous game), takes a liking to him and becomes his close friend. But the plot thickens: Williams and Lefty fall in love with the same woman, the nurse Elinor. When Lefty discovers that she is the girl Williams loves, he treats her with indifference, deciding to sacrifice himself for his friend. Meanwhile the two leave for Nicaragua to fight the local guerrillas. Williams, tough but timid, asks the subtler Lefty to intercede with Elinor and declare his love to her. It is the irony of fate. Lefty declares Williams's love for Elinor with a heavy heart; but she confesses that she loves him, Lefty. A misunderstanding ensues: Williams believes Lefty has double-crossed him and quarrels with him. The battle against the revolutionary troops begins. Lefty is a co-pilot (he cannot fly alone because, again ingloriously, he failed to get his wings); the plane is hit and goes down. Lefty saves himself and the wounded pilot. Meanwhile Williams, overcoming his jealousy, comes to the aid of his friend lost in the jungle; but he, too, is wounded, and Lefty, demonstrating his valor to himself and to the world, skillfully flies the plane back to the base. All ends well: Lefty is joined with Elinor beneath the condescending gaze of Williams, and definitively cancels his fault.

Again, one is shown strong but weak men: all the male characters are good, yet fragile. Lefty's life is a series of failures; the only endeavor in which he is successful is love, where he succeeds thanks to his clumsiness (even in the last sequence, he is unable to find the right gear in the jeep that carries the woman he has won). Panama, on the other hand, is a disaster with women; and he is tied to Lefty by a suspicious camaraderie: they wrestle, venting their homosexual tensions, both for fun and for real. The men are timid and whiney. There is just one bad guy, Lefty's cruel comrade in arms who constantly reminds him of his failures; but even in this case, one will discover that it is only a provocative way of bringing out the man in him. "You needed it, you had lost your sense of humor," the former enemy, now friend, tells Lefty with his last breaths. And it is somewhat the moral of the film and of Capra's cinema. This is perhaps the director's most "rightist" film, at least from the standpoint of the outer wrapping: an exaltation of American "imperialism" in South America, a surprisingly topical representation of guerrilla warfare in Nicaragua (where the "bandits" have flags like Jolly Rogers), a nationalistic rhetoric. But here, too, the style is that of a comic strip, of the "heroic series" where the guerrillas closely resemble the old, familiar Indians. And the cowboy Panama is a sort of *Luciano Serra Pilota* (a famous Fascist Italian film about a pilot hero).

Dirigible. Lieutenant Jack Brandon, a U.S. Navy pilot, is studying the use of dirigibles for exploration. Another officer, Frisky Pierce, opts instead for airplanes. The two friends enter into a subtle competition. Jack asks Frisky to go along with him on an expedition—in a dirigible—to the South Pole: Frisky's plane is to be hooked to the belly of the dirigible and go off on brief exploratory flights. But Frisky's wife, Helen, begs Jack to leave her husband home. Jack obliges her with a pretext, but Frisky interprets his action as a gesture of envy on the part of Jack, jeaolous of his fame. In any case the dirigible's attempt fails: the airship runs into a snowstorm and goes down. The crew is rescued but the venture is finished. A long time will pass before another dirigible can be built. So, the firey Frisky picks up the ball and sets out in his turn for the pole, this time in a plane. He carries a letter in which his wife asks for a divorce because of his too-frequent absences and his disorderly life. (Of course, Helen has asked him to read the letter only after he has completed his mission). Frisky and the explorer Rondelle fly over the pole. Then the young officer rashly tries to land, but the plane crashes in the snow. The fliers must face days of difficulty, cold, and hunger, during which Frisky gives proof of authentic heroism. At the last minute, when all seems lost, Jack arrives with a new dirigible and saves the crew. What is more, he saves Frisky's love: he does not read the bitter letter to his temporarily snow-blinded friend, he invents a new version on the spot. Back home, Jack is greeted by the fame of men and the gratitude of Helen, who has naturally repented.

The mechanism has been perfected at this point and does not change with respect to *Submarine* and *Flight*. The "heroes" are all losers (Frisky because he has run unnecessary risks; Jack because he ends up alone, as usual; Helen because she has shown herself to be stupid and superficial). Then there are the themes, which will return later: the airplane amid the snows of *Lost Horizon*; and the newspaper headlines, the stylistic and narrative element so typical (one is tempted to say, obsessive) of this director who once worked the streets as a newsboy.

SERIALITY

Submarine, Flight, and *Dirigible* are three adventure films, epics of the U.S. armed forces centering on male friendship regularly upset by the presence of a woman: three sequels, one would say, or three episodes of a television series *ante litteram*, were it not for the fact that the names (but not the characteristics) of the characters change. In these works Capra again reveals his acute interest in contemporary events and in technical progress: one of the constants of this "serial" trilogy is in fact the presence of a modern means of transportation—a submarine, an airplane, a dirigible—that becomes a modernist and futurist metaphor of mobility and transformation. The mechanical object, however, is also the protagonist of a material catastrophe (it sinks, is shot down, or crashes) connected with a personal catastrophe (betrayal by a woman or, apparently, by a friend) that can be overcome only by a major effort. Nevertheless, the most intense and melodramatic moments—connected also to the presence of the romance—are often relieved by delicate comic touches, lines or gags that alleviate the viewer's emotional tension, peparing him or her for a new climax.

The genre of war and adventure stories built around buddies was begun by Paramount in 1927 with *Wings* by William A. Wellman, a highly successful film that won an Academy Award the following year. Capra apparently stuck to the model, but there are important changes, beginning with the interest shown in the action. The spectacularity of certain sequences filmed on site (for instance the aerial maneuvers in *Flight* and *Dirigible*) is sought because it meets the needs of the epic and contributes to the glorification of the courage and skill of American sailors and pilots. Nevertheless the action scenes are never gratuitous and they do not represent the true fulcrum of interest, for Capra prefers to underscore the consequences of such events on the conscience of his two protagonists. In particular, the director senses that the involvement of the audience is deeper when the screen presents situations that are credible not only on the level of the diegesis, but also and above all in their emotional responses: "Drama is choices, drama is a man having to choose this or that—the more difficult the choice, the more intense the drama. And when he makes one choice, it's failure, it's tragedy; you make another choice, it's victory.... You tell drama through people" (Schickel, 188-189).

Both protagonists, at a certain point in the story, find themselves divided between faith to their friend and love for a woman, long remaining incapable of deciding which relationship is preferable and hence of understanding themselves. The woman is a marginal character, a pretext for the two male heroes to face their own consciences and their own deepest desires and feelings: in Capra's films even heroic warriors must undergo the same difficult process of revision and maturation that distinguishes characters otherwise so different socially, such as fallen women. In *Submarine* Bob falls in love with Jack's wife, who has lured him by pretending to be single; in *Flight* both protagonists love the nurse, Elinor; in *Dirigible* it is Holt who secretly loves his friend's wife. In each case the woman becomes an obstacle to be overcome in order for the tie between the two men to be strengthened: thus she can be removed as an traitress (*Submarine*) or integrated into the male friendship when one of the two (Holt) sacrifices himself for the happiness of the other.

The friends/rivals are already fully characterized in *Submarine*, so that in the two films that follow they will continue to change. Graves is the handsome young man of action—exuberant, jocular, easy with women, impulsive, adventurous; Holt instead personifies the mature friend—more sedate and rational, responsible and proud but also generous to the point of personal sacrifice. The bond of affection central to the plot, then, becomes the friendship between two men united by courage but endowed with different and complementary characters. Used to coming to each other's aid, they are united in a relationship that recalls that between father and son, with continuous role changes. The constant physical interaction between the two is not devoid of elements of repressed homosexuality—pats on the back, fists that become embraces, shoves and kicks are never lacking—signalling an emotionality whose more ambiguous aspects are made to seem "virile." Graves and Holt, furthermore, become protagonists of an unusual romance as conventional stylistic elements are reinterpreted in a modern key.

The Romantic Hero and the Antiromantic Purpose

The romantic hero is traditionally a member of the warrior class (here represented by the Navy and Marine Air Corps) capable of performing great deeds (saving a sunken submarine, conquering the South

Pole, combatting the rebels in Nicaragua). Still characterized as a human being (he does not have supernatural gifts), in reality he proves capable of actions that make him superior to other men. The world in which he moves is fantastic, made up of mysterious, fairy-tale landscapes (the depths of the sea, the jungle, the eternal snows of Antarctica): "Romance ... lacks a strong sense of biological time, and continuity is a function of an eternal ideal, an almost platonic cultural conception of beauty and courtesy transcending time and space" (Poague, 65).

Capra's approach to the world of romantic idealism, however, is original and personal. His heroes not only ride modern steel hippogryphs and fight real wars; they also present a weak dimension unknown to their archetypes. America in the thirties, in fact, lacked the moral certainty and purity of ideals that were still possible in the Middle Ages. The two superheroes carry out tasks at the limits of the superhuman in the search for a symbolic grail and for recognition of their valor. But Capra intervenes in the traditional formula, inserting the opposition, *right grail vs. wrong grail*. The romantic hero, that is, is placed before an anti-romantic purpose, as he must learn to seek the good of others (the right grail) before his own success (the wrong grail): the trophy may be obtained only through personal sacrifice and the renunciation of glory. This argument goes against the current with respect to the pictures being made at the time, in which the recurrent message is that of reaching one's own goals at all costs and by any means, legal or illegal, without acknowledging obsolete ethical or juridical norms (exemplary in this sense is the sweeping success of gangster movies). For Capra, on the contrary, dreams torn away from reality can be destructive, especially when they estrange one from the sense of the community. However, the same thing happens in such films as *Arrowsmith, SOS Iceberg,* and so on.

Like the cynical characters, the romantic dreamers of his films also fail when they try to assert their own personalities while ignoring their responsibilities toward others: "total selfhood is thus as wrong as the total lack of selfhood characteristic of mobs, and what is needed is personal integrity within the context of personalist communities, families, and neighborhoods, or even military units" (Poague, 94). In *Dirigible* this is particularly evident. Frisky and Brandon are the friends competing for the conquest of the South Pole, but Frisky sets himself a mistaken goal— glory—placing it even before his marriage and thus risking to lose his wife, who prefers the more mature Brandon. When the plane crashes, however, Frisky's individualistic dreams vanish, revealing a new, true hero capable of sacrificing himself for others and of admitting his own defeat without giving in (half-blind, he tries to lead his companions to safety). And when Brandon, who had already tried unsuccessfully to reach the Antarctic, undertakes a second journey on the trail of his friend, the noble goal (saving human lives) becomes a guarantee of the success of the enterprise.

As always, Capra is aware of the difficulties present even in the most generous resolution, and in fact offers two conclusions. Frisky gives up his dreams of glory but wins back his wife: he "rejects his overly romantic notions of glory in favor of the kind of comic family value, domestic rather than heroic, that is at the heart of Capra's personalist vision." Brandon instead finds himself famous, but alone, amid a crowd of strangers who celebrate him, "and the grim look on his face reminds us of the pain that goes along with being a responsible being in a realistic universe" (Poague, 65). The conclusion is thus ambivalent: without integrity there cannot be happiness, but integrity does not always assure happiness.

CATASTROPHE, TRAGIC SUBENDING, AND HAPPY ENDING

In these films the protagonist's faith in the goodness and soundness of his undertaking finds support in his strength of character and, at the same time, builds it. Capra's heroes usually reject an ethic of submission and in the end succeed in overcoming all obstacles. Nevertheless the accent is placed prevalently on the effort and on the momentary lack of confidence that precede the final victory. Capra is acutely aware that beyond all dreams and personal aspirations lies a reality that is often harsh and frustrating: thus he shows not so much his heroes' moment of triumph—always dangerously transitory—as their crises, weaknesses, worries, personal doubts, and failures. Even a film with such a deceptively optimistic title as *It's a Wonderful Life* takes place entirely in this dramatic dimension, and Bailey's reconciliation with himself and with the community takes up only a few minutes of the finale.

Even when dealing with a "heroic subject" Capra does not lose his sensitivity toward evil and day-to-day labors, be they physical, moral, or mental. The heroic adventure, the conquest of the world and of the self, are possible thanks to the virtue, obstinacy, courage, generosity, and perseverence that the director advocates and on which Hollywood bases the ideal image of the American people. These gifts, however, are put to a tough test: the intimate drama of the hero who clashes with a disappointing reality is underscored and made more acute (and spectacular) by the presence of a concomitant material catastrophe which, by reversing the protagonist's destiny, seems to end the film. This is the moment of the tragic subending, usually foreshadowed by minor premonitory failures: although it is a constant element of Capra's filmmaking, it has been unjustly overlooked by traditional criticism, which has classified the director's films as "fantasies of goodwill." On more attentive examination, however, the happy ending that characterizes Capra's finales (it is almost a trademark) appears to be an artificial solution for personal tragedies and collective catastrophes so serious as to be otherwise unresolvable. A cumbersome obscure side, in reality, is present in every hero, every story, every dream.

Most of Capra's brilliant movies, in fact, follow a similar course: day-to-day events—minimal or fundamental, usual or unusual, funny or painful—inevitably lead the hero toward an experience destined to disturb his existence, compelling him to reconsider his certainties and placing him in an unstable and frustrating condition. The catastrophe, which momentarily becomes the ultimate meaning of the whole story, appears in diverse forms and on various levels of seriousness, so that its resolution becomes more or less plausible. An attempt can be made to trace a typological description of this device, which becomes a constant stylistic component of Capra's films: it should be borne in mind, however, that the tragic subending is never built upon a single painful experience, but results from a mixture of different kinds of catastrophe.

A type of catastrophe contemplates the sudden dissolution of important emotional ties. The hero may be repudiated by his original family (Andy in *That Certain Thing*, or Birdie in *The Younger Generation*), finding himself suddenly destabilized and deprived of his traditions, existential background, and moral and economic support. The future becomes more uncertain than ever. Elsewhere the relation threatened is marriage, an institution that seems to have become obsolete and is frequently denied (*Platinum Blonde, Broadway Bill, Riding High*) or betrayed (*Submarine*). In general, for Capra—who has Catholic, peasant, Italian origins—the family is a fundamental experience in everyone's life and is truly essential to society and the individual. Each person becomes a father, mother, son, daughter, brother, sister, husband, or wife, really or metaphorically filling roles that define him or her in relation to other individuals. Yet the director cautions that not even blood ties are secure: the bond with parents, for instance, paradoxically can be constructed only in the sphere of an acquired economic and mental independence; and marriage can succeed only as long as one finds the right person, without letting oneself be dragged along by passion and instinct. Catastrophe can take on the subtle but intense forms of the existential drama, as happens to those characters who, unsatisfied by their socio-economic condition, their role, or their social mask, work a substantial (physical and psychological) transformation that allows them to lead a new life until events break up the carefully constructed simulacre, often revealing the void or the insecurities that lurk behind the bright façade. Molly and Apple Annie succeed in being ladies only for a day; Kay Arnold and Stew Smith are incapable of keeping up their laboriously acquired patina of middle-class respectability, and so must abandon the world of luxury; and Florence Fallon is no longer able to distinguish the extent to which falsehood has crept into her existence.

Elsewhere the catastrophe is not caused by the hero, but by selfish, wicked, corrupt, and cynical individuals ready to manipulate single persons or whole crowds for their wretched economic or political ends: thus Deeds is put away as crazy, and Smith and Doe are unjustly accused of fraud by the true culprits.

Last but not least is the more material catastrophe, usually tied to a physical event that transcends the will and control of the protagonists. These are all particularly spectacular events capable of upsetting not only the life of a single individual, but the existence of vast groups of people, especially where economic questions are concerned (as indeed occurred with the Wall Street Crash). Examples include the collapse of the banks in *American Madness* and *It's a Wonderful Life;* the fire in *Rain or Shine* and *The Miracle Woman;* and the sinking of the submarine and the crashing of the aircraft in the "Wings" Trilogy.

Generally speaking, the catastrophe implicates, threatens, or overwhelms those values which Capra officially acknowledges and to which he usually seems to render homage in his films: disquieting doubts torment the consciences of his heroes, compelled to live in a world that no longer respects anything or anyone. The solutions that Capra usually proposes in his happy endings are sometimes credible, but at other times forced or decidedly utopian and artificial; what unites them is the combative attitude of the hero who, after innumerable hesitations and uncertainties, decides to fight, ready to commit all his resources in order to overcome every difficulty. Sometimes his tenaciousness, courage, and ingenuity alone are able to redeem his existence (*That Certain Thing, Rain or Shine*); but at other times the action of others is required, be they the woman loved (*Platinum Blonde, Mr. Deeds Goes to Town, Mr. Smith Goes to Washington*) or the man loved (*The Miracle Woman*), family members (*You Can't Take It with You*) or a more or less vast crowd of friends and acquaintances—of those little people who often become fundamental to the solution of the more difficult cases (*American Madness, It's a Wonderful Life, Meet John Doe*). In any case the moment of the nightmare, preceded by experiences of painful failure, is fundamental, constituting a dramatic peak that will always come back in Capra's narrative gear: the happy ending needs a catastrophe, the epicenter of the earthquare prepares the positive reversal and the resolution of the comedy.

It would seem that the catastrophe is presented in order to be recomposed, so that man might assert himself even when life is not simple, demonstrating his greatness. For this reason critics have always considered these moments a prerequisite of the peace-making resolution presented in the finale. Capra, however, never allows an easy optimism; consequently one is compelled to reread the tragic subending, which become the true endings, escaping the director's control and acquiring dynamics of their own, capable of questioning the whole ideology of the film with their apparently sour note. As Pechter observes, "this convention of the happy ending seems, on a closer look, to be curiously quarantained in Capra's films, and the observance of it has often been strangely perfunctory."[1]

The films of the "Wings" Trilogy demonstrate how Capra arrives at the construction of the dramatic peak, subsequently resolving it in a happy ending that never succeeds in being altogether conventional. At the beginning of *Submarine*, Dorgan gets tangled in a rope tied to a bomb that has been dropped in the sea. Heedless of the danger, Bob dives in and sets him free in a gesture that immediately characterizes the intensity of the relationship between the two men. The second intensely dramatic moment is the betrayal perpetrated by Dorgan's wife with Bob. The relationship threatened, however, is the men's friendship, not the marriage. When the two lovers are discovered it is not the woman who despairs most (as would be logical), but Bob, who exclaims: "How can I ever face my pal again?" After these two antecedents the film can more rapidly reach its climax with the sinking of the submarine in which Bob remains trapped. Dorgan is the only one who can save him, but he is tormented by jealousy. The immaculate, fearless hero, the champion of

---

[1] William S. Pechter, "American Madness," in Richard Glatzer and John Raeburn, *Frank Capra, the Man and His Films*, 180-1.

the Navy, the romantic knight,[2] abandons the stereotype and reveals himself to be a common man who must face, with his reason and his heart, the primitiveness of his deepest feelings. At this moment the noble member of the warrior class thinks not of the other men shut up in the submerged coffin, but only of his friend/enemy.

In these sequences the editing is particularly rapid and effective for the purposes of suspense, switching from the desperate attempts to rescue the crew, to images of the crowd gathered on the pier, to interiors of the submarine, to shots of Jack walking restlessly over the newspapers that carry the news of the tragedy. The end result is a double involvement of the viewer, who alternately identifies with the growing desperation of the trapped crew (the result of the material catastrophe) and the dramatic incapacity to come to a decision, which torments Jack (and is the fruit of a personal catastrophe). After interminable minutes comes the painful decision to depart, but it must be understood that this occurs only after the discovery of the univocal guilt of Jack's wife: the viewer remains in doubt concerning what the outcome of the choice would have been had the discovery not been made. Discomfort over this solution, moreover, is sharpened by the fact that earlier it had been Bob who had saved his friend's life. Jack's dilemma, on the other hand, is potentially unsolvable, because the faith placed in his friend and that placed in his wife are mutually exclusive: it becomes necessary to qualify one of the two objects of love as "unworthy." The male friendship is reconfirmed in the happy ending: in the last scene the two men go off arm in arm along the beach of a tropical isle, ready to explore and conquer a reign from which women will inevitably be excluded.

In *Flight* the forewarnings of catastrophe concern instead Lefty Phelps who, it will be recalled, scores a touchdown for the wrong team in that crucial Harvard versus Yale football game. Joining the Navy in search of redemption, on his first solo flight he is is unable to take off: the plane bursts into flames, but Pierce, his instructor and friend, saves his life.

---

2 Carney, Chapter 1, "Frank Capra and American Romanticism," 3.

The metaphor underlying the entire film will be that of the wrong direction and the incapacity to "take off," that is, to fulfill one's potentials and overcome one's limits.

If Lefty's failures are technical, Panama experiences a personal failure when he discovers that Elinor, the nurse he wants to marry, is actually in love with Lefty. Panama is unable to accept this defeat in love, as he is convinced that it is the outcome of a deception by his friend. While engaged in a military action in Nicaragua, Lefty's plane crashes. This catastrophe could resolve the situation, dramatically eliminating his rival in love; but Capra prefers to avoid easy and unlikely solutions because he is more interested in exploring human feelings. Panama does not impulsively or readily rise to the occasion; he remains torn for a long time between hurt pride and affection for his friend. This time, too, the indecision is drawn out until the woman resolves the situation by exculpating her lover: "He never made love to me, I made love to him." Panama can thus set out in search of Lefty, confirming the nobility of his feelings. But Lefty too must accomplish a personal redemption: this occurs when he flies his wounded companion to safety during the rescue operation, succeeding even in landing on one wheel. To symbolize the fact that he has matured, once again completing the old king/new king cycle, this time it is Panama who gets out of the plane to run off and vomit (as Lefty had done before), revealing for the first time an unsuspected weakness.

In *Flight* even the happy ending contains a melancholic note: the two newlyweds, Lefty and Elinor, set out in reverse (once again going the wrong way), and it is Panama who puts them on the right track, shouting "that way!" The old king is still the wisest, but he is alone, left out of the life of the new couple. This ending is taken up again in *Dirigible*, when Holt parades through the exultant crowd: framed from above, flattened against the seat of the car that carries him in triumph, he creates an image that keeps the viewer from rejoicing too much in the happy conclusion.

Dirigible too hinges on the friendship between two men made rivals by the action of a woman: the wife of Pierce, an ace flyer, asks Jack, the official of a dirigible, not to involve her husband in the attempt to conquer the South Pole. This time it is Graves who doubts his friend, believing that his exclusion from the expedition is caused only by the latter's desire to monopolize the glory. His principal fault therefore remains his excessive narcissism, which drives him to neglect the value of human relations, and particularly of matrimony. Convinced that his wife would wait ten years for him, he cannot imagine that she is confiding her desperate solitude to Jack at that very moment. Jack sets out to conquer the pole alone, but the dirigible is destroyed during a storm (a first failure). Frisky is sent with his plane to rescue him. Shortly thereafter the aviator leaves again with the explorer Rondelle, but when they reach the pole the plane crashes on the ice. This catastrophe is doubly dramatic, because it is caused not by an unforeseeable event (an accident at sea, a revolution in a foreign country), but by the pilot's own irresponsible boldness. The hero must walk a long gauntlet of purification and redeem himself by learning to think of others and struggling for their survival. Frisky is required to combat not hot-headed revolutionaries, but "man's greatest enemies: hunger and cold." His battle becomes a metaphor of the daily struggle of the millions of unemployed and homeless created by the Depression; and salvation comes from mutual aid, from the willingness to help others while sacrificing one's own interests. These are particularly touching scenes that never lapse into sentimentalism, because the characters always remain credible and true, maintaining their dignity, courage, and irony even in the most adverse circumstances. As Emilio Cecchi states, "Capra knows how to deal with the horrible without sweetening it, and in any case without it becoming revolting, a quality of which he makes use with vaster and deeper effects when, from the interpretation of physical horror, he transports it to the moral."[3] The days during which the snowblinded Frisky wanders over

---

[3] Emilio Cecchi, "Frank Capra," *Bianco e Nero* (April 1937): 121; my translation.

the ice drawing his sled are a painful passage but one that is necessary in order for the hero to acknowledge the fundamental values of generosity, charity, and abnegation. Only when this spiritual pilgrimage is completed can his friend and savior arrive, who with a new dirigible and a noble purpose will finally succeed in conquering the new frontier.

As time passes the happy ending will become increasingly affected and formal, revealing a truly profound uneasiness and bitterness even if these qualities are still often denied by the director on the conscious level. In *Mr. Deeds Goes to Town,* for instance, the happy ending is preceded by a tragic subending (when Deeds is accused of being mentally ill). *Mr. Smith Goes to Washington,* which presents a very similar character, creates the dramatic climax with an overwhelming, intense rhythm, only to overturn it in a happy ending that is unexpected and too quick to remain in the consciousness of its viewers. The finale of *Meet John Doe* is entirely "out of whack" with respect to the construction of the rest of the film; but in this case it is Capra himself who acknowledges his incapacity to find a conclusion at once credible and satisfying.

So, although the director repeatedly proclaims his faith in the happy ending, one must carefully consider the brusque changes of style and the constant presence of evil in order to understand how Capra feels the full weight and effort of everyday life, in addition to the fragility and corruptibility of traditional values and institutions. The usual discrepancy between the complexity of the antitheses established in the film and the facility with which they are reconciled becomes, in short, an alarm signal that urges the revision of the concept of Capracorn. Even *It's a Wonderful Life* takes on a dramatic connotation usually overlooked by the critics. In particular, it should be underscored that the final solution is possible only thanks to the intervention of an angel, *a deux-ex-machina,* as ordinary reality lacks a satisfactory response to Bailey's anxieties and frustrations.

A RE-READING OF CAPRA'S PATRIOTISM

In the light of what we have seen so far I would like to suggest that the cliché regarding Capra's patriotic attitude also be revised. With this purpose in mind I shall point out the presence of off-key frames even in his apparently more rhetorical sequences.

The director claims with conviction to have the "stuff of the patriot," and his films seem to confirm this statement. In *The Strong Man* (1926) Harry Langdon is a Belgian soldier who, after the armistice, goes to America as the assistant of his former enemy, the German Zandow, and there learns to pledge allegiance to the Stars and Stripes. Military parades and patriotic hymns return in *Flight*, *Rain or Shine*, and *Dirigible*. Longfellow Deeds stops, emotionally moved, in front of Grant's Tomb, reminding one that only in a country like America an unknown young man from Ohio can become President; while Jefferson Smith admires the Lincoln Memorial with equal devotion, reciting the famous Gettysburg Address etched in the marble.

Capra's patriotism, however, is never blind, fanatical, or aggressive: it is a sincere, traditional, naïve sentiment based on solidarity and on faith in the great myths of freedom and democracy. In his films, which have the declared goal to "say thanks to America," the director always remains attentive, alert, lucid, and critical. In other words, love for his adopted country does not keep him from recognizing the ills present in that society—ills sometimes so deeply rooted as to leave little room for hope. In this case, too, therefore, it is essential not to stop at the director's own declarations or at consolidated critical judgments: as always Capra requires a more careful investigation.

Submarine, for instance, was made in cooperation with the U.S. Navy to relaunch the latter's image. The film is thus dedicated "to those heroes of the deep, who brave the winds of the sea and the treacherous depths—to the men of the Submarine Service." The tone of the caption is maintained throughout the picture, and the men of the Navy are always defined—with a rhetoric that is bombastic but also naïve in its emphasis—with glorious appellatives, such as "the mighty men-of-war." As the submarine sinks, the captain encourages his crew, reminding them, "Whatever happens, act like men"; and later on, when all hope seems lost, brandishing a loaded pistol, he repeats: "Let's pass out like men. Who'll be number one?" Yet the trapped men are not readily courageous: they all have their fears and their weaknesses (one of them, feeling himself suffocate, opens the last oxygen tank, quickly finishing it). And if numerous divers try to reach the submarine with the air tube (with laudable courage), the only one capable of accomplishing the feat (namely, Jack) is paralyzed by anger and jealousy. In *Submarine*, therefore, the epic hero shows weaknesses that, even if they are understandable, are in contrast with the customary moral fiber of the character of the Navy officer.

The following film, *Flight*, goes even further. Lefty Phelps joins the Marine Air Corps in search of redemption, but during his first flight he feels ill: back on the ground, he has to vomit, but the flag-lowering ceremony stops him in his tracks. The images of the glorious American flag alternate with point-of-views of a bucket that Lefty wants to reach as soon as he can. A strident contrast is thus created between the long shots of the symbol of all America's ideals and values, and the close-ups of Lefty's tormented face. Then when Lefty's plane goes down in Nicaragua, Steve, the pilot, is wounded and in the end dies. Lefty decides at that point to burn the plane, but the camera shoots in detail the symbol painted on the fuselage: an eagle with wings spread perched on the globe with the inscription *semper fidelis* above its head. As is known, *Flight* is traditionally considered Capra's most politically conservative film because it seems to support an imperialistic image of America as the bearer and guarantor of peace; but if one thinks of these two sequences, or of the fact that the Lobo bandits launch their attack on the fallen plane waving the pirate flag, one realizes that Capra's rhetoric is not devoid of irony: war becomes a dangerous game played by reckless and irresponsible adults.[4]

Dirigible, finally, revolves around another characteristic aspect of American culture, the spirit of frontier conquest. As there are no more frontiers to be conquered on the American continent, the new frontier is extended to the ends of the earth, thus defining the image of a country that stops at nothing. Yet here too is an element of disturbance. It is the motive that makes Frisky leave: the hero is not interested in the glory of his country or in the possibilities connected with the conquest. His goal is fame alone, and his narcissism seems almost to negate the possibility of a true heroism in contemporary America. The motto "South Pole or bust" makes the event pure spectacle, distancing it from the noble ideals of the pioneers of long ago. In another sequence of the film, it is Jack who sets out for Antarctica; when the dirigible flies near the Statue of Liberty, the commander salutes it at attention with a free and easy "Good-bye, Lady." Immediately afterward a telegram announces the arrival of a storm that will cause the airship to crash at sea. The approval and support of the great homeland (symbolized in the imaginary salute to the statue) are no longer sufficient guarantees of success. America in the 1930s had lost the sense of omnipotence that had characterized the expansionistic phase after World War I, to discover with painful astonishment its own weaknesses. Of these Capra became the interpreter, going as far as to conceive a film that carries onto the screen the most recent catastrophe (the Wall Street Crash) and the madness that it determined. From private stories (always set in a highly realistic social context) the director's gaze shifted to history.

---

[4] Regarding Capra's patriotism, Joseph McBride writes in an interesting manner about his "vulnerability." Capra is contradictory, torn between enthusiasm and anxiety, and suffers considerably during the HUAC era (see the chapter, "The Judas Pain," 561).

from *Platinum Blonde*

CHAPTER 6

FAMILY CONFLICTS

WHEN THE FAIRY-TALE FAILS: THE DARK SIDE OF THE HAPPY FAMILY

If *That Certain Thing* was the capitalist fairy-tale of social ascent realized and celebrated, acknowledged and made part of the establishment, *The Younger Generation* is Capra's first film to give complete expression to the dark side of that movement. While treating of the same
theme the two works are thus specular, that is, equal and opposite: the
American dream of the former is transformed into the American Nightmare of the latter.

The Younger Generation is a film full of contaminations (it is fable,
family drama, social and ethnic drama ...) testifying to Capra's versatility
in integrating myth and modernity, traditional narrative models and
contemporary subjects. Taken from *It Is to Laugh,* a theatrical drama by
Fannie Hurst, the film narrates the rise to success of a young Jew, Morris
Goldfish, who moves his family from the Lower East Side to the elegant
Park Avenue. Economic prosperity does not coincide with domestic
serenity, however, and the young man finds himself alone when his
father dies and his mother decides to leave him to follow her daughter.

The plot follows the story of the Goldfish family from the early years
of the century until the end of the twenties; in particular it focuses attention on Morris, the elder son, who grows up feeling the shame of immigration and of his family's misery. He wagers all on social redemption
and in the end becomes a wealthy antique dealer. Now the family is well
off, but the old joy has disappeared. Morris changes his name from
Goldfish to Fish to mask his Jewish origin and moves his family from the
Lower East Side to an elegant apartment on Park Avenue.

Morris's sister, Birdie, is in love with Eddie, a young singer and musician (the three, one has seen, grew up together). But Morris objects:

he holds the family's good name in the highest consideration, and to complete his social escalation he plans to marry the daughter of a millionaire, Kahn. Notwithstanding his veto, Birdie marries Eddie. The latter, however, is unwittingly involved in a robbery (he unknowingly covers the crime, improvising a street concert in front of a jewelry shop where, aided by the small crowd that gathers, the bandits go about their work undisturbed). Eddie is arrested. Birdie is unjustly driven out of Morris's house. Sadness descends on the Goldfish family. Papa Goldfish gives himself no peace and goes back every now and then to the old neighborhood, where he was miserable but happy. And he slowly expires. On his deathbed he ends up reconciling with the family: Mama Goldfish, Morris, Eddie; and the grandchild is born in the meantime.

The family saga had begun with *Long Pants*. Here it bursts onto the screen in full force. Capra projects onto the "younger generation" his personal experience as an immigrant, the American myth of success and social advancement, and the petit-bourgeois, popular common sense that will be the leitmotif of Capracorn. "Money ain't good for nothing, Mama, if it can't buy happiness": so says the elderly Papa Goldfish to his wife, with sound patriarcal wisdom, when confronted with his son's economic success and the pruderies of social escalation; and the line holds the moral of all later Capra (the peak will be *You Can't Take It with You*). In this story of changing American society seen through the history of a Jewish family from the early years of the century until the late twenties (the eve of the Crash), Capra constructs a popular fresco, more in the manner of old popular prints than of comic strips. The result is a well-rounded realism that sometimes dissolves in a sketch but often stands out forcefully in its sharp contrasts, its marked chiarosuro. Capra's realism surfaces above all in the first part, in which the camera investigates, with the methods of documentary filmmaking, the social environment of poor neighborhoods in the early part of the century. The exteriors, especially (there is a very intense sequence in which the mother runs, followed by the crowd, toward the house in flames) give the film a flavor of genuineness. It is in this first part of popular interiors and exteriors that the liveliest aspect of the plot is developed, initially from the standpoint of the children (the younger generation). One will see them grow together with their contradictions, which create the air of the lower-class family saga. The saga closely resembles that of early-twentieth-century Manhattan in Coppola's second *Godfather*, or of the Po River Valley in Bertolucci's *Novecento* (the Goldfish contain both the Dalcos and the Berlinghieris).

The second part of the film, in contrast—when the children have grown up, with their different decisions and prospects in life—is built on interiors, on a more theatrical family drama, a more conventional ethic based on noble sentiments and the longing for an unrepeatable golden age. This time the atmosphere recalls *The Jazz Singer*, especially in certain constituent elements such as the generational conflict, the Judaism of the father, and the theme of the hit song (so similar are the two works that one may think the scriptwriters sought, in this mixed silent film/talky, to repeat *The Jazz Singer*'s successful recipe). The result is a schizophrenic air accentuated by the mixed technique, which makes the movie a fascinating hybrid. The mixture of live sound, silence, and added sound makes the directing, too, a bit schizophrenic. The latter unfolds on two levels: in the silent part it relies heavily on gestures and on the baldness of the captions; in the part accompanied by sound, it revolves more around the articulation of the dialogue and the development of the characters. The silent part emphasizes vision, the self-sufficient strength of the image; the part with sound discovers the word. Capra again seems divided but intrigued by the two techniques (two worlds, two eras): silent film declining, talkies coming on strongly. And that of the talkies is "the younger generation."

FAMILY AND MERCHANDISE: AT THE BASES OF CAPITALISM

The Younger Generation recalls the structure and theme of Shakespeare's *Merchant of Venice*. Both works concern mercantile society and capitalism, and both point out that "it is not just being a capitalist that is significant, but the kind of capitalist you are" (Poague, 37). Morris's economic rise involves the whole family, but its effects on the single individuals are different. Julius Goldfish, the father, prefers talk to selling pots and pans. In the initial scene the camera discovers him joking with his friends, and when his wife goes looking for him to put him to work, he responds with a quip: "Mama says that money talks, but I tell her it ain't never said 'Hello, Mr. Goldfish'." Like all the characters in the film, Julius is immediately well characterized, both visually and morally. He is the typical Jew with a vest, a long beard, and a *yarmulka*; but the viewer notices above all his capacity to interact socially and to joke even about money. The development of the narrative will confirm these initial sensations: once he has settled into the new house, his only moments of true serenity will be those in which he lovingly plays with his daughter Birdie (once again, as Carney notes, the activity of play) or dreams of his past life (dream activity). Affluence in itself is not a motive of joy for him, and the new status seems to confirm his earlier suspicion that "money ain't good for nothing" (compare *You Can't Take it With You*). True happiness resides in the warmth of the family, the affection of friends, and in human relations in general. His last smile before dying will be for the birth of his grandchild, "a Goldfish all over" (in clear contrast with Morris, who has even changed his surname), whose presence will guarantee the perpetuation of the dynasty.

Birdie, his daughter, at that point is psychologically and emotionally close to Julius, almost replacing the mother at his side and forming a new couple not devoid of Oedipal ambiguities. Her love for Eddie Lesser, a childhood friend, is disliked by her brother, as it would compromise his image in the upper-class society of which he is now part. In this respect the story recalls the contrasted love of Shakespeare's Romeo and Juliet, but the comic obstacle here derives not from old family quarrels, but from modern class conflicts. Capra, furthermore, reserves for the young lovers a happy ending that is missing in the original drama: the lovers will overcome every difficulty, they will marry and have a child, a visible sign of the "fertility" of their love. Birdie is able to make the right decision: her investment is emotional; she does not seek to enter the beau-monde through a marriage of convenience; she remains faithful to her first love, even when this means having to abandon the comfortable life assured to her by her brother. Like her father, she acknowledges that the true values of life are not riches or worldly glory, but human relations; furthermore she shows the same distancing humor as Julius when she ironically claims that "Morris could sell anything— even society."

Mama Goldfish, on the contrary, is clearly obsessed by money and its possibilities, and even her emotional choices are oriented with these concerns in mind. Though certainly fond of her husband, she nevertheless considers him inept in business; whereas Morris, who sells all the papers given to him, is the object of her love and attention and the repository of all her ambitions of socio-economic improvement. Morris reveals from childhood an extraordinary talent for making good gains: a new King Midas, he changes everything he touches into gold. The sequence that visualizes this ability in an exemplary way is that of the burning of the house on the Lower East Side: Morris comes out with a large sack over his shoulder and shrewdly answers his mother, who scolds him for the danger he has run, "But look at all I saved, Mama— now we can have a fire sale!" (Here is another fire, by the way, likewise material and symbolic: a basic "catastrophe" at the beginning of the film). Down through the years, from his first second-hand furniture shop the young man will go on to buy a large antique shop and, as is known, a house on Park Avenue. The process in itself certainly would not be blameworthy for Capra if it did not imply a progressive ethical and spiritual decline. Blinded by his aspirations, Morris does not hesitate to tread on the feelings and needs of his loved ones: thus he obstructs Birdie's relation with Eddie (embodying the anticomic) and prevents his father from receiving his friends. In short he is determined to make his family into "real people" whether they like it or not, and every move must be calculated to contribute to his personal success.

Both Shylock and Morris fail in the end and lose their families precisely because "they would not risk putting family first" (Poague, 36).

Both the usurer and the antique dealer, that is, reveal the human inadequacy in their blind and exclusive faith in the mercantile ideal. In Morris, particularly, faith in success remains the only feeling left, and to break this scheme would mean total destabilization for him. Obsessive capitalism, the pursuit of wealth for its own sake, are signs of spiritual lifelessness and moral sterility: Morris's destiny therefore cannot be other than isolation and abandonment.

That Capra does not attack capitalism in itself, is clear: to A.B. Charles in *That Certain Thing* he opposes Molly; to Potter in *It's a Wonderful Life* he opposes Bailey; and to Morris he opposes Eddie. The latter, desperate because he lacks the money necessary to marry Birdie, accepts the attractive proposal to play in front of a jewelry store and finds himself involved in a robbery: after attempting to escape and marrying Birdie, he turns himself in to the police. The lesson he had to learn is, not to give in to prospects of easy money: money must be earned honestly, day by day. Once out of jail he will manage to become a fairly successful composer and proprietor of a shop selling musical instruments. Eddie is the "good capitalist" who works passionately and does not forget the importance of family affections: he will be flanked in the shop by his wife.

ROOTS

So the basic problem intrinsic to the socio-economic escalation of the immigrant (or of anyone else) lies in the parallel potential revolution of family and interpersonal relations. Julius misses his old friends and jealously keeps his yarmulka under his pillow: wearing it at night allows him to dream of his happy past. He feels lonely and depersonalized in his new home; outside the ghetto he no longer finds the strength to laugh and joke (and hence to express his own vitality). His incapacity to fit into his new world, however, seems more a matter of ethical coherence than of actual inadequacy, even if some scenes show that, as an immigrant, he did not know how to read or write in English. Morris on the contrary tries every way of repressing his past existence in order to reconstruct a new identity for himself, one in which his ethnic origins are no longer important. To complete the metamorphosis he will go so far as to repudiate his father's surname: Goldfish will become Fish, breaking the last and most cumbersome tie with the past (not only the recent past of the Lower East Side, but also the religious, cultural, and moral past of his ancestors and his people). The viewer is confronted with a phenomenon common to Morris, Birdie, Capra, and every other immigrant—namely, the "process of creation of an individual identity within an unstable, fluid society."[1]

Morris seemingly manages to recompose his new ego, but in doing so he repudiates his family and the entire Jewish tradition. Birdie, in contrast, appears as the heroine, for she continues to respect family and community relations. A deeper examination, however, reveals some ambivalence in the portrait of the two young poeple: although the girl represents the values that Capra officially supports (the family), Morris is the figure on which the director's attention focuses. The paradox that burdens the narrative is therefore the following: the American Dream fulfilled (represented by Morris's career) brings not only the attainment of greater freedom and independence, but also the dangerous corollaries of isolation, abandonment, alienation, and destabilization (Morris loses everything in the attempt to re-create his identity). The alternative to this movement, however, seems to be a pale stasis, a remaining anchored to one's past without making any true progress. Carney points out in this connection that the daughter represents a real danger: "to remain smothered within the bosom of nuclear family and never be able to move beyond it, or beyond one's past" (54).

Certainly Capra and the film are torn between faith in the reactionary values of family stability and social responsibility and the individualistic dream of radical change and personal autonomy. But whereas in *That Certain Thing* the passage from a state of dependence to one of autonomy came off perfectly, here the accent is placed on the effort, the

---

[1] Carney, 53. See also Max Lerner, *America as a Civilization* (New York: Simon & Schuster, 1957).

pains, and the anxieties of those who become their own fathers outside the protective system of the family and the community. Tormented by doubts about his own human and professional capacities, Capra soon discovered the dark side of the ideal archetype of exceptionality and individualism he pursued, as well as the fears of the naked and exposed ego. These inner conflicts are brought out in *The Younger Generation*.

Unlike Carney, I believe that a possible positive solution is represented in the humane path of the daughter. Indeed, if one turns again to psychoanalysis and the roots of the fairy tale, one finds two common *topoi*: : "brother and sister " and "the two children". In the various versions of the former fable, brother and sister leave their father's home and set out in the world, but an evil spirit transforms the boy into an animal while his sister remains human. The girl represents the superior mental functions (the ego and superego, which is partly constituted by the interiorization of the teachings of the parents), whereas her brother, dominated by the id, pursues the immediate gratification of his needs. His sister tries to stop him, until it becomes impossible to do so and, drinking at an enchanted spring, the boy is transformed into a fawn (that is, he loses his human appearance). In order for the spell to be broken, the fawn must be hunted for three days, which happens in the end. But the sister also must be initiated in a superior form of existence: the passage from childhood to adult life takes place when she gives birth to a child.

In *The Younger Generation* Birdie maintains close ties with her father and her ghetto friends: she is witty and gay, but she is also rational and aware that the true joys of life do not lie in the irresponsible pursuit of material pleasures. Her behavior is marked by a kindness and a sense of responsibility toward other people motivated by the ego and superego; whereas Morris, who also seems to worry about the welfare of his family, in fact seeks only his own pleasure. What he does for others is always subordinated to his climb to success, and if he keeps his father with him it is only because it would be socially unbecoming to have relatives in East Road. What redeems one as a human being is the care one shows for those one loves; but Morris lacks this. So if Birdie reaches maturation by integrating the forces of id, ego, and superego, the same cannot be said of her brother, who remains trapped in the gilded cage constructed by his own indomitable drives. Morris is the immigrant who goes forward detaching himself from his past, but this repudiation leads to catastrophe. Birdie instead manages to integrate these two contrary trends in an existence that is successful from all points of view: she symbolically breaks away from her old family, constituting a new nucleus (she becomes a wife and mother), and at the same time she maintains deep emotional ties with her parents, avoiding dangerous identity crises.

OEDIPAL CATASTROPHES

In Capra's films the metaphor of maternal fertility is often contrasted with that of paternal sterility, regardless of whether the story concerns true mothers (Ma Smith, Penny Sycamore, Ma Mitchell, Mrs. Bailey, and Sophie Moretta) or women with maternal attitudes (Mrs. Higgins in *The Miracle Woman,* Mrs. Meredith in *Mr. Deeds*). In any case they are the warm, beating heart of the family, and they embody all sorts of virtues. "They are generally kind, concerned, and ... too busy holding their family together to worry about themselves" (Poague, 86). These characters recall Sara Capra, a very important presence in the life of the director, who in his autobiography remembers her as a "patient, strong, and solid woman."

At various times Capra found himself entirely dependent upon his mother who, replacing his prematurely deceased father, became the true nucleus of the family. In a world that seemed to disintegrate every day, risking to overwhelm him, she was the only firm point he could grasp onto. "I tenderly loved my strong and courageous mother; I loved her even if I was well aware that I counted very little in her estimation—and she had every reason" (Capra, 22). Elsewhere Capra will go so far as to declare, "I have no identity, no fatherland, only a motherland."[2] Inevitably, the presence of a mother, together with that of a father, became one

---

[2] From a TV interview: Gian Piero Brunetta and Luciano Mingozzi, *Storie di cinema e di emigranti,* RAI 1 (Italian television), 1984.

of the more significant presences in the existence of his characters, even though it preserved a recurrent ambivalence. The negative double, the Mr. Hyde that is hidden in each of us (and that returns in the dichotomy of good father vs. bad father and good capitalist vs. bad capitalist), therefore also touches the "mothers," giving rise to women used to thinking only of themselves. The archetype is constituted by Mama Goldfish, who will be followed by Mrs. Strong in *Ladies of Leisure*, Mrs. Schuyler in *Platinum Blonde*, Mrs. Jackson in *Bitter Tea*, and Ma Jones in *Here Comes the Groom*. What unites them is their wealth or an irrepressible aspiration to material well-being: "they are generally more than willing to sacrifice their children for the sake of material gain and social status" (Poague, 87).

From the very beginning it is clear that Mama Goldfish, in a certain sense, supports and feeds her son's unconscious desires to replace the father figure at her side, often praising him in a comparison in which the father loses his primacy. In one of the first scenes, when the boy returns home after selling his newspapers, the woman embraces him enthusiastically: "I wish Papa was such a good businessman like you." After the burning of the house, seeing her son appear with a sack full of objects, with satisfaction she expresses a certainty regarding his destiny: "Some day, Papa, Morris will be a *big* businessman like you ain't." Her obsession with socio-economic advancement will be fulfilled, in effect, thanks not to her husband but to her son, and a caption ironically warns that "A mother's prophecy uually comes true ... !" Thus the rise to success is joined with the gradual substitution of Morris for his father: in a montage sequence one sees the signs of the Goldfish shops change in rapid succession, concluding with "Antiques Morris Goldfish Importer," which sanctions the father's exit from the scene. The domestic drama has been played out: Morris now guides the life of his family members, and, usurping his father's position, makes the latter an obedient child while augmenting his mother's prestige.

One scene in particular foreshadows this definitive passage of command. Morris returns home, his mother embraces him (as would a wife on the return of her husband); he jokes and makes her close her eyes: when she reopens them she finds a splendid diamond bracelet. In the succession of playful frames, of fillips and faked embarrassments, the protagonists appear as a real couple of lovers, perfectly at ease in the environment that surrounds them and that represents the symbolic fruit of their relation. The father is definitively deposed in the next scene when, at the table, his wife explains to him why Morris has changed his surname. Birdie explicitly underscores the latent significance of the announcement with a bitter toast: "Goldfish is dead, long live Mr. Fish." The king is dead, long live the king!

Poague notes that "Morris realizes that something is wrong in this Oedipal relationship, that this kind of maternal domination should not be" (38): nevertheless, he does not find energy enough to escape his mother's control. Back from a dinner at the Kahn home, Morris embraces his mother in the foyer: his father stands somewhat aloof, and on his shoulders has the shawl handsomely embroidered by his wife. The son has an instinctive reaction of disgust to this sight: it is less an aesthetic problem (a man dressed as a woman) or one of roles (in family affairs the mother has a stronger role than the father), than an ethical one. The shawl represents "both the cause and the result of Morris's dedication to money and status" (Poague, 39). Unconsciously Morris is disturbed by what he sees represented: a man wrapped by his mother in a suffocating attention for things, more than for human relations. "What the shawl stands for ... is a dehumanizing dedication to things rather than people (when Mama puts the shawl on Papa she tells him how happy he should be to have such a nice house and such nice furniture)" (39). At the end of the film the mother goes away wearing the old shawl (and hence symbolically re-embracing the old traditional values), while Morris, alone in front of the fireplace, wraps himself up in the emboidered shawl , admitting his personal defeat (the empty house is just a cold tomb). It is one of Capra's most bitter unhappy endings. In the final sequence showing Morris's room, over which threatening shadows stretch like the bars of a prison, social catastrophe and family catastrophe come together.

DOMESTIC CONFLICTS: *PLATINUM BLONDE*

Reporter Stew Smith is assigned a gossip-column job on the breakup of an engagement in the wealthy Schuyler home. But the assignment becomes something larger: Stew saves the family from a blackmail scheme and marries Anne, the Schuyler daughter to whom the inheritance will go. With a certain reluctance, he moves into the Schuyler home. Here he is uncomfortable: he is "Anne's husband" to his acquired family; he is "the Cinderella man" for his former colleagues, who deride him. To win them back, he organizes a party at the Schuyler's without the latters' knowledge. When the proprietors return, a fight breaks out: Stew understands that that world is not made for him and falls back on more amenable shores. He returns to his former friends and to his old flame Gallagher, whom he finally discovers he has always loved.

The press, the family, and class obsessions are typical ingredients that fit together in a film that has gone down in history above all for the myth of the platinum blonde Jean Harlow—a personality who passes like a meteor through Capra's sky. The male star, Robert Williams, also passed through briefly (he unfortunately died just after the film's release). By this time the newspaper has become a distinctive feature of Capra's subjects and editing (the headline of a newspaper sums up complex events simply, while the newspaper environment creates the idea of a world in movement, the nascent society of information). It should be borne in mind that the newspaper is the center of American civilization in Superman comics, too; and Clark Kent, Jimmy Olsen, and Lois Lane are the avant-garde of a twentieth century on the march. This is why the reporter—Clark Gable in *It Happened One Night*, Bing Crosby in *Here Comes the Groom*—is the modern hero. Capra's class obsessions appear pathological at this point, and they are not resolved in this case: Stew Smith will go back to his old flame in spite of the conventions of matrimony (which here are transgressed, as they will be in

Broadway Bill). The film's most lasting impression, however, regards the set design, the depth of the filmic space, and the way in which the camera investigates these leisure-class interiors. The camera rummages around, perhaps with the eyes of the investigative journalist, recording, judging, and suspecting.

Platinum Blonde begs an analysis of the genre of comedy—another genre indirectly influenced by the conventions of the Production Code, in effect at the time. In this instance recourse will be made to the work of Leland Poague, which is particularly useful in this specific connection. "Comedy [is] a highly conventional form both in its structure and in its contents, which derive directly from archaic rites and myths that have been endlessly repeated with only superficial changes." According to Poague, Capra's success can be traced to his use of the classical formula reworked and adapted to his own talent and means. "Capra celebrates the human virtues of fertility, maturity, integrity, and community, and he does so in a fully committed, deeply humanistic, and completely cinematic manner" (Poague, 45). In the dark days of the Depression, when death, poverty, and desperation triumphed, the capacity to celebrate faith in the comic strength of fertility and of the sense of adequacy seemed to consolidate the director's popularity. Poague's interpretation is interesting, but it glances over the dark side of comic movements, considering them less the fruits of a choice and of a precise world view than as an integral part of the stylistic conventions adopted. In reality, comedy does provide predetermined forms and contents; nevertheless artistic freedom survives in the final result—that is, in the emphasis given to the two opposite poles, *fertility* vs. *sterility*, *life* vs. *death*. Through the conventions and traditions of the genre, the author can successfully photograph contemporary society—perhaps snapping (by chance, in spite of himself) also the "off-key photograms" of which I have spoken. In *Platinum Blonde*, for instance, the use of the conventions of Attic comedy to explore contemporary society is particularly interesting. The protagonist of this film is the hero par excellence on the screens of the time—the newshawk—who here passes from a symbolic death (in the loss of identity that follows his marriage with Anne Schuyler) to an ethical resurrection (his wedding with Gallagher) linked to his exit from conventional worlds (he becomes a playwright).

EVERYDAY CLAUSTROPHOBIAS

Platinum Blonde opens on the chaos of the editorial offices of a newspaper, the *Post*, where Stew Smith is immediately characterized as a confident performer: heedless of the screams of the chief who is looking for him, he remains well hidden behind a screen to play with a puzzle. As Bergman points out, "the newspaper office was a great place in Depression films.... Newspapermen, by definition, were after scandal; their corruption was less a matter of graft (phony expense accounts, perhaps) than a corruption of communication. They lied" (Bergman, 21). The two main journalistic trends of the early thirties, in fact, are contraries: on one hand were the serious political commentaries; on the other, the more successful strategy of sensationalism. Readers sought and demanded explanations capable of justifying the confused events of the time; soon, however, concern for the spread of evil became morbid curiosity for every form of scandal—crime, adultery, and above all corruption. In 1930-33 *shysters*—cynical, corrupt big-city characters—populated American screens. Their presence denounced the weakness and amorality of the individual, but also mirrored the faults and ethical laxness of the entire community. Furthermore the city (especially New York) became at once a longed-for goal (greater possibilities of work) and the center of all sorts of evil (the high unemployment rate, the spread of crime and corruption). "Never has cynicism been so attractively embodied as it is in the shyster ... a lovely good bad guy who revels in an atmosphere of corruption. The shyster became an important character type in the problem film ... in three basic guises: as a mouthpiece lawyer, as a crooked politico, and as an amoral newshawk" (Roffman and Purdy, 31).

The audience's attitude toward these new characters in effect is extremely ambiguous, and even "their makers delighted in the rogues they were attempting to condemn" (Bergman, 18). The newshawk, in particular, enjoyed popular favor and encouraged identification: he is characterized as a potentially "common" man immersed in a ceaseless struggle with the difficulties of daily life, ideally in the pursuit of what is "rotten" in the country even if he himself is not always irreprehensible. Good rhetoric, lack of constraint, astuteness, self-confidence, humor, and cynicism are the qualities that allow him to survive and to control people and events. During the period of silent pictures few films had dealt with the problem of the power of the press: if the hero was a reporter, he customarily had to fight the bad guys and save the heroine. The Wall Street Crash and the Depression, however, generated a greater demand for realism (favored by the parallel advent of sound) and of a more accurate investigation of the everyday: the newshound thus became the protagonist of numerous productions. Newspaper titles and former journalists were utilized by the movie industry, which soon pinpointed an evident affinity between the public image of the reporter and that of the shyster, by virtue of which the former wound up being an integral part of the dishonest world he condemned in his articles. Like the private investigators who invaded the screens later, the reporters explore reality, try to denounce the guilty, but also lie and cheat, trampling on every ethical code and social rule that stands in the way of a good scoop, while maintaining their caustic and brilliant humor. The discovery (or invention) of a scandal unites both the editor-in-chief and the common reporter: the truth is assiduously sought after, but it is not indispensable.

In *Platinum Blonde* ace reporter Stew Smith is an accurate representative of the category, although the more unethical features of the character have vanished. When, at the beginning of the film, he is sought out because he is the only one capable of writing an article on the broken engagement in the Schuyler home, Smith boldly responds that he could do so without leaving the office. Even though they are the eyes and conscience of the people, the gossip columnists not only are capable of rendering private lives public (responding to the American conviction that the desire for privacy means that there is something to hide), they also know how to invent news if necessary. Constantly in search of a scoop, racing against time and his rival colleagues, Smith is well characterized not just visually (through his beat-up hat and slovenly clothes, or typical gestures such as the feet on the desk), but verbally as well. The rapid use of slang and vernacular reflect a tendency toward movement, essential in a world where the social immobilism of the aristocracy and the economic paralysis of banks and industry are the roots of all ills. The machine-gun bursts of the gangster hero are replaced by the rapid-fire lines that often leave Dexter, the Schuyler family lawyer, literally with his jaw hanging, stiffened as he is by attitudes and mental schemes generated by the arid snobism and stale social conventions of high society.

Generally speaking, *Platinum Blonde* gives prominence to the visuality of Capra's style, where the editing, the depth of focus, and the changes in shooting angle work together to underscore the conversation between the characters, bringing it alive emotionally for the audience. For Capra the camera, substantially, must show the characters, their states of mind, and their relations—all factors that are revealed by the language. Dialogues and verbal confrontations often distinguish the key scenes and are followed by physical actions: the camera underscores their nuances and underlying meanings, amplifying their significance. Although one-fourth of Capra's films are drawn from theatrical works, the emphasis given to words never renders them "low" or "redundant."

Smith's easy verbosity goes hand in hand with a skill in managing, overcoming, and modelling physical spaces, their vastness and their rigidity. The fluidity and plasticity of the protagonist's movements seem to refer to a unique capacity to overcome architectural and social barriers with equal dexterity: in contrast, the stiff, measured movements of the Schuylers make them prisoners of their own world. Smith will continue to enter and leave the camera's field of vision with nonchalance and to creep fancifully through the spaces between the characters, while the Schuylers often appear seated (hence "immobile") or at the margins of the frame (just as their real importance in society is marginal), enclosed in a narrow space that they are unable to violate. The metaphor of space is constantly repeated in the *mise-en-scène*: the sets of the Schuyler home, in particular, are constructed by creating plays of bars, gates, and cages, in addition to contrasts of black and white.

During these years Capra seemed to make careful use of physically large and socially complex spaces, attempting to give a symbolic context to the movements of the protagonist who, although he can sometimes aspire to privacy, often finds himself compelled to live a public life and hence to come to grips with the collectivity. The use of vast spaces, furthermore, allowed Capra and Walker to move the camera around with more freedom and creativity and to take shots with greater depth of field.

In *Platinum Blonde*, Smith and Anne are the only ones endowed with three-dimensionality (in Anne's case it is only partial), whereas the upper class is frozen in a two-dimensional iconography that reduces them to the dusty portrait of a sterile, decadent world whose relations, conventions, and values no longer have reason to exist. "Smith's movements are literally 'eccentric' whereas those of almost all the characters around him are 'concentric'" (Carney, 142): the explosive power of Smith's behavior distances him from the stereotypes that constitute the existential hub of the parvenu aristocracy. The space, therefore, is not just scenography and choreographic possiblity, but also a metaphor for personal and collective values. The Schuyler home becomes a claustrophobic universe, a gilded prison like the room of Morris Fish. The imaginative and creative hero, the brilliant, bold, and unconstrained reporter, here becomes "Anne Schuyler's husband," "Mr. Schuyler," a "gigolo," the "Cinderella man" who ends up in the papers, going from newswriter to newsmaker (here is the prototype of Mr. Deeds and Mr. Smith). But when the details of his life appear in the headlines, it means that his destiny has more than a merely private meaning, because it represents the destiny of the community. By accepting to settle down with Anne in the Schuyler home, Smith suffocates that spirit of independence and mobility that had made him alive, becoming "a bird in a gilded cage." In his new environment he is a stranger who will never manage to assimilate upper-class customs and conventions (for instance he refuses to wear a tuxedo and go to the parties): the two classes are irreconcilable.

A gleam of the independence of former days survives in the moments in which Smith leaves room to the imagination and to his eccentricity in childish gestures: as when he gives Binji a punch in the nose, or plays on the floor, or teaches the butler to make an echo in the foyer. None of these actions, however, is a valid solution to the basic problem, which is that of his momentary adhesion to a sterile, immature, and unproductive life style (his play gets bogged down). Notwithstanding the apparently spirited tone of the narrative, therefore, Capra repeatedly places the accent on the force of the sterile elements and on the discomfort and comic inadequacy of the hero inserted in the upper-class world. "Sterility," to use Poague's term, triumphs up to the last minute, in which Smith's rebellion will come to a head thanks to the constant nearness and aid of Gallagher. The girl, in fact, encourages him to begin his play starting out not from the description of distant worlds, but from his own experience of life in the Schuyler household.

Alone, the imaginative and strong-willed hero is vulnerable and incomplete; but the reciprocal recognition between the working woman and the protagonist enriches the experience of both. Smith decides to leave his wife and build a new family with Gallagher, giving her a new femininity; Gallagher instead helps Smith to fulfill himself both professionally (as a writer) and as a man (that is, a happy husband). Every form of material wealth is rejected in favor of the power of imagination and creativity: in his miserably furnished two-room apartment, with his clothes in tatters, seated at the typewriter and with Gallagher relegated to the kitchen, Smith is again the lively, confident man of the beginning, who refuses the alimony check offered by Dexter (who also receives a punch). This is the moment of the conventional resurrection: life returns and flourishes with the announcement of the new wedding, the fertility of which is foreshadowed by the completion of the comedy.

Smith, then, is an invitation to hope: nevertheless his symbolic death serves as a reminder that in Depression days the most just and effective solution is not passive acceptance of upper-class immobility, but a renewed faith in the middle-class resources of hard work and ingenuity. The road will not be so easy as it was in *That Certain Thing,* and success may not come immediately; yet the individual must remain faithful to his potential and develop his talents, even if the powers of imagination cannot settle class conflicts but, indeed, must find expression outside the social system (as playwright, Smith will make the real world a work of art). The "genteel formula" that will guarantee the success of *It Happened One Night* therefore enjoys an early triumph in *Platinum Blonde:* the vivacious, creative spirit of the middle class, after various difficulties, overwhelms the stale rules, stupid prejudices, and frozen amorphous attitudes of an upper class which, drained of all enthusiasm, merely perpetuates an obsolete tradition.

The archetypal conflict between fertility and sterility and the spectre of the Crash are represented also in the two female antagonists, Anne Schuyler and Gallagher: worlds apart physically, socially, spiritually, and emotionally, they present Smith with the problem of a complex choice that is ethical and social as well as comic and erotic. Anne is the *femme fatale,* the most sensual, irresistible woman of the world. She is the "thoroughbred" whose beauty overshadows the presence of Gallagher, the draft horse, more trustworthy but less striking. Wrapped in extremely elegant clothing, she exerts a very strong erotic appeal on Smith; but from an emotional point of view she is cold and calculating. What drives her to marriage is not love, but the desire to transform the reporter into a little gentleman (and his resistance makes the challenge even more exciting). Gallagher, on the contrary, is physically neutral for Smith; but because she truly loves him, she is the right woman for him.

The scenes in which Stew declares himself to the two women paint a good picture of the contrast between the sterility of the one and the fertility of the other, once again binding together character and environment. When he asks Anne to marry him, Smith is in the garden of the Schuyler home: the two lovers (who are not, however, the true comic lovers) find themselves behind an electrically lighted fountain, and the artificiality of the situation corresponds well to the artfulness of Harlow. Thus, "the things that should come naturally, including love, are forced and foreign" (Poague, 42). Notice here the same elements of the forthcoming Code, which inadvertently creates new narrative formulas and linguistic stereotypes, as in this famous scene. During another party Smith, now married to Anne, is sitting alone in the garden when Gallagher comes up behind him wearing a soft, elegant white dress, the moonlight (a natural light) in her hair. Seeing her, Smith exclaims: "Gallagher, what have you done to yourself?" What has changed is not so much the girl's appearance as the perception he has of her. Cinderella has become a princess; the ugly duckling, a swan.

Anne is a cool, empty, sterile beauty; for this reason her ideal environment is the marble of the Schuyler home. Gallagher, in contrast, is a lively, generous woman and is duly recognized as such in a green (and hence fertile) context. The solution of the conflict, with the victory of Gallagher (played by Loretta Young), comes about unexpectedly but very successfully. During the Depression years (but also in the Roosevelt era) the working woman who through her labor constructed an economic independence all her own, certainly proved to be a more suitable companion than the woman of luxury, accustomed to living in well-provided leisure thanks to the family income or the labors of her spouse. Although she might have been less attractive than the sexy heiress, she was certainly the only person capable of encouraging and supporting her partner in moments of difficulty. To do so, however, she had to "change clothes," to wear a different "social mask." Gallagher, in fact, considered "a pal" by her colleagues, reappropriates her femininity only when she casts off the (real and metaphorical) guise of the reporter and puts on a sophisticated evening gown that allows her to win Smith. The final scene will show her happy in the kitchen frying eggs for the future writer, even if it is she who inspires the story.

The declaration she receives is quick and concise: "I love you. I have always loved you. I want to marry you." It reflects not the romantic love or the overwhelming passion of which every woman dreams, but a love that has grown over time, based on respect and trust: a love made of solidarity, which may allow the middle-class couple to survive even in the midst of the difficulties of the Depression. If on one hand Smith foreshadows the character of Peter Warne in *It Happened One Night*, on the other Gallagher is the prototype of the independent, strong, wise woman-in-love who will see the hero through his repeated identity crises—in the manner of Babe Bennett in *Mr. Deeds Goes to Town*, Saunders in *Mr. Smith Goes to Washington*, and Anne Mitchell in *Meet John Doe*.

ESCAPE FROM THE FAMILY: *BROADWAY BILL*

No discussion of family catastrophes would be complete without a mention of *Broadway Bill*, a film that presents the collapse of the traditional values of the family as the fundamental nucleus of the American Myth. Dan Brooks is a horse-trainer who marries one of the daughters of the magnate J.L. Higgins. He also tries, unsuccessfully, to manage a paper mill belonging to his father-in-law, after which he goes back to horses, not without causing a controversy in the family. He takes his horse, *Broadway Bill*, and his faithful helper, Whitey, and tries to win a famous race. Hence begin the adventure of *Broadway Bill* and the misadventures of Dan and his friends, such as the Colonel, a pleasant, penniless swindler. The only member of the family to follow Dan is his sister-in-law Alice. With her help Dan solves various problems: a lack of funds (resolved with an intrigue of the Colonel), a cold the horse has, the ruthless competition of his adversaries. Finally the race begins. *Broadway Bill* out-distances all the competitors and crosses the finish line first, but then collapses, killed by the fatigue and the stress. As the horse is buried near the track where he won his epic race, Dan receives the uncheerful news from home: his wife has asked for a divorce, his father-in-law has practically fired him. But the faithful and discrete Alice remains; and when Dan finally notices her, he goes to pick her up at the Higgins house, announcing his arrival loudly: a stone breaks the window of the formal drawing room where the whole family is gathered (it is the signal of his love).

This is the prototype of today's "black stallions." Broadway Bill is a poor horse who fights against rich horses, like his master Dan Brooks. Both are strong but unfortunate (the horse gets sick, the man ends up in jail), and both play out on the track the needs for moral and social revenge they have accumulated in public life. The horse race as social redemption will return with the figure of the penniless Sinatra in *A Hole in the Head*. The object from which the protagonists escape at breakneck speed at the race track is Higginsville (which closely recalls Pottersville in the daydream-nightmare of George Bailey), the economic and family empire of the magnate Higgins. Higginsville is a "little monarchy" (this is Dan's accusation), where money and boredom both abound: in a spirited sequence all the members of the Higgins family eat at the same pace, lifting the food from their plates with identical movements. Broadway Bill, instead, paws the ground with *joie-de-vivre*. For this reason the struggle between Dan and Higgins, and between Broadway Bill and Gallant Lady (the favorite horse) is a fight to the death; and the horse will sacrifice himself (another sacrifice, another hero), his death settling the class contrast and mending the broken threads of affection.

Around these motifs of revenge swirls the babel of comic and semi-comic expedients, which reaches a peak in the two sequences of the "oral media," or more precisely, of the opinion leaders: when Colonel Pettigrew spreads the (false) rumor that the Duboy horse is the favorite, and when the chance bet of an eminent figure in the hospital leads to a rash of bets on Broadway Bill. In both cases, as in *American Madness*, the message is amplified and deformed in its various passages until it becomes an aberrant mass phenomenon. Instead of a bank, this time a race track is the center of the world.

CHAPTER 7

AMERICAN DREAMS, AMERICAN NIGHTMARES

ESCAPE FROM AND RECONCILIATION WITH THE FAMILY: *IT HAPPENED ONE NIGHT*

Another typical escape from the family halted by an improbable final reconciliation is that of Ellie Andrews (Claudette Colbert) from the the yacht of her millionaire father in *It Happened One Night*. Ellie's gesture carries a charge of liberating, if dramatic (and metaphorical) transgression with respect to the security of middle-class values. All will be resolved in the most classical of happy endings (marriage and another "escape," that of Ellie toward the car of Peter Warne, played by Clark Gable); but which is the "true" finale, the conventional one of the marriage, or the tragic subending in which Peter, back from the city, encounters Ellie who, escorted by the police (the protected, secluded prisoner of her class) surrenders her dream and returns home? Perhaps "reconciliation" is not possible.

Ellie, a young, spoiled heiress, gets engaged to a frivolous young man, King Westley, only to spite her father. The latter, to induce her to give up her intention, locks her in the cabin of his yacht; but the exuberant Ellie escapes and dives into the sea. Later, on a Greyhound from Miami to New York, she meets Peter, a penniless reporter who has just been fired by his boss. An adventure of travel and love ensues. Ellie's suitcase is stolen. Peter is forced to help her, partly because he realizes that Ellie is the girl about whom the papers have been talking and he is thinking about an outstanding scoop (her father is organizing a gigantic manhunt to find her). The two travel by bus, car, and thumb, splitting meager meals, doughnuts, and bedrooms (but in the motel room, to avoid misunderstandings, a blanket is made into a partition jokingly called "the wall of Jericho"). Naturally, they fall in love.

One night, while Ellie is sleeping, Peter nips up to New York to convince the editor of his newspaper to give him another chance—and some money. But the girl wakes up while he is away, believes that Peter has just used her to his own advantage, and, disappointed, calls her father and abandons the adventure. When Peter returns, he meets Andrews' cars, which have picked up the prodigal daughter. And the newspaper editor fires Peter for the umpteenth time. Preparations are made for the wedding, but Ellie's father, the old fox, has understood that his daughter is not in love with her fiancé and intercedes in Peter's favor. At the last moment, as she is about to say "I do," Ellie escapes toward a car waiting for her at the end of the driveway. Shortly thereafter the "wall of Jericho" will come tumbling down.

"A simple story for simple people": this is the slogan pronounced by Clark/Peter, a reporter in search of a story to tell. And it is also the formula of Riskin's script and Capra's movie, one of the better known and more widely studied. Thomas Schatz (*Hollywood Genres*) and Wes Gehring (*Screwball Comedy and the Comic Anti Hero*) address the problem of whether or not it belongs to the screwball comedy genre; Andrew Bergman and Robert Sklar discuss its importance in the context of Depression films. Also interesting is the comparison that can be made between Riskin's script and the story from which it is drawn, *Night Bus* by Samuel Hopkins Adams, which in turn reflects the language of films of the early thirties.[1] Here too are recurrent themes: the reporter, the contrast of status, the *coup de scène* during the wedding (it will return in *Here Comes the Groom*), etc. But the miracle of success lies in small, simple, and unpredictable secrets: Clark Gable's thumb and Claudette Colbert's calf when they are hitch-hiking, a doughnut with its hole, a bus travelling along the East Coast.

The typical theme of the Cinderella man or woman (which we have seen more than once at this point), reappears. In the typical middle-

---

[1] See, William Kittredge and Steven M. Krauzer, eds. *Stories into Film* (New York: Harper and Row, 1979).

class story a young heiress—pretty, spoiled, restless, and single—lives a bored life until the moment at which, on a whim or following an argument with her father, she escapes from her gilded cage. The girl is partially incapable of understanding the life of the outside world, and her attitudes are largely inadequate. In the course of her adventures, however, she invariably encounters a penniless, fanciful, and enterprising young man. The hero is the Cinderella man, without a social position and material assets, but rich in personal charm, kindness and initiative. The two comic lovers find themselves at the center of unforeseeable and absurd situations, which they manage to confront only thanks to imagination. Misunderstandings and disguises abound, as do moments of "acting within the acting": typical is the scene in which the two protagonists are compelled by circumstances to pretend they are man and wife.

An important change, with respect to the comedies of earlier years, is that the wealthy are not the greedy speculators responsible for the Wall Street Crash, but pleasant, amusing personages often characterized by peculiar but innocuous behavior. The screwball comedy, in fact, presents a story and a society in which social conflicts manage to be healed. The two lovers, after overcoming a thousand difficulties, declare their love and can marry with the blessing of the wealthy parent. In marriage the hero is integrated in the dominant class, which he regenerates by virtue of his comic initiative, his vitality, and his optimistic, easygoing view of life. Those who acknowledge the established order, in short, will see their dreams both of social mobility and of romantic love, crowned. For the women the message is even more explicit: romantic love and marriage are better than wealth, careers, and independence. Submission and faithfulness to one's husband are the only guarantees of happiness.

Screwball comedies are comic versions of the artful and worldly family melodramas filmed in the years after World War I. The characters are led to the threshold of social disorder, but they stop in time. The centrifugal and explosive movement of the comedies of the early thirties is replaced by a powerful centripetal and implosive force, which manages to convey every energy, character, and event toward an ideal central nucleus: the established system (both in society and in the family). When the lively young hero recognizes the legitimacy of the power of the dominant classes he is welcomed into them and wind up benefiting by those prerogatives which had been precluded to them before.

A RECONCILIATION OF THE CLASSES?

In *It Happened One Night* one finds all these new narrative processes, along with numerous elements taken up from Capra's earlier productions. After the fiasco of *The Bitter Tea of General Yen,* the director preferred to return to those stylistic devices which had once assured him success.

Originally, Peter Warne was to be a painter in Greenwich Village, a variation on Jerry Strong in *Ladies of Leisure.* Ellie, on the other hand, was simply a wealthy, spoiled, and bored heiress. Capra revisse the characters, to give them greater depth and make them more appealing to the audience. So substantial changes were made. Peter became an attractive reporter, whose contempt for the snobbish world of the upper class makes him very similar to Stew Smith in *Platinum Blonde,* but with a substantial difference. In addition to the usual impertinence, rough and resolute manners, and somewhat vaunting courage, the reporter slowly reveals unsuspected veins of idealism and the same dreamy character that will distinguish Capra's future heroes, Deeds and Smith. The two reporters, furthermore, share the pose of cynic; but Stew Smith's cynicism is an integral part of the character (the newshawk), whereas Peter Warne's is more the fruit of a choice by one who has discovered the inadequacy of the real world with respect to his dreams and his romantic expectations (he recalls having been "sucker enough to make plans").

Peter is an anomalous reporter also because he is unusually tired of the newspaper world: his heart conceals a poet who drives him to write articles in blank verse, getting him fired. This latent sensitivity, joined to his intolerance for his social role, are the same as those of Kay Arnold, a lady of leisure who no longer wants to be a gold digger; or Jerry Strong, a wealthy playboy tired of being such. The reporter-rich girl-poor girl love triangle is the same as in *Platinum Blonde*, but the two female characters are here joined in Ellie. Stew Smith had to deal with the problem of a choice that was ethical and social as well as erotic; Peter Warne experiences an even deeper confusion, meeting a women who refuses to let herself be classified according to the stereotypes he assigns to her and indeed uproots them with her unpredictability.

The character of Ellie is also modified: she is no longer an unbearable, bored, and spoiled brat, but an heiress who is bored precisely because she is spoiled, a girl who is petulant because she has never truly known the reality of life (a bit like Anne Schuyler). Imprisoned by the false expectations of those who surround her, she lacks the opportunity to discover who she really is. Peter treats her as a spoiled brat—and in the beginning she conforms to his prejudice—but away from the gilded and urban world of the wealthy, Ellie reveals unsuspected qualities of humor, exuberance, and inventiveness.

People, in short, are too multifaceted to be closed in a definition: and the propellent force in the film is precisely the theme of recognition. As Poague underscores, "Peter and Ellie learn about selfhood and about each other, and they learn to go beyond the false stereotypes that obstruct such self discovery. Every incident in the film serves to define and reveal character" (Poague, 156). In a structure typical of the comedy of errors, Peter and Ellie must unmask their true identities before themselves and others. Although their differences are not so profound as those of Megan and Yen in *Bitter Tea*, they experiment a similar movement in the collapse of old prejudices and preconceptions thanks to the clarifying force of love. A correct perception of the self seems to be achieved more readily in the sphere of a love story that ends in marriage, which is a cause of vulnerabilities in the mutual revelation but also the crowning of the romantic dream within the bounds of a social institution.

Peter is the hero representative of the middle class. Endowed with fantasy and unusual powers of imagination, he also has direct knowledge of the facts of life: and as the story unfolds he will try to communicate his notions to the upper-class snob girl. From the outset he diverts himself with conviction into a new role—of the uncompromising, good-natured teacher, willing to teach his eager pupil all he knows about life. His lessons do not express complicated philosophies, but pragmatically teach Ellie how to find pleasure in simple, everyday gestures (he teaches her the "correct" way to dip her doughnut in her coffee), or how to get by on a few dollars and a great deal of cheek (he rents just one room, pretending to be the girl's husband); or else they reveal the psychology of gestures (the lessons on how a man undresses himself, or how to hitch-hike). The revolutionary point is that Ellie is eager to learn and confronts the new experiences enthusiastically: the "shrew," in short, is happy to let herself be "tamed." That she is economically dependent on her man makes her even more vulnerable. Hers is not a pose or a pretense, and the viewer gradually becomes aware of the pleasure that simple gestures and common actions give her. As she herself confesses, Ellie has always lived under the control of tutors and governesses: the journey from Miami to New York is her first opportunity to unleash the energies that so far had remained latent, and that will make her a companion adequate to the needs of Peter (who of course is looking for "a real woman").

At the beginning of the film the two protagonists are in clear contrast, symbolizing in a typical manner the latent strife between middle and upper class: he scorns the fatuous and conceited world of the wealthy; she is both repelled and attracted by the brusque, resolute manners of this common man. The conflicts of the film do not conceal any sort of class judgment: they are quarrels dictated by stubbornness and pride, family skirmishes that end with the return of the prodigal child to the fold, and with the father/author figure welcoming the new couple with open arms (the motive of the quarrel that leads to Ellie's escape is significant, for instance: the girl argues with her father because he wants to impede her marriage with King Westley, an ace pilot).

Even Mr. Andrews, in reality, turns out to be completely different from the many impediment-fathers encountered earlier in Capra's films (not only in Capra's: Connolly repeated the role in *She Couldn't Take It* by Tay Garnett, Purnell Pratt did it in *Red Salute* by Sidney Lanfield, Claude Gillingwater in *There Goes My Heart* by Norma McLeod). He opposes the marriage not because the pretender is poor, but because he considers him "a scoundrel" (a moral judgment that regards the man, not his status). But in the end he clearly prefers as his son-in-law a young man who is penniless but resourceful and strong of character, like Peter, to the wealthy but idle Westley, more interested in money than in Ellie. Mr. Andrews, moreover, is a new capitalist, different from A.B. Charles or from the Schuylers. Significantly, he is shown in constant motion. While he pursues his daughter by plane or car his words are always "faster, faster," indicating an energy of which there was no trace in the stale, paralyzed world of the Schuylers, portrayed just three years earlier. Presumably this is the same energy that, applied to the working world, has made him so successful in business.

So one has an optimistic, post-Depression romance that proposes a social pact, a "corporative" settlement of class conflicts. The "fall of the wall of Jericho" is certainly a sexual metaphor; but it is also a metaphor for a pulling down of class barriers. Here it is the prototype of the (impossible?) reconciliation of the two families in *You Can't Take It with You*. Peter Warne's class leap is not "for a day," as in *Lady for a Day*. It is an individual and collective socio-political agreement. Does this mean that the scenario is completely optimistic and consolatory? Is one looking at a genuinely "happy" ending? Once again hope is not disjoined from the awareness and memory of evil.

DISQUIETING PRESENCES

In this picture Capra and Riskin employ the conventional devices of the middle-class narrative, adding significant changes that make the plot less sugary than it might seem. The narrative, first of all, no longer takes place in the sophisticated drawing rooms of the wealthy, but in the streets of an America still scarred by the Depression. And the people who surround the protagonists are no longer aristocratic snobs and dandies, but common men of every sort (there is the good guy, but also the bad guy). The world that is created on the screen, in short, is not a special and distant place, but a real universe that seems to represent and contain the whole of American social life: for just this reason the signs of evil are so disquieting. The city, for instance, takes on a more specifically negative power. Although it does not harbor the shysters typical of earlier films, it nonetheless represents an environment suited only to a stale, conceited character like Westley: Peter and Ellie, true and alive, are placed in the natural frame of the country and even in the final scene will crown their love not in a luxurious apartment, but in a humble motel.

In the films that follow, beginning with *Mr. Deeds Goes to Town*, the city increasingly becomes a symbol of wickedness and corruption and the center of the forces of evil. The picaresque journey through the country, however, is not idealized: the bus is uncomfortable and "two-thousand miles is a long way," as the driver points out. All kinds of characters are present in the four-wheeled microcosm, and others come from the "outside" world: almost all have a particular role for the purposes of the message, and many constitute precisely those sour notes that ring like alarm bells even in the more serene moments. During a first, brief stop, for instance, a thief steals Ellie's suitcase, leaving her with just a few dollars. The episode is a narrative expedient that works on several levels. First of all, it is a comic device: Peter, suspicious of the man's furtive approach to the suitcase, keeps an eye on him; but the girl, believing she is the object of so much attention, reacts by striking a funny, annoyed pose. On a metaphorical plane, after the theft Ellie can truly begin a new life, free from all ties with the past. In her progress toward freedom she needs the concrete help and moral support of someone more expert than she: hence she must face a new form of dependence. More directly, finally, the episode warns of the presence of dangerous characters in everyday encounters. The people around one, in short, are not all reliable, humanity is not all good, one's neighbor is not necessarily trustworthy: a few sequences further on, Peter and Ellie will be picked up by a motorist who, at the first opportunity, goes off with their suitcase. The Good Samaritan proves to be a trickster accustomed to plundering naïve passers-by: brotherly love, kindness, and altruism truly seem an impossible dream. Even the reporter, usually a cunning man of the world, has been deceived. This time, though, his reaction is quicker: after a rapid pursuit and a physical clash off camera, he returns victorious with his trophy ... and the car. In such a cruel world it seems necessary to trust in the right of might, to be ready to strike first if one does not want to yield.

Together with fear, the other obsessive presence throughout the journey is hunger—a hunger that Capra seems to have carried over from the times of *That Certain Thing*. It is the hunger of a mother who, on the bus, faints from privation while her son explains that "she hasn't eaten since yesterday," and desperately reveals their personal tragedy: "Mom hoped to find work in New York" (the spectre of unemployment is still a motive of distress). But Peter and Ellie also are hungry. The girl wants to buy a chocolate bar, but Peter does not let her, because it costs too much: people, he seems to say, have to learn to live according to their means and face the bad times while waiting for the good. During their shared breakfast, the reporter tells Ellie: "eggs, toast, milk, and coffee: that's what the house offers." Even sandwiches are too expensive for their finances.

Fear and hunger come together in the haystack scene. The two protagonists have improvised a bed from some sheaves of hay: the night is calm and silent, but the atmosphere, notwithstanding the suffused lighting, is anything but romantic. The abandoned wheel of a wagon towers in the background (progress no longer makes advances), the trees cast spectral shadows, and the moonlight is faint. Ellie complains, "I'm dying of hunger": hers is no longer the whim of a spoiled girl, but an authentic physical torment still present in the viewers' memory. Peter tries to paint the situation in less dramatic colors, speaking of "auto-suggestion," but Ellie retorts: "I'm hungry and I'm scared." The reporter tries a word-play: "Try to dispel your hunger with your fear"; but the answer is desperate: "I don't have enough fear to dispel my hunger." What might have been an amusing exchange of quips (as would have occurred, for instance, if Colbert's tone had been capricious or annoyed) instead conveys an intense dramatic character, thanks to the sincere suffering that Ellie expresses. A last bitter reference to hunger is made when the two reach the gas station. Peter tries to convince Ellie to eat raw carrots, but the girl decides to try to get the motorist who has driven them that far to offer her lunch. The reporter ironically comments, "You'd even give him a kiss for a steak, wouldn't you?" But his quip once again does not hit the mark as he had hoped, because the girl simply responds, "Of course: I'm hungry!" It is as though hunger has suddenly swept away every form of decency and shifted the limits of morality.

So it would be wrong to believe that a film like *It Happened One Night* denies the importance of money only because it calls for the reconciliation of the penniless reporter with the millionaire heiress in the end. On the contrary, money counts, and not having any doubtlessly renders life more difficult. Not all situations can be resolved by fantasy and improvisation. The climax, in this sense, is reached in the scene near the river, when Gable advises the girl to telegraph her father. Ellie makes fun of him: "Have you become scared?" but he responds, imperturbable: "No, I've become wise: the prospect of fasting isn't cheerful." In the end Peter is actually compelled to try to sell his love story with Ellie to the newspaper in order to marry her; as he will remind his editor-in-chief, "I can't marry a woman without a penny in my pocket." What could have been represented as just a carefree, picaresque adventure therefore ends up giving both protagonists a more correct—and therefore less romantic and illusory—perception of the reality that surrounds them. Ellie learns that outside of her world she no longer has any control over people and situations; she discovers she is no longer the princess to whom every privilege is due: to take a shower she has to stand in line like everyone else, surrounded not by servants but by ruffled, ill-mannered women. When she finally returns to her father, she seems an older, disillusioned woman, not a young girl excited by an "escapade": "That's enough, I wasn't able to find my happiness; it doesn't matter, I won't look for it anymore. I give up." Her wedding with Westley is to be celebrated no longer as a whim, but out of inertia, because of the failure of a transgressive and creative idea of life. And the most off-key frame of the film, in fact, is the sullen look of Ellie, escorted by the police, glimpsed by Peter from the car. A brief but intense picture of anguish.[2]

AMERICAN NIGHTMARES, *AMERICAN MADNESS*

Even in the more optimistic films, therefore, the American Dream sometimes slips into an American Nightmare. Even in Peter and Ellie's bus, in the long night of their disappearance. But the film which best of all expresses the American nightmare's reality, is *American Madness*.

Thomas Dixon is the enlightened president of the Union National Bank. Against the opinion of his board of directors, he insists on granting loans based more on the character of the client than on economic guarantees. But a perverse mechanism is being constructed behind his back. While he devotes all his energies to his work, his wife yields to the advances of the wicked teller Cluett (who has a $50,000 debt with a gangster and is drawn by the latter into a scheme to rob the bank). To give himself an alibi, Cluett arranges to be with Dixon at the moment of the hold-up. The suspicions therefore fall on Matt Brown, the other

---

[2] *It Happened One Night* is crucial to Joseph McBride's book. It "happened" in a paradoxically difficult moment of Capra's life, when the director felt insecure and ill. The film marked a turning point in Capra's career: the beginning of "the catastrophe of success." "But at this critical point in his career, Capra faced his future secretly crippled by fear" (McBride, 314): just after *It Happened One Night* and its "accidental" success, Capra became weak and anxious. As I already pointed out, McBride is carried away by this psychoanalytic reading, but it is true that 1934 was a turning point for Capra, as it was for U.S. film history. Because McBride reads too much of Capra's life into his work, he reaches such conclusions as the following: "Riskin and Capra portrayed the rich much more sympathetically in *It Happened One Night* than they did in *Platinum Blonde*, perhaps because they themselves were becoming wealthy men" (306).

teller of the bank, an ex-convict who has won Dixon's trust. Word of the robbery gets out (the rumors make the sum grow from $100,000 to $500,000 to $5,000,000), and people rush to the bank windows to take out their savings. Dixon tries to check the flow of money, which is ruining the bank. He is alone: neither his co-directors nor his board of trustees is willing to run a personal risk in order to help him. But the faithful and grateful Matt calls Dixon's friends, those whom he has helped, and asks them to put their savings into the bank. The friends rush to his aid and with their prompt response convince the other directors, too, to defend the bank. Meanwhile the police nab Cluett, who is really behind the robbery. The bank is safe.

Bourgeois drama, film noir, Rooseveltian comedy: the bank is the center of the world, its golden navel; the safe is like a shrine, the rite of its closure or of its robbery is sacred. A scaled-down copy of American society, the Union National Bank reproduces not only its "madness," but also its sketches (of petty office workers and switchboard operators like in Camerini's films), its dark conspiracies (the adultery of the director's wife), and its crimes (the mystery story). And Capra's camera dwells at length on this world to be discovered: it tracks from beneath the table of the board room to the legs of the girls on the stairs and among the lines of the crowd at the windows. And it looks down, taking part in, but also detached from and somewhat ironic about, the world's collective folly.

American Madness is a lucidly critical film that ranges from social drama to detective story to comedy, directly and forcefully revealing the fears and panic created by the New York Stock Exchange crash. Its acute analysis of the catastrophe that overwhelmed not only the economy, but also American values, is conducted by Capra with a skill that reveals his full maturity as an author. Robert Riskin's subject focuses attention on a hero who is rather improbable in the historic context of his time: a banker. (Although there are many supporting characters in Hollywood films, like Grant Mitchell in *One More Spring*, in order to emphisize the banker as a figure of integrity). What is more, Tom Dixon is also a sort of contradiction in terms, because as the story develops he is clearly represented as a populist banker. Dixon in fact is the president of the Union National Bank (the very concept of union—in the sense of federation of autonomous entities—belongs to the nineteenth century), whose directors are counting on a merger with New York Trust (which instead represents the concentration of economic power). Capra does not want to attack banks and bankers in general, so much as the way in which they often work: in short there is a right way and a wrong way of being a banker.

The directors are typical representatives of selfish, unscrupulous conservative finance of the pre-Keynesian type. They explicitly recall those who contributed to the stock market crash with their obsolete economics, under the Hoover Administration. Interested above all in the immediate accumulation of wealth and in personal gain, they are unable to understand the potential implicit in the policy of Dixon, whom they paradoxically judge a liberal. Dixon, the hero, was modelled after two real figures, the brothers Amedeo Peter and Attilio Henry Giannini, the sons of Italian immigrants in California. In 1904 Amedeo founded the Bank of Italy—which would later become the Bank of America—in San Francisco. His system of management was completely new and, at least in appearance, fairly risky: small branches were opened in various cities, in the attempt to attract small and medium savers. Loans were granted to private citizens (for instance, to buy a house on monthly installments) and small firms, requesting only minimal guarantees: what counted was the validity of the purpose and the character of the applicant. In 1930 Transamerica Corporation, the bank's finance company, was the most powerful firm of its kind in the world: Giannini encouraged public participation in his corporation and helped his employees become stockholders thanks to a profit-sharing plan.[3]

---

[3] See Edward Buscombe, "Notes on Columbia Pictures," cit. See also Bob Thomas, *King Cohn* (New York: G.P. Putnam, 1967), and Brian Taves, "Studio Metamorphosis. Columbia's Emergence From Poverty Row," in Robert Sklar and Vito Zagarrio (eds.), *Frank Capra. Authorship and the Studio System*, cit.

His brother Attilio took an interest in cinema and worked with several independent studios between the two world wars. Columbia was established thanks also to a $100,000 loan from him, and the banker remained a member of the executive council even after Joseph Brandt was liquidated by the Cohn brothers. While most of the banks that invested in the movie industry were attracted by the real estate (the chains of theaters), Giannini was interested in making movies: Columbia, in fact, was one of the few studios that did not possess its own theater chain.

The two brothers were estranged from the New York banking establishment, with whom they were very unpopular. In 1935 Amedeo Peter supported the Banking Act introduced by Roosevelt, convinced that reinforcement of the Federal Reserve Bank and measures of government control were preferable to the uncontrolled predominance of Wall Street. Then in 1936 he supported the re-election of the Democratic President in a period in which the conservative financiers considered him a real threat to their interests: by helping small business and farmers, the Gianninis came into line with the policy of the New Deal.

Dixon seems to follow a similar strategy, but it must be pointed out that in this film Capra is torn between the individualist positions of nineteenth-century populism and the interventionist economic principles of the New Deal. On one hand the banker believes that the cause of the Depression can be traced to the selfishness and greed of those who accumulate money, keeping it out of circulation and impeding its use in the strengthening of industry. The problem therefore can be solved only by keeping purchasing power high. On the other hand, the decision to loan money on the basis of character is typical of the agrarian, populist America of the nineteenth century (it will also be the moral of *It's a Wonderful Life*). On the ethical-ideological level the film's theme thus becomes "the conflict between a resolute individual, full of goodwill toward his fellow men, and the forces of disunity and corruption who would create and exploit social dislocations for their own benefit."[4] The Depression is presented incisively: premonitory signals are accumulated from the outset, even if they are often attenuated by the brilliant context created above all by the dialogue. In one of the first sequences Matt has just distributed the cash to the cashiers when he asks one of them to lend him $10. His colleague refuses, first playfully singing, "I can't give you anything but love," but then reminding him, "Didn't you hear a Depression is on?" Matt, in reality, is well aware of the current situation: in fact he cannot marry Helen, Dixon's secretary, precisely because of their economic difficulties. The position of assistant accountant would be the only solution for the young couple.

In another scene a cashier jokes with a colleague: "See you in the breadlines!" while a young woman discovers with disappointment that she cannot cash a check because it is uncovered. Fundamental for establishing the narrative movements as well as the social and cultural context in which the film takes place, is the first encounter between Dixon and the board of directors. The board is led by Mr. Clark, the typical evil capitalist in Capra: fat and with a perennially smoking cigar. He reads to his colleagues the list of those who have benefited from loans and financing: they are humble names and professions, small businessmen who have nothing to do with the large firms that in real life dominated the American market during the thirties. Clearly, for Dixon the bank is not a speculative concern, but an enterprise with personal character—almost a living appendix of his person. To it alone he has devoted his efforts and his energies, neglecting even his wife. His refusal of the merger has a strictly private motivation, more than an ideological one: "Why should I turn over this bank to somebody else? I've worked for twenty-five years night and day to build it up."

His care for the small laborer and the intermediate saver and his faith in strength of character and in the ultimate goodness of the American way of life are not, however, the only elements that Dixon shares

---

[4] John Raeburn, "American Madness and American Values," in Glatzer and Raeburn, 57-58.

with Rooseveltian politics. His attentive and sensitive attitude and the personal relationship he establishes with his clients and employees are similar to that of the President toward the great mass of voters. Dixon reminds the directors that his account holders trust in him as a man, not only as an important social figure: "They're my friends. They're looking at me for protection, and I'm not working on them." His concern makes him a sort of father figure in what can be considered a big family. Inside the bank the virtues most appreciated prove to be personal qualities such as sensitivity, tact, and respect, more than courage or heroism. Moreover, that the banker is always so present in the life of his clients (contrary to the Hoover Administration in the twenties) will guarantee him a minimum of trust on the part of some of his protégés when the time comes.

In the sequence under examination Capra seems to want to underscore that Dixon's policy is not just a form of charitable philanthropy. The banker is also a skillful manager who can proudly boast of the effectiveness of his action: "How many losses has this Bank taken in the last twenty-five years? I tell you: not a single one!" Dixon's policy would therefore seem to prove valid both from an ethical viewpoint and in terms of economic advantage. Nevertheless he cannot close his eyes to what is going on in contemporary society: thus, when one of the directors tries to cut him short recalling that "Conditions are changed. Banks today have got to be careful and you're more liberal than ever," Dixon is not intimidated and begins a long tirade maintaining that "We've got to keep the money in circulation before we get this country back to prosperity." The catastrophe, however, impends threateningly. This time it is an experience that overwhelms not only the lives of the single heroes, but the existence of an entire crowd: "The fearful and panicked mob is the objectification of the profound anxiety felt by everyone in this society" (Raeburn, 61).

Cyrill Cluett's gangster creditors convince him to tamper with the automatic lock mechanism on the bank's armored safe. In this way they easily manage to get their hands on $100,000, but during their escape the night guard is killed (the first victim of the catastrophe). Word of the theft rapidly spreads, and the sum reported increases from one report to the next. The people, seized by panic, run to the bank to withdraw their savings. In re-creating on the screen a dramatic scene from the life of just a few years earlier, Capra clearly expresses his perplexities and anxieties about those same people he customarily seemed to esteem and exalt. In connection with *The Miracle Woman* I have already observed how he deeply feared the depersonalization of the individual in modern mass society. Capra thinks very highly of the single individual, underscoring the uniqueness and preciousness of his personality. Furthermore he is also convinced, as John Doe will say, that "it is the character of these millions of molecules that mold the character of a nation." Society for him is made in the image of the individual; thus it is essential that the honest man succeed in converting the entire community to his vision.

But the director is also aware that the individual often loses his capacity to think autonomously in the crowd, becoming exploitable and dull-minded and losing sight of everyday values. Individual freedom then becomes a danger, too, because the reactions of the unguided crowd are unpredictable and unstoppable. "Individual man, under the pressure of the Depression, was becoming mass man, and mass man was irrational, cruel, and uninterested in the value of the community" (Raeburn, 65). One false rumor is enough to transform and stun the mass which, without judgment and a will of its own, is dragged on by its own actions. The crowd is not a simple background to the action, but an active protagonist of considerable depth. And the hero-mob conflict, which is also the self-society conflict, often generates the dynamics of the narrative. The crowd bursts into the life of the protagonist with a negative power: it is the community which, with its conventions, impedes the fulfillment of the outsider-hero; it is the angry mob that disowns its benefactor; it is the curious and gossipy neighborhood that makes all forms of privacy impossible; and it is the thick-headed mass that allows itself to be deceived by false idols (the miracle woman) and continues to crucify the real heroes (John Doe).

In this context Capra's populism is clearly contradictory. According to the original populist ideology of the nineteenth-century agrarian Midwest, the common people are always right and never do wrong, as they are guided by the purest motives. In a Manichaean vision evil is incarnated in bankers, lawyers, politicians, and intellectuals—in short, in all those who move in the corrupt microcosm of the city. The mythicized heroes are Christ (who may be glimpsed behind John Doe) and Lincoln (protagonist of Ford's *Young Mr. Lincoln*), innocent victims of intolerance and of totalitarian power. The ideals supported are those on which the American homeland was originally established: hard work, simplicity, purity of heart, trust in the capacities of the individual, the family, the community, and democracy. All these ideals, in effect, are present in Capra's films, although I have demonstrated that they also show a deep, hidden dark side.

The populist world view is realized in the small town or in the country, which constitute topoi in the Deeds-Smith-Doe trilogy. Yet evil lingers even in Capra's small communities, perhaps in the guise of the envious and curious neighbor, or in the betrayal (real or apparent) of those one believed to be friends. One can therefore conclude that Capra wanted to believe in the populist ethic, but was also aware that the "people" are capable of rapidly denying those same principles they usually affirm.

As Charles Alexis de Tocqueville has pointed out, freedom of conduct is one of the greatest strengths and weaknesses of American society. If on one hand it allows the individual maximum liberty, on the other it provides the basis for a large mob to usurp power, to the prejudice of reason.

During the bank run, Dixon tries to calm and reassure the people, but in vain: his words are jeered as a human tide washes over him. Even the phone calls made in the effort to obtain loans prove useless: his policy line seems to fail, his trust in the people proves misplaced. What is more, the financial drama is flanked by that of the presumed betrayal of his wife with Cluett. Just as the mob for an instant loses faith in its leader and benefactor (and, of course, in traditional values and institutions), so Dixon feels a sense of loss and doubt toward Matt (who, when accused, refuses to reveal where he was at the time of the robbery), toward his wife (whose embarrassment seems to confirm the betrayal), and toward his own people (who have abandoned him). And whereas before the banker had been characterized by unconstrained, energetic movements, by convincing and effective speech (like Stew Smith), by presence of spirit, and by the capacity to control people and events, now he is reduced to a mannequin paralyzed by the collapse of faith in his ideals. Fallen into a state of painful apathy, disappointed by everything and everyone, sitting silent and inert, Dixon even reaches the point of contemplating suicide. The camera follows his movements carefully as he opens a desk drawer to put away his wife's photograph: a brief dolly followed by a rapid tracking shot focus the viewer's gaze on the gun that lies in the drawer. The suicide is not carried out, but the very fact that it hovers as a disquieting presence in the life of an honest man attached to sound values, seems to underscore the unpredictability and the seriousness of the consequences of an unsuccessful act of faith. The hero has been defeated, and his strength, his energy, are not sufficient to raise him from his state of prostration. His strength will be restored by his friends, by the many Joneses whom he has helped and who now (as in the finale of *It's A Wonderful Life*) run to deposit their savings, confirming their confidence in him. Comforted by this demonstration of trust and by his wife's declaration of love, the banker comes back to life and is able even to convince the board of directors to invest their money. This time a good "madness"—contrary to that which had caused the bank run—seems to capture the humblest clients and the bosses both; as Mr. Clark (previously Dixon's most indomitable adversary) says, "When everybody goes crazy, I'll go crazy too."

American Madness seems then to wed the dramatic picture of contemporary events (and the sense of disorientation, confusion, and apprehension typical of the time) with a message of hope for the future:

Capra does not maintain, as Hoover did, that "prosperity is just around the corner," but proclaims instead that "the only thing to fear is fear itself": the future battle cry of the New Deal. Yet though it ends on a note of confidence and optimism, the film portrays an America that does not leave much room for hope. The proof is in the film's "form" and in Capra's "style."

CONTEXT AND STYLE

American Madness represents a fundamental stage in Capra's filmmaking, partly because of the stylistic maturity reached by the director. Nevertheless, the judgment of Donald C. Willis, who reduces the film to "a pure technical exercise, a successful if rather hollow one, with the characters strictly agents of the tricky plot" (Willis, 132), seems inadequate. In Capra's oeuvre form is always strictly subordinated to content and to the transmission of the message. Most of the stylistic decisions, furthermore, aim at underscoring the reactions, feelings, and thoughts of the protagonists: the camera is placed at the service of the character and is never exhibited gratuitously. *American Madness* is a good example of Capra's style in this sense.

The plot of the film is inserted in a circular structure. The facts are concentrated in just three days, and the first and last sequence reiterate the rite of the opening of the armored safe. The safe is the central fetish around which the American madness revolves, being the very emblem of capitalism. Apparently it is a massive, solid mechanism, the impregnable stronghold of the U.S. economy: and yet it is also something extremely slow in its movements, which appear inadequate and syncopated with respect to the frenetic rhythm of the lives of the bank and of Dixon. The automatic lock mechanism, furthermore, seems to give it a life of its own. Often shot with a series of gates and grates before the camera, it constitutes a sort of shrine, entrance to which is reserved for just a few adepts, making it an institution that is difficult to approach. This bastion can nevertheless be conquered the moment a traitor sabotages it from within.

The stock market crash demonstrated that American capitalism was rotten to the core, and the guilty were openly identified as the bankers who "failed through their own stubborness and their own incompetence," as Roosevelt recalled in his inaugural address. So, it probably is not coincidental that the cause of the catastrophe in *American Madness* is Cyrill Cluett, the head cashier, who tampers with the timer that opens the safe.

One of the last sequences repeats the usual opening rite: the bank is safe now, and order seems to have been reestablished. Nevertheless, the line that Matt tosses at the cashiers about the fact that the day before they "ran for their money" seems aimed at pointing out how delicate and precarious the newly regained equilibrium really is. The gap between wisdom and madness, order and disorder, is so small that it constitutes a threatening presence that hangs over everyday life.

The parallel between good and evil, right and wrong, confidence and desperation, tranquility and panic is skillfully constructed in two other sequences realized with the use of long tracking shots. At the beginning of the film Matt hands out cash to the cashiers, going from window to window with one of them. While they push the carts with the money the two are followed by the fluid movements of the tracking shot: their conversation continues without interruption, the mood is relaxed, and the situation is under control. Nothing special is happening. Later, however—during the bank run—we see Dixon running along the same route, trying to give rapid and precise instructions to each of the cashiers. This time the movements of the camera using the tracking shot are no longer homogeneous and invisible, but rushed and "dirty," re-creating all the urgency of the moment with their speed.

Generally speaking, the pace of the film conforms perfectly to that of the action: for the first time Capra uses accelerated tempo, that is, a pace one-third faster than normal. During a screening, in fact, the director noticed that the action seemed to proceed too slowly, running the risk of boring the audience. So he changed the pace of filming: the actors were compelled to act more quickly, and rapid cuts were prefered to cross-fades (widely used at the time, but requiring longer dead times). The actors' lines, furthermore, are often interrupted or made to overlap each other, just as occurs in reality: another major change with respect to the custom of speaking in complete sentences, as was current in theater. In this circumstance a fundamental contribution was made by the sound technician Ed Bernds, who used microphones concealed on the actors' bodies. In any case Capra skillfully exploited sound since the beginning in a creative way, realizing—also thanks to Riskin—lively, colloquial dialogue very close to reality.

But atmosphere is not created by words alone: often ambient noise can underscore what happens on the screen, making the action even more convincing and effective. In the hold-up scene, for example, the human voices, but even the echoes of the steps, the squeaking of the mechanisms, the wheels of the carts, the doors opening and closing, create a sense of isolation, violated sacrality, and suspense in clear contrast with the cheeerful confusion of the noises of the bank during the day. Even more effective is the use of noise during the bank run. When a small crowd begins to form, one hears only the sound of the hurried steps of the people running to the windows. Soon, however, the crowd grows to the point that it is no longer possible to hear and distinguish single individuals: one hears only an undecipherable buzz that constantly grows in volume, sprinkled now and then with desperate cries or angry exclamations. Capra succeeds in rendering the movements of the individual extras intense and meaningful by adequately instructing them regarding their hypothetical motive in each given scene.

But editing remains the means Capra uses most often to create the desired effects in the viewer's heart: "the frequency of cutting in Capra demonstrates an intensity of interest corresponding to the emotional magnitude of a given scene in its given context.... Cutting tends to increase during moments of emotional and ethical significance, when our own interest and ethical curiosity reach a peak" (Poague, 112). In *American Madness* Capra uses editing not only to give the film a fast pace, but also to portray "the dissipation of rationality under stress, and the concomitant growth of a mob psychology as panic begins to take over."[5] The switchboard operator at the bank rashly begins to spread the news of the robbery: in just a few minutes in montage sequence one sees a series of close-ups and medium shots that make it possible to follow the spread of the news and its distortion. This extraordinary sequence is multifunctional. The short lines exchanged by the characters re-create the growing sense of doubt, uncertainty, and, finally, panic; as one of them says: "That's the trouble nowadays, you don't know whom you can trust." The central problem is therefore the loss of confidence in institutions and in traditional values, destabilization and uncertainty regarding one's own destiny. The characters' faces, their dress, the accents of their voices show they belong to all ages, classes, and ethnic groups (there is the Japanese, the Jew...). In historical reality, those most dramatically hit by the Depression were in fact the small and medium savers, the men-on-the-street who lacked any sort of technical-financial notion and allowed themselves to be overwhelmed by the collective madness of stock-market speculation. Many of these faces, finally, are shot from unusual angles, and with an expressionistic use of light: in this case the unusual stylistic choice is intended to render the sense of disorientation, instability, anomaly, and disorder implicit in the film's title.

Another kind of peculiar shot is a sort of "semi-point-of-view (à la Bogart in *The Maltese Falcon*, for instance): the principal character is shot from behind at the center or at one side of the frame, while a fundamental event takes place in front of him that focuses his and our attention and that could have been shot, for example, in point-of-view. This kind of shot differs, however, from the point-of-view by virtue of a very particular characteristic. Whereas in the point-of-view the identification between the spectator's viewpoint and the protagonist's is made implicit and invisible, in the "semi-point-of-view" it is given prominence and declared. Spectator and actor participate—being on

---

[5] R. Glatzer and J. Raeburn, eds., 64.

the same side —in the vision of an event that closely regards both; but at the same time, with this technique, they succeed also in maintaining a distance from the events on the screen. Witness in this connection Dixon's attempt to calm the angry crowd during the bank run. After making his way with difficulty through the crowd, the banker mounts the steps of the staircase leading to the mezzanine, and from that improvised pulpit tries to control the growing panic. His speech is not shot from the point of view of the crowd—that is, placing him before his audience—but in a counterfield that is maintained throughout the scene and that includes Dixon himself, from behind, at the center of the frame.

From the style of *American Madness,* then, comes the strongest transgression of Capracorn, which is based also on stylistic elements: on the "intermediate" style, on the "axial" editing, on the disapperance of the camera, on a reassuring and comforting filmic narrative. Here, instead, the photography is nervous and neurotic, the accelerated tempo creates anxiety, the mob scenes disturb us with images of an America populated by "zombies," as in Ford's *The Grapes of Wrath* or in *Meet John Doe.*

The Tragic Dimension of American Culture

The final homage to *Meet John Doe* brings us back to the most well known period of Capra's filmography. After *It Happened One Night* we have to face what we can define the "classic" Capra. From *Mr. Deeds Goes to Town* to *It's a Wonderful Life*, our director builds his most famous masterpieces. But even there, it is easy to try a different reading of Capra's films, too easily canonized and superficially analyzed. Even there, we can find evidences of those "tragic dimensions of American culture" Robert Sklar discusses in the foreword to this volume.

The best demonstratiuon is *Meet John Doe*, an atypical film about mass society that mixes demagogy, Christian parables, apparent antiauthoritarianism, and unconscious authoritarianism. A pessimistic examination of the uneven struggle between man and the system, it is the story of a hobo who is transformed with the help of the mass media into a popular and influential hero and who is then betrayed and abandoned by the same faceless mob who initially exalted him. Not surprisingly, it is the only film of his long career for which Capra was unable to resolve the ending. *Meet John Doe* makes plain the nature of the fissure that had marred the American model. Not only is the film unable to reconcile what had become an irreconcilable dichotomy; it is a gloomy mirror of a society of sheep at the mercy of an aberrant system.

The American Dream assumes the connotations of a nightmare, not only through the specter of the war seething in Europe, but also through the unconscious collapse of the optimistic structure of Capra's discourse and the explosion of vaster contradictions within the American system: mass control mechanisms, information manipulation systems, and forms of social stratification. John Doe lives no more and no less than the same recurrent fable (that of *Lady for a Day*) of momentary and chance happiness; but this time the same daydream is a bad dream filled with ghosts —the phantoms of that "fascism of the spirit" of which Nollte and Fromm speak, a fascism with many faces, a death wish, a need to flee from freedom that highlights the parallels between the portrayal of the masses in this film and the mass control techniques of the German Nazi Party. *Meet John Doe* provides a warning of the crisis-to-come, the crisis of the Capra model and more generally of the New Deal. The fact that Capra shot five different versions of the film's finale demonstrates that the narrative he had schematized no longer worked. What is missing is the magnificent Capra/Riskin sense of plot, where everything builds toward the final suspense. The "dramatic pinnacles" do not lead toward resolution, but writhe instead in the bowels of a "cursed" film.

However, some traces of this pessimistic vision are clear also in the easier comedies of the 30s: let us think about the anguish of the Depression and the corruption of society in *Mr. Deeds Goes to Town*; the corruption of politics and James Stewart fainting—after he's defeated in the Senate—in *Mr. Smith Goes to Washington*; the class conflicts in *You Can't Take It With You*; the war and racial conflicts at the beginning of *Lost Horizon* and the anguishing end of the Utopia in the same film.

Later, in the 40s, let us think about the huge tragedy of the war represented in the famous series of *Why We Fight*; the subtle metaphors of horror and madness hidden behind the comedy genre in *Arsenic and Old Lace*; the existential problems of Frank Sinatra in *A Hole in Head*; the contradiction of the American Dream exploding in *Pocketful of Miracles*; and above all the large nightmare we have already emphasized in *It's a Wonderful Life*, whose title sounds ironical like Fellini's "sweet" life.

Is Capra an *auteur*? A re-reading of Capra must try a reconsideration of certain points of style, of his typical way of making films. Capra's brand of authorship[1] is not that of "New Hollywood" authors, as it does

---

[1] See John Caughie, *Theories of Authorship* (London: Routledge & Kegan Paul, 1981); Peter Wollen, *Signs and Meaning in the Cinema* (London: Secker & Warburg, 1969 [1972]). Nick Browne, "Rhétorique du Text Spéculaire," *Communications*, 23 (Paris: Seuil, 1975); Edward Buscombe, "Ideas of Authorship," *Screen* 14.3 [Autumn 1973]); Jean Luc Comolli, "Vingt Ans

not take poetics as a priority. It is a defense of the role of the director with respect to the film industry; an awareness of the art/merchandise mixture that that industry imposes; a use of craft (as opposed to art) to express a world; and a consciousness of cinema as a group effort. Screen-writer, director of photography, star, and character actors, a smoothly efficient crew and the "usual" cast of characters, all dependable talents: this is the solid platform that allowed Capra to ride the wave of success throughout the 1930s and that subsequently—with ups and downs - carried him through to the masterful *It's a Wonderful Life*. During these years Capra earned his right to be called an auteur. The "name above the title," as his autobiography boasts, is not that of the star or the Studio, it is the director's. His is the signature above the film's credits. This does not mean, however, that Capra claimed an artistic "aura": he stated on more than one occasion that his goal was not to make art, but to create a well-made product within the boundaries of an industry and the context of a group in which the contributions of co-workers and crew were decisive factors. Hence his primary concern was not to produce works of art, but to claim leadership within the studio system and to exert the autonomy of choice granted him by studio executives. To a director, top billing means freedom of movement. To the Studios it means that the director's name guarantees more ticket sales than the name of the star. Capra was party to the convergence of interests that permitted Hollywood directors to come out of anonymity, to move from pure craftsmanship toward a more exacting professional, decision-making presence.[2] He was the first director of "old Hollywood" who thought of himself as an author, and even in a careful reading of what at times is a narcissistic autobiography written with the wisdom of hindsight, one can isolate a constant search for autonomous creative space in his progress as a director. In Capra's eyes the recognition (in the sense of both fame and honor) of having his name above the title after

---

Après: le cinéma américain et la politique des auteurs," *Cahiers du Cinéma* 172 (November 1965).

[2]Tino Balio, ed., *The American Film Industry* (Madison: University of Wisconsin Press, 1976).

having been at the bottom of the social ladder, is an affirmation that the original American Dream had been achieved. The notion of auteur therefore had personal significance as well as historic and economic importance vis-a-vis the Hollywood production-system ethic of the self-made man. Perhaps Capra did not have the "Lubitsch touch," he is not a Hawks, or a Ford,[3] and he is not to be found in the lists of "Politique des auteurs" in *Cahiers du Cinéma* or in the auteurist theory of Andrew Sarris.[4] Nevertheless, he owns another kind of "touch", that one Robert Riskin was sometimes angry about:[5] a deep consciousness of the *comedie humaine*, a mature knowledge of the structure of narration and emotions, a precise vision of the world, a *Weltanschauung*.

And even in terms of style, although he's not a director using the camera movements in an "acrobatic" way, such as Welles or Hithcock, he shows a clear talent in his directorial job, in his *mise en scène*.

But this is another story, as Billy Wilder would say.... And I postpone this debate to my next book. On Frank Capra.

---

[3]Robin Wood, *Howard Hawks* (London: Secker & Warburg, 1968); Jean Loup Bourget, *John Ford* (Paris: Editions Rivages, 1990); Lindsay Anderson, *About John Ford* (New York: McGraw Hill, 1981).

[4]Andrew Sarris, *The American Cinema: Directors and Directions, 1929-1968* (New York: E.P. Dutton, 1968).

[5]In a famous anecdote, Robert Riskin, tired of the "Capra's touch" the audience devoted to the director, send him a completely blank script: "Put your famous touch on this...."

1922
FULTAH FISHER'S BOARDING HOUSE
Director: Frank Capra; *Screenplay*: Walter Montague (from the poem *The Ballad of Fultah Fisher's Boarding House* by Rudyard Kipling in *Departmental Ditties and Other Poems*, 1899); *Cinematographer*: Roy Wiggins; *Cast*: Mildred Owens (Anne of Austria), Ethan Allen (Salem Hardicker), Olaf Skavian (Hans); *Producer*: Fireside Productions; *Distribution*: Pathè; *Runtime*: 12'

1926
THE STRONG MAN
Director: Frank Capra; *Assistant Director*: J. Frank Holiday; *Screenplay*: Frank Capra, Arthur Ripley, Hal Conklin, Robert Eddy, Harry Langdon (from a story by Arthur Ripley); *Cinematographers*: Elgin Lessley, Glenn Kershner; *Editor*: Harold Young; *Titles*: Reed Henstis; *Cast*: Harry Langdon (Paul Bergot), Gertrude Astor ("Lily" of Broadway), Priscilla Bonner (Mary Brown), William V. Mong (Parson Brown), Robert McKim (Roy McDevitt), Arthur Thalasso (Zandow); *Producer*: Harry Langdon; *Distribution*: First National; *Runtime*: 60'

1927
LONG PANTS
Director: Frank Capra; *Screenplay*: Arthur Ripley, Robert Eddy; *Cinematographers*: Elgin Lessley, Glenn Kershner; *Cast*: Harry Langdon (the boy), Gladys Brockwell (his mother), Al Roscoe (his father), Alma Bennett (the Vamp), Priscilla Bonner (Priscilla), Frankie Darro (Harry as child), Betty Francisco (the blond girl who fight with the Vamp); *Producer*: Harry Langdon; *Distribution*: First National; *Runtime*: 60'

1927
FOR THE LOVE OF MIKE
Director: Frank Capra; *Screenplay*: Leland Hayward, J. Clarkson Miller (from a story by John Moroso titled *Hell's Kitchen*); *Cinematographer*: Joy Boyle; *Cast*: Claudette Colbert (Mary), Ben Lyon (Mike), Ford Sterling (Herman Schultz), George Sidney (Abraham Katz), Hugh Cameron (Patrick O'Malley), Richard "Skeets" Gallagher ("Coxey" Pendleton), Rudolph Cameron (Henry Sharp), Mabel Swor (Evelyn Joyce); *Producer*: Robert Kane; *Distribution*: First National; *Runtime*: 73'

1928

THAT CERTAIN THING

Director: Frank Capra; *Screenplay*: Elmer Harris (according to some sources, from a story by Frank Capra); *Cinematographer*: Joseph Walker; *Art Director*: Robert E. Lee; *Editor*: Arthur Roberts; *Cast*: Viola Dana (Molly Kelly), Aggie Herring (Maggie Kelly), Ralph Graves (A. B. Charles Jr.), Burr McIntosh (A.B. Charles), Carl Gerard (Secretary Brooks), Sydney Crossley (Valet); *Producer*: Harry Cohn for Columbia Pictures Corporation; *Distribution*: Columbia Pictures Corporation; *Runtime*: 69'

1928

SO THIS IS LOVE

Director: Frank Capra; *Assistant Director*: Eugene De Rue; *Screenplay*: Elmer Harris, Rex Taylor (from a story by Norman Sprinter); *Cinematographer*: Ray June; *Art Director*: Robert E. Lee; *Editor*: Athur Roberts; *Cast*: Shirley Mason (Hilda Jenson), William Collier (Jerry McGuire), Johnnie Walker ("Spike" Mulligan), Ernie Adams ("Flash" Tracy), Carl Gerard (Otto), William H. Strauss ("Maison" Katz), Jean Lavery (Mary Malone); *Producer*: Harry Cohn for Columbia Pictures Corporation; *Distribution*: Columbia Pictures Corporation; *Runtime*: 60'

1928

THE MATINEE IDOL

Director: Frank Capra; *Assistant Director*: Eugene De Rue; *Screenplay*: Elmer Harris, Peter Milne (from a story by Robert Lord and Ernest S. Pagano); *Cinematographer*: Phillip Tannura; *Art Director*: Robert E. Lee; *Editor*: Arthur Roberts; *Cast*: Bessie Love (Ginger Bolivar), Johnnie Walker (Don Wilson), Lionel Belmore (Colonel Bolivar), Ernest Hilliard (Wingate), Sidney D'Albrook (J. Madison Wilberforce), David Mir (Eric Barrymaine); *Producer*: Harry Cohn for Columbia Pictures Corporation; *Distribution*: Columbia Pictures Corporation; *Runtime*: 66'

1928

THE WAY OF THE STRONG

Director: Frank Capra; *Screenplay*: William Counselman, Peter Milne; *Cinematographer*: Ben Reynolds; *Cast*: Mitchell Lewis (Handsome Williams), Alice Day (Nora), Margaret Livingston (Marie), Theodore von Eltz (Dan), William Norton Bailey (Tiger Louise); *Producer*: Harry Cohn for Columbia Pictures Corporation; *Distribution*: Columbia Pictures Corporation; *Runtime*: 61'

1928

SAY IT WITH SABLES

Director: Frank Capra; *Assistant Director*: Joe Nadel; *Screenplay*: Dorothy Howell (from a story by Frank Capra and Peter Milne); *Cinematographer*: Joseph Walker; *Art Director*: Harrison Wiley; *Editor*: Arthur Roberts; *Cast*: Melene Chadwick (Helen), Francio X. Bushman (John Caswell), Margaret Livingstone (Irene Gordon), Arthur Rankin (Doug Caswell), June Nash (Marie Caswell), Alphonse Ethier (Mitchell); Edna Mae Cooper (Maid); *Producer*: Harry Cohn/Frank Capra Production for Columbia Pictures Corporation; *Distribution*: Columbia Pictures Corporation; *Runtime*: 70'

1928

SUBMARINE

Director: Frank Capra; *Assistant Director*: Buddy Coleman; *Screenplay*: Dorothy Howell (from a story by Norman Springer); *Cinematographer*: Joseph Walker; *Editor*: Arthur Roberts; *Cast*: Jack Holt (Jack Dorgan), Dorothy Revier (Bessie), Ralph Graves (Bob Mason), Clarence Burton (Submarine Commander), Arthur Rankin (boy); *Producer*: Harry Cohn for Columbia Pictures Corporation; *Distribution*: Columbia Pictures Corporation; *Runtime*: 93'

1928

THE POWER OF THE PRESS

Director: Frank Capra; *Assistant Director*: Buddy Coleman; *Screenplay*: Sonya Levien (form a story by Frederick A. Thompson); *Cinematographers*: Chet Lyons and Ted Tetzlaff; *Art Director*: Harrison Wiley; *Editor*: Frank Atkinson; *Cast*: Douglas Fairbanks Jr. (Clem Rogers), Joybna Ralston (Jane Atwill), Mildred Harris (Marie), Philo McCullough (Blake), Wheeler Oakman (Van), Edwards Davis (Mr. Atwill), Del Henderson (Johnson); *Producer*: Jack Cohn/ Frank Capra Production for Columbia Pictures Corporation; *Distribution*: Columbia Pictures Corporation; *Runtime*: 62'

1929

THE YOUNGER GENERATION

Director: Frank Capra; *Assistant Director*: Tenny Wright; *Screenplay*: Sonya Levien (from the play *It is so Laugh* by Fannie Hurst); *Cinematographer*: Ted Tetzlaff; *Editor*: Arthur Roberts; *Cast*: Jean Hersholt (Papa Goldfish), Rosa Rosanova (Mama Goldfish), Lina Basquette (Birdie), Ricardo Cortez (Morris), Rex Lease (Eddie), Martha Franklin (Mrs.Lesser), Sid Crossley (Butler), Julia Swayne Gordon (Mrs. Striker), Julianne Johnston (Irma Striker), Jack Raymond (Pinsky); *Producer*: Jack Cohn/Frank

Capra Production for Columbia Pictures Corporation; *Distribution*: Columbia Pictures Corporation; *Runtime*: 75'

1929
THE DONOVAN AFFAIR

Director: Frank Capra; *Assistant Director*: Tenny Wright, *Screenplay:* Dorothy Howell, Howard J. Green (from the play by Owen Davis); *Cinematographer*: Ted Tetzlaff; *Art Director*: Harrison Wiley; *Editor*: Arthur Roberts; *Cast*: Jack Holt (Inspector Killian), Dorothy Revier (Jean Rankin), Agnes Ayres (Lydia Rankin), William Collier Jr. (Cornish), John Roche (Jack Donovan), Fred Kelsey (Carney), Hank Mann (Dr. Lindsey), Wheeler Oakman (Porter), Virginia Browne Faire (Mary Mills), Alphonse Ethier (Peter Rankin), Edward Hearn (Nelson), Ethel Wales (Mrs. Linsey), John Fallace (Dobbs); *Producer*: Harry Cohn/Frank Capra Production for Columbia Pictures Corporation, *Distribution*: Columbia Pictures Corporation; *Runtime*: 83'

1929
FLIGHT

Director: Frank Capra; *Assistant Director*: Buddy Coleman; *Screenplay*: Howard J. Green (from a story by Ralph Graves); *Cinematographers*: Joseph Walker, Joseph Novak (*Aerial Photography*: Elmer Dyer); *Art Director*: Harrison Wiley; *Editors*: Ben Pivar, Maurice Wright, Gene Milford; *Sound*: John Livadary, Harry Blanchard; *Cast*: Jack Holt (Panama Williams), Ralph Graves (Lefthy Phelps), Lila Lee (Elinor), Alan Roscoe (the Major), Harold Goodwin (Steve Roberts), Jimmy De La Cruz (Lobo Sandino); *Producer*: Harry Cohn/ Frank Capra Production for Columbia Pictures Corporation; *Distribution*: Columbia Pictures Corporation; *Runtime*: 110'

1930
LADIES OF LEISURE

Director: Frank Capra; *Assistant Director*: David Selman; *Screenplay*: Jo Swerling (from *Ladies of the evening*, a play by Milton Gropper); *Titles*: Dudley Early; *Cinematographer*: Joseph Walker; *Art Director*: Harrison Wiley; *Sound*: John P. Livadary, Harry Blanchard; *Editor*: Maurice Wright; *Cast*: Barbara Stanwyck (Kay Arnold), Ralph Graves (Jerry Strong), Lowell Sherman (Bill Standish), Marie Prevost (Dot Lamar), Gorge Fawcett (Mr. Strong), Johnnie Walker (Charlie), Juliette Compton (Claire Collina), Charles Butterworth (man at party); *Producer*: Harry Cohn/Frank Capra Production for Columbia Pictures Corporation; *Distribution*: Columbia Pictures Corporation; *Runtime*: 98'

1930
RAIN OR SHINE

Director: Frank Capra; *Assistant Director*: Sam Nelson; *Screenplay*: Jo Swerling, Dorothy Howell (from the play by James Gleason and Maurice Marks); *Cinematographer*: Joseph Walker; *Art Director*: Harrison Wiley; *Editor*: Maurice Wright; *Music*: Bakaleinikoff; *Sound*: John P. Livadary, E. L. Bernds; *Cast*: Joe Cook (Smiley Johnson), Louise Fazenda (the "Princess"), Joan Peers (Mary Rainey), William Collier Jr. (Bud Conway), Dave Chason (Dave), Adolph Milar (Foltz), Nella Walzer (Mrs. Conway), Edward Martindale (Mr. Conway), Nora Lane (Grace Conway), Tyrrell Davis (Long Hugo Gwynne), Tom Howard (Amos K. Shrewsbury), Clarence Muse (Nero), Alan Roscoes (Dalton), *Producer*: Harry Cohn/Frank Capra Corporation; *Distribution*: Columbia Pictures Corporation; *Runtime*: 87'

1931
DIRIGIBLE

Director: Frank Capra; *Assistant Director*: Sam Nelson; *Screenplay*: Jo Swerling, Dorothy Howell (from a story by Commander Frank Wilber Wead); *Cinematographer*: Joseph Walker (*Aerial Photography*: Elmer Dyer); *Editor*: Maurice Wright; *Sound*: Edward Bernds; *Cast*: Jack Holt (Jack Brandon), Ralph Graves (Frisky Pierce), Fay Wray (Helen), Hobart Bosworth (Louis Rondelle), Roscoe Karns (Sock McGuire), Clarence Muse (Clarence); *Producer*: Harry Cohn/Frank Capra Production for Columbia Pictures Corporation; *Distribution*: Columbia Pictures Corporation; *Runtime*: 102'

1931
THE MIRACLE WOMAN

Director: Frank Capra, *Screenplay*: Jo Swerling, Dorothy Howell (from the play *Bless You Sister* by John Meehan and Robert Riskin); *Cinematographer*: Joseph Walker; *Editor*: Maurice Wright; *Sound*: Glenn Rominger; *Cast*: Barbara Stanwyck (Florence Fallon), David Manners (John Carson), Sam Hardy (Hornsby), Beryl Mercer (Mrs. Higgins), Charles Middleton (Simpson), Eddie Boland (Collina), Thelma Hill (Gussie), Aileen Carlyne (Violet), Al Stewart (Brown), Harry Todd (Briggs); *Producer*: Harry Cohn/Frank Capra Production for Columbia Pictures Corporation, *Distribution*: Columbia Pictures Corporation; *Runtime*: 91'

1931

PLATINUM BLONDE

Director: Frank Capra; *Screenplay*: Jo Swerling, Dorothy Howell, Robert Riskin (*Dialogues*), from a story by Harry E. Chanler and Douglas W. Churchill; *Cinematographer*: Joseph Walker; *Editor*: Gene Milford; *Sound*: Edward Bernds; *Cast*: Loretta Young (Gallagher), Robert Williams (Stew Smith), Jean Harlow (Anne Schuyler), Walter Catlett (Binji), Louise Closser Hale (Mrs. Schuyler), Halliwell Hobbes (Smythe), Reginald Owen (Dexter Grayson), Edmund Breese (Conroy), Donald Dillaway (Michael Schuyler); *Producer*: Harry Cohn/Frank Capra Production for Columbia Pictures Corporation; *Distribution*: Columbia Pictures Corporation; *Runtime*: 82'

1932

FORBIDDEN

Director: Frank Capra; *Screenplay:* Jo Swerling (from a story by Frank Capra); *Cinematographer:* Joseph Walker; *Editor:* Maurice Wright; *Song: Cupid's Holiday* by Irving Bibo and Pete Fylling; *Sound:* Edward Bernds; *Cast:* Barbara Stanwyck (Lulu Smith), Adolphe Menjou (Bob Grover), Ralph Bellamy (Al Holland), Dorothy Peterson (Helen Grover), Thomas Jefferson (Wilkerson), Charlotte V. Henry (Roberta), Oliver Eckhardt (Briggs), Halliwell Hobbes (florist); *Production:* Harry Cohn/Frank Capra Production for Columbia Pictures Corporation; *Distribution:* Columbia Pictures Corporation, *Runtime:* 87'

1932

AMERICAN MADNESS

Director: Frank Capra; *Assistant Director*: Charles Coleman; *Cameraman*: Andre Barlatier; *Screenplay*: Robert Riskin; *Cinematographer*: Joseph Walker; *Art Director*: Stephen Gossom; *Editor*: Maurice Wright; *Sound*: Edward Bernds; *Cast*: Walter Huston (Thomas Dickson), Constance Cummings (Helen), Pat O' Brien (Matt), Gavin Gordon (Cluett), Kay Johnson (Phyllis Dickson), Robert Ellis (Dude Finlay), Sterling Holloway (Oscar), Edwin Maxwell (Clark), Constance Cummings (Helen), Arthur Hoyt (Ives), Robert O'Connor (Inspector), Jeanne Sorel (Cluett's secretary); *Producer*: Harry Cohn/Frank Capra Production for Columbia Pictures Corporation; *Distribution*: Columbia Pictures Corporation; *Runtime*: 75'

1933

THE BITTER TEA OF GENERAL YEN

Director: Frank Capra: *Assistant Director*: Charles C. Coleman; *Screenplay*: Edward Paramore (from the novel by Grace Zaring Stone); *Cinematographer*: Joseph Walker;

Editor: Edward Curtis; *Music*: W. Frank Harling; *Sound*: Edward Bernds; *Cast*: Barbara Stanwyck (Megan Davis), Nils Aster (General Yen), Gavin Gordon (Dr. Strike), Walter Connolly (Jones), Toshia Mori (Mah-Li), Richard Loo (Captain Li), Lucien Littlefield (Mr. Jackson), Clara Blandick (Mrs. Jackson), Helen Jerome Eddy (Miss Reed), Emmett Corrigan (Bishop Harkness), Moy Ming (Dr.Lin), Ella Hall (Mrs. Hansen), Martha Mattox (Miss Avery), Arthur Gillette (Mr. Pettis), Miller Newman (Dr. Mott), Arthur Johnson (Dr. Shuler), Jessie Perry (Miss Reid), Jessie Arnold (Mrs. Blake), Adda Gleason (Mrs. Bowman), Daisy Robinson (Mrs. Warden); *Producer*: Walter Ranger/Frank Capra Production for Columbia Pictures Corporation; *Distribution*: Columbia Pictures Corporation; *Runtime*: 88'

1933
LADY FOR A DAY
Director: Frank Capra; *Assistant Director*: Charles C. Coleman; *Cameraman*: Andre Barlatier; *Screenplay*: Robert Riskin (from the novel *Madame La Gimp* by Damon Runyon); *Cinematographer*: Jospeh Walker; *Screenplay*: Stephen Gossom; *Editor*: Gene Havlick; *Costume Designerer*: Robert Kallock; *Sound*: Edward Bernds; *Musical Director*: Bakaleinikoff; *Cast*: May Robson (Apple Annie), Warren Williams (Dave the Dude), Guy Kiblee (Judge Blake), Blenda Farrell (Missouri Martin), Ned Sparks (Happy McGuire), Jean Parker (Louise), Walter Connolly (Count Romero), Barry Norton (Carlos), Robert Emmet O'Conner (Inspector); *Producer*: Harry Cohn for Columbia Pictures Corporation; *Distribution*: Columbia Pictures Corporation; *Runtime*: 95'

1934
IT HAPPENED ONE NIGHT
Director: Frank Capra; *Assistant Director*: Charles C. Coleman; *Screenplay*: Robert Riskin (from the story *Night Bus* by Samuel Hopkins Adams); *Cinematographer*: Joseph Walker; *Art Director*: Stephen Gossom; *Editor*: Gene Havlick; *Music*: Louis Silver; *Costume Designer*: Robert Kallock; *Cast*: Clark Gable (Peter Warne), Claudette Colbert (Ellie Andrews), Walter Connolly (Alexander Andrews), Roscoe Karns (Oscar Shapeley), Alan Hale (Danker), Ward Bond (bus driver), James Thomas (King Westley); *Producer*: Harry Cohn/Frank Capra Production for Columbia Pictures Corporation; *Distribution*: Columbia Pictures Corporation; *Runtime*: 105'

1934
BROADWAY BILL
Director: Frank Capra; *Screenplay*: Robert Riskin (from a story by Mark Hellinger); *Cinematographer*: Joseph Walker; *Editor*: Gene Havlick; *Sound*: Edward Bernds; *Cast*:

Warner Baxter (Dan Brooks), Myrna Loy (Alice), Walter Connolly (J.L.Higgings), Clarence Muse (Whitey), Raymond Walburn (Colonel Pettigrew), Margaret Hamilton (Edna), Douglas Dumbrille (Eddie Morgan), Jason Robards (Arthur Winslow); *Producer*: Harry Cohn/Frank Capra Production for Columbua Pictures Corporation, *Distribution*: Columbia Pictures Corporation; *Runtime*: 90'

1936

MR.DEEDS GOES TO TOWN

Director: Frank Capra; *Assistant Director*: C. C. Coleman; *Screenplay*: Robert Riskin (from the novel *Opera Hat* by Clarence Budington Kelland); *Cinematographer*: Joseph Walker; *Art Director*: Stephen Goosson; *Costume Designer*: Samuel Lange; *Music*: Howard Jackson; Sound: Edward Bernds; *Special Effects*: E. Roy Davidson; *Editor*: Gene Havlick; *Cast*: Gary Cooper (Longfellow Deeds), Jean Arthur (Babe Sennett), Lionel Stander (Cornelius Cobb), Walter Catlett (Morrow), Douglas Dumbrille (John Cedar), George Bancroft (McWade), Raymond Walburn (Walter), H.B. Warner (Judge Walzer), Franklin Pangborn (taylor), Mayo Methot (Mrs. Semple), Margaret Seddon and Margaret McWade (Amy and Jane Faulkner, sisters "pixilated"); *Producer*: Frank Capra for Columbia Pictures Corporation; *Distribution*: Columbia Pictures Corporation; *Runtime*: 115'

1937

LOST HORIZON

Director: Frank Capra; *Assistant Director*: C. C. Coleman; *Screenplay*: Robert Riskin (from the novel by James Hilton); *Cinematographer*: Joseph Walker (*Aerial Photography*: Elmer Dyer); *Art Director*: Stephen Goosson; *Costume Designer*: Ernst Dryden; *Music*: Dimitri Tiomkin; *Musical Director*: Max Steiner; *Editors*: Gene Havlick, Gene Milford; *Cast*: Ronald Colman (Robert Conway), Jane Wyatt (Sondra), Thomas Mitchell (Henry Barnard), Sam Jaffe (big Lama), Edward Everett Horton (Alexander P. Lovett); John Howard (George Conway), H.B. Warner (Chang), Margo (Maria), Isabel Jewell (Gloria Stone); *Production*: Frank Capra for Columbia Pictures Corporation; *Distribution*: Columbia Pictures Corporation; *Runtime*: 132'

1938

YOU CAN'T TAKE IT WITH YOU

Director: Frank Capra; *Assistant Director*: Art Black; *Screenplay*: Robert Riskin (from the play by Gorge S. Kaufman and Moss Hart); *Cinematographer*: Joseph Walker; *Art Director*: Stephen Goosson; *Costume Designer*: Bernard Newman and Irene; *Music*: Dimitri Tiomkin; *Musical Director*: Morris Stoloff; *Editor*: Gene Havlick; *Cast*: Jean

Arthur (Alice Sycamore), Spring Byington (Penny Sycamore), James Stewart (Tony Kirby), Edward Arnold (Anthony Kirby), Lionell Barrymore (grandfather Vanderhof), Mischa Auer (Kolonkhov), Ann Miller (Essie Carmichael), Dub Taylor (Ed Carmichael), Samuel S. Hinds (Paul Sycamore), Donald Meek (Poppins), H. B. Warner (Ramsey), Halliwell Hobbes (Mr. DePinna), Mary Forbes (Mrs. Anthony Kirby), Eddie Anderson (Donald), Lilion Yarbo (Rheba), Harry Davenport (Judge); *Production*: Frank Capra for Columbia Pictures Corporation; *Distribution*: Columbia Pictures Corporation; *Runtime*: 127'

1939
MR. SMITH GOES TO WASHINGTON
Director: Frank Capra; *Assistant Director*: Arthur S. Black; *Screenplay*: Sidney Buchman (from a story by Lewis R.Foster, *The Gentleman from Montana*); *Cinematographer*: Joseph Walker; *Editing Effects*: Slavo Vorkapich; *Art Director*: Lionel Banks; *Costume Designer*: Dimitri Tiomkin, *Musical Director*: M.W. Stoloff; *Sound*: Ed Bernds; *Editors*: Gene Havlick, Al Clark; *Cast*: James Stewart (Jefferson Smith), Jean Arthur (Clarissa Saunders), Claude Rains (Senator Paine), Edward Arnold (Taylor), Thomas Mitchell (Dizz), Eugene Pallette (Chick McGann), Guy Kibbee (Governor Hopper), Beulah Bondi (Ma Smith), Porter Hall (Senator Monroe), Astrid Allwyn (Susan Paine), Ruth Donnelly (Emma Hopper), William Demarest (Bill Griffith), Grant Mitchell (Senator McPherson), H. V. Kaltenborn (himself); *Producer*: Frank Capra for Columbia Pictures Corporation; *Distribution*: Columbia Pictures Corporation; *Runtime*: 128'

1941
MEET JOHN DOE
Director: Frank Capra; *Assistant Director*: Arthur S. Black; *Screenplay*: Robert Riskin (from a story by Richard Connell and Robert Presnell); *Cinematographer*: George Barnes; *Editing Effects*: Slavo Vorkapich; *Art Director*: Stephen Goosson; *Costume Designer*: Natalie Visart; *Music*: Dimitri Tiomkin; *Musical Director*: Leo F. Forbstein; *Sound*: C. A. Riggs; *Special Effects*: Jack Cosgrove; *Editor*: Daniel Mandell; *Cast*: Gary Cooper (Long John Willoughby), Barbara Stanwyck (Anna Mitchell), Edward Arnold (D.B. Norton), Walter Brennan (Colonel), James Gleason (Henry Connell), Spring Byington (Mrs. Mitchell), Rod La Nocque (Ted Sheldon), Regis Toomey (Bert Hansen), Warren Hymer (Angelface), Sterling Holloway (Dan), Gene Lockhart (Mayor Lovett), Farrell MacDonald (Sourpuss Smithers); *Producer*: Frank Capra for Columbia Pictures Corporation; *Distribution*: Columbia Pictures Corporation; *Runtime*: 125'

1942

PRELUDE TO WAR (part one of the series WHY WE FIGHT)

Director: Frank Capra; *Screenplay*: Eric Knight, Antony Veiller; *Voice Over*: Walter Huston; *Music*: Alfred Newman; *Editor*: William Hornbeck; *Producer*: Frank Capra for War Department; *Runtime*: 53'

1943

THE NAZIS STRIKE (part two of the series WHY WE FIGHT)

Directors: Frank Capra, Anatole Litvak; *Screenplay*: Eric Knight, Anthony Veiller, Robert Heller; *Voice Over*: Walter Huston, Anthony Veiller; *Music*: Dimitri Tiomkin; *Producer*: Frank Capra for War Department; *Runtime*: 42'

1943

DIVIDE AND CONQUER (part three of the series WHY WE FIGHT)

Directors: Frank Capra, Anatole Litvak, *Screenplay*: Anthony Veiller, Robert Heller; *Voice Over*: Walter Huston, Anthony Veiller; *Music*: Dimitri Tiomkin, *Editor*: William Hornbeck; *Producer*: Frank Capra for War Department; *Runtime*: 58'

1943

THE BATTLE OF BRITAIN (part four of the series WHY WE FIGHT)

Director: Anthony Veiller; *Screenplay*: Anthony Veiller; *Voice Over*: Walter Huston, Anthony Veiller; *Music*: Dimitri Tiomkin; *Editor*: William Hornbeck; *Producer*: Frank Capra for War Department; *Runtime*: 54'

1944

THE BATTLE OF RUSSIA (part five of the series WHY WE FIGHT)

Director: Anatole Litvak; *Screenplay*: Anatole Litvak, Anthony Veiller, Robert Heller; *Voice Over*: Walter Huston, Anthony Veiller; *Music*: Dimitri Tiomkin; *Editor*: Walter Hornbeck; *Producer*: Frank Capra for War Department; *Runtime*: 80'

1944

KNOW YOUR ALLY: BRITAIN

Director: Anthony Veiller; *Screenplay*: Anatole Litvak; *Voice Over*: Walter Huston, Anthony Veiller; *Musical Director*: Dimitri Tiomkin; *Music*: Cyril Mockridge; *Titles*: Consolidated Film Industries; *Producer*: Frank Capra for War Department; *Runtime*: 45'

1944

THE NEGRO SOLDIER

Director: Stuart Heisler; *Screenplay*: Carlton Moss; *Musical Director*: Dimitri Tiomkin; *Music*: Howard Jackson, Al Glasser, Paul Horgan, Meredith Wilson and Earl Robinson; *Cast*: men and women of Armed Forces of the United States, Captain Colin Kelly, Sergeant Meyer Levin, Sergeant Dorie Miller, William Broadus (Jim), Berta Wolford (Mrs. Bronson); *Producer*: Frank Capra for War Department; *Runtime*: 43'

1944

THE BATTLE OF CHINA (part six of the series WHY WE FIGHT)

Directors: Frank Capra, Anatole Litvak, *Screenplay*: Anthony Veiller, Robert Heller; *Voice Over*: Walter Huston, Anthony Veiller; *Music*: Dimitri Tiomkin; *Editor*: William Hornbeck; *Producer*: Frank Capra for War Department; *Runtime*: 67'

1944

TUNISIAN VICTORY

Directors: Frank Capra, Hugh Stewart; *Screenplay*: J.L. Hodson, Anthony Veiller; *Voice Over*: Leo Glenn, Anthony Veiller; *Musical Director*: Dimitri Tiomkin; *Music*: Dimitri Tiomkin; *Cast*: Bernard Miles (voice of British soldier), Burgess Meredith (voice of the american Infantryman); *Producer*: Frank Capra for War Department; *Runtime*: 76'

1944

ARSENIC AND OLD LACE

Director: Frank Capra; *Assistant Director*: Jesse Hibbs; *Screenplay*: Julius J. and Phlip G. Epstein (from the play by Jopseph Kesserling); *Cinematographer*: Sol Polito; *Art Director*: Max Parker; *Music*: Max Steiner; *Editor*: Daniel Mandel; *Special Effects*: Byron Haskin, Robert Burks; *Cast*: Cary Grant (Mortimer Brewster), Priscilla Lane (Elaine Harper), Raymond Massey (Jonathan Brewster), Peter Lorre (Dr. Einstein), Josephine Hull (Abby Brewster), Jean Adair (Martha Brewster), Edward Everett Horton (Mr. Witherspoon), John Alexander (Teddy Roosevelt Brewster), James Gleason (Lt. Rooney); *Producer*: Frank Capra for Warner Brothers; *Distribution*: Warner Brothers; *Runtime*: 118'

1945

WAR COMES TO AMERICA (part seven of the series WHY WE FIGHT)

Director: Anatole Litvak; *Screenplay*: Anatole Litvak, Anthony Veiller; *Voice Over*: Walter Huston, Anthony Veiller; *Music*: Dimitri Tiomkin; *Editor*: William Hornbeck, *Producer*: Frank Capra for Army Pictorial Service; *Runtime*: 67'

1945

KNOW YOUR ENEMY: GERMANY

Director: Gottfried Reinhardt; *Screenplay*: Gottfried Reinhardt, Anthony Veiller, Ernst Lubitsch; *Voice Over*: John Beal, Anthony Veiller, *Producer*: Frank Capra for Army Pictorial Service; *Runtime*: 52'

1945

KNOW YOUR ENEMY: JAPAN

Directors: Frank Capra, Joris Ivens, Edgar Peterson; *Screenplay*: Irving Fallace, Edgar Peterson, John Huston, Joris Ivens; *Voice Over*: Walter Huston, Jean Beal, Anthony Veiller; *Musical Director*: Dimitri Tiomkin; *Titles*: Consolidated Film Industries; *Producer*: Frank Capra for Army Pictorial Service; *Runtime*: 63'

1945

YOUR JOB IN GERMANY

Director: Ted Geisel; *Voice Over*: John Beal; *Musical Director*: Raoul Kraushaar; *Music*: Dimitri Tiomkin; *Titles*: Consolidated Film Industries; *Producer*: Frank Capra for Army Pictorial Service; *Runtime*: 15'

1945

TWO DOWN, ONE TO GO

Director: Frank Capra; *Screenplay*: Anthony Veiller; *Voice Over*: Anthony Veiller; *Producer*: Frank Capra for Army Pictorial Service; *Runtime*: 9'

1946

IT'S A WONDERFUL LIFE

Director: Frank Capra; *Assistant Director*: Arthur S. Black; *Screenplay*: Frances Goodrich, Albert Hackett, Frank Capra, Jo Swerling from the story by Phlip Van Doren Stern *The Greatest Gift*); *Cinematographers*: Joseph Walker, Joseph Biroc; *Art Director*: Jack Okey; *Costume Designer*: Edward Stevenson; *Music*: Dimitri Tiomkin; *Sound* : Richard Van, Clem Portman, *Special Effects*: Russel A. Cully; *Editor*: William Hornbeck; *Cast*: James Stewart (George Bailey), Donna Reed (Mary Hatch), Lionel Barrymore (Hanry Potter), Henry Travers (Clarence, the guardian angel), Thomas Mitchell (oncle Billy), Beulah Bondi (Mrs. Bailey), Ward Bond (Bert), Frank Faylen (Ernie), Gloria Graham (Violet), H.B. Warner (Gower), Todd Karns (Harry Bailey), Samuel S. Hinds (Mr. Bailey); *Producer*: Frank Capra for Liberty Films; *Distribution*: RKO; *Runtime*: 129'

1948

STATE OF THE UNION

Director: Frank Capra; *Assistant Director*: Arthur S. Black; *Screenplay*: Anthony Veiller, Myles Connelly (from the play by Howard Lindsay and Russell Crouse); *Cinematographer*: George J. Folsey; *Art Directors*: Cedric Gibbone, Urie McCleary; *Music*: Victor Young; *Costume Designer*: Irene; *Editor*: William Hornbeck; *Cast*: Spencer Tracy (Grant Matthews), Katharine Hepburn (Mary Matthews), Van Johnson (Spike McManus), Adolphe Menjou (Jim Conover), Angela Lansbury (Kay Thorndyke), Charles Lane (Blink Moran), Irving Bacon (Buck Swenson), Lewis Stone (Sam Thorndyke), Margaret Hamilton (Nora); *Producer*: Frank Capra for Liberty Films; *Distribution*: Metro-Goldwin-Mayer; *Runtime*: 124'

1950

RIDING HIGH

Director: Frank Capra; *Assistant Director*: Arhuir Black; *Screenplay*: Robert Riskin, Melville Shavelson, Jack Rose from a story by Mark Hellinger (remake of *Broadway Bill*); *Cinematographers*: Gorge Barnes, Ernst Laszlo; *Art Directors*: Hans Dreider, Walter Tyler; *Costume Designer*: Edith Head; *Music*: Johnny Burke, James Van Heusen; *Musical Director*: Victor Young; *Editor*: William Hornbeck; *Cast*: Bing Crosby (Dan Brooks), Colleen Gray (Alice Higgins), Charles Bickford (J.L. Higgins), William Demarest (Happy McGuire), Raymond Walburn (Professor Pettigrew), Margaret Hamilton (Edna), Percy Kilbride (Pop Jones), Ward Bond (Lee), Douglas Dumbrille (Eddie), Gene Lockhart (J.P. Chase); *Producer*: Frank Capra for Paramount Pictures Corporation; *Distribution*: Paramount Picture Corporation; *Runtime*: 112'

1951

HERE COMES THE GROOM

Director: Frank Capra; *Assistant Director*: Irving Asher; *Screenplay*: Virginia Van Upp, Liam O' Brien, Myles Connolly (from a story by Liam O' Brien and Robert Riskin); *Cinematographer*: George Barnes; *Art Directors*: Hal Pereira, Earl Hedrick; *Music*: songs by Johnny Mercer, Hoagy Carmichael, Jay Livingston, Ray Evans; *Musical Director*: Joseph J.Lilley; *Editor*: Ellsworth Hoagland; *Cast*: Bing Crosby (Pete Garvey), Jane Wyman (Emmandel Jones), Alexis Smith (Winifred Stanley), Franchot Tone (Wilbur Stanley), James Barton (Pa Jones), Robert Keith (Gorge Degnaan); Jacques Gencel (Bobby), Beverly Washburn (Suzi), Walter Catlett (McGonigle); H. B. Warner (oncle Elihu); *Producer*: Frank Capra for Paramount Picture Corporation; *Distribution*: Paramount Pictures Corporation; *Runtime*: 113'

1956

OUR MR. SUN (n.1 of the series BELL SYSTEM SCIENCE SERIES)

Director: Frank Capra; *Screenplay*: Frank Capra; *Cinematographer*: Harold Wellman; *Animation*: United Productions of America; *Editor*: Frank P. Keller; *Cast*: Eddie Albert (the story writer), Lionel Barrymore (voice of "Father Time"), Dr. Frank Baxter (Dr. Research), Marvin Miller (voice of Mr. Sun), Sterling Holloway (voice of "Chloro Phyll"); *Producer*: Frank Capra for Frank Capra Productions; *Distribution*: Bell Telephone; *Runtime*: 59'

1957

HEMO THE MAGNIFICENT (n.2 of the series BELL SYSTEM SCIENCE SERIES)

Director: Frank Capra; *Screenplay*: Frank Capra; *Cinematographer*: Harold Wellman; *Animation*: Shamus Cullane Productions; *Editor*: Frank P. Keller; *Cast*: Frank Baxter (Dr. Research), Richard Carlson (the story writer), Sterling Holloway (Jim), Marvin Miller (voice of Hemo the Magnificent); *Producer*: Frank Capra for Frank Capra Production; *Distribution*: Bell Telephone; *Runtime*: 59'

THE STRANGE CASE OF THE COSMIC RAYS (n.3 of the series BELL SYSTEM SCIENCE SERIES)

Director: Frank Capra; *Screenplay*: Frank Capra, Jonathan Latimer; *Cinematographers*: Harold Wellman, Ellis Carter; *Animation*: Shamus Cullane Productions; *Editors*: Frank P. Keller, Raymond Snyder; *Cast*: Frank Baxter (Dr. Research), Richard Carlson and the puppets of Bill and Cora Baird; *Producer*: Frank Capra for Frank Capra Productions; *Distribution*: Bell Telephone; *Runtime*:59'

1958

THE UNCHAINED GODDESS (n.4 of the series BELL SYSTEM SCIENCE SERIES)

Director: Frank Capra; *Screenplay*: Frank Capra, Jonathan Latimer; *Cinematographer*: Harold Wellman; *Animation*: Shamus Cullane Productions; *Editor*: Frank P. Keller; *Cast*: Frank Baxter (Dr. Research), Richard Carlson (the story writer); *Producer*: Frank Capra for Frank Capra Productions; *Distribution*: Bell Telephone; *Runtime*: 59'

1959

A HOLE IN THE HEAD

Director: Frank Capra; *Assistants Director*: Arthur Black, Jack R. Berne; *Screenplay*: Arnold Shulman; *Cinematographer*: William H. Daniels; *Art Director*: Eddie Imazu;

Costume Designer: Edith Head; *Music*: Nelson Ridde (songs: "High Hopes" and "All my Tomorrows" by Sammy Cahn and Jimmy Van Heusen); *Editor*: William Hornbeck; *Cast*: Frank Sinatra (Tony Manetta), Edward G. Robinson (Mario Manetta), Eddie Hodges (Ally Manetta), Eleanor Parker (Mrs. Rogers), Carolyn Jones (Shirl), Keenan Wynn (Jerry Marks), Thelma Ritter (Sophie Manetta); *Producer*: Frank Capra for SinCap Productions; *Distribution*: United Artists; *Runtime*: 120'

1961
POCKETFUL OF MIRACLES
Director: Frank Capra; *Assistants Director*: Arthur S. Black; *Screenplay*: Hal Kanter, Harry Tugend, Jimmy Cannon (from a story by Damon Runyon and from screenplay of LADY FOR A DAY by R. Riskin); *Cinematographer*: Robert Bronner; *Art Directors*: Hal Pereira, Roland Anderson, *Costume Designer*: Edith Head, Walter Plunkett; *Music*: Walter Scharf (song: "Pocketful of Miracles" by Sammy Cahn and James Van Castle); *Sound*: Hugo Grenzback, Charles Grenzbach; *Editor*: Frank P. Keller; *Cast*: Glenn Ford (Dave the Dude), Bette Davis (Apple Annie), Arthur O'Connell (Count Romero), Hope Lange (Queenie Martin), Peter Falk (Joy Boy), Thomas Mitchell (Judge Henry Blake), Edward Everett Horton (Butler), Ann Margaret (Louise); *Producer*: Frank Capra for Franton Productions; *Distribution*: United Artists; *Runtime*: 136'

1964
REACHING FOR THE STARS
Director: Frank Capra; *Screenplay*: Frank Capra; *Cast*: Danny Thomas (the interviewer), *Producer*: Frank Capra for Graphic Films Corporation; *Distribution*: Martin-Marietta Corporation; *Runtime*: 19'

INDEX

ABOUT THE AUTHOR

Vito Zagarrio is an accomplished film director and film scholar. He is a professor at the University of Rome 3 and teaches for American University programs in Italy (such as NYU in Florence). He is the author of several books on both Italian and American cinema. He has also been a visiting professor at Indiana University, Bloomington, and at Nortwestern University.

Professor Zagarrio's recent publications include: *Regie. La messa in scena del grande cinema italiano* (Rome: Bulzoni, 2010); *Carlo Lizzani. Un lungo viaggio attraverso il cinema* (Venice: Marsilio, 2010); *Quentin Tarantino* (Venice: Marsilio, 2009); *L'immagine del fascismo. La revisione del cinema e dei media nel regime* (Rome: Bulzoni, 2009); *"Primato": Arte, cultura, cinema del fascismo attraverso una rivista esemplare* (Roma: Edizioni storia e letteratura, 2007); *Overlooking Kubrick* (Rome: Dino Audino, 2006); *John Waters* (Milan: Il castoro, 2005); *Cinema e Fascismo. Film, modelli, immaginari* (Venice: Marsilio, 2004); and *L'anello mancante. Teoria e storia dei rapporti tra cinema e televisione* (Turin: Lindau, 2004).

He has directed three feature films: *La donna della luna* (*Young Distance*) (1988), *Bonus Malus* (1993), and *Tre giorni d'anarchia* (*Three Days of Anarchy*, 2006), as well as several documentaries and TV shorts. In 1991 he received a David Award for the first HDTV film with the Eureka standard, *Un bel dì vedremo*. He has founded Italian film festivals in Rome and Ragusa (Sicily), and is one of the main organizers of the Pesaro film festival.

Saggistica

Taking its name from the Italian–which means essays, essay writing, or non fiction–*Saggisitca* is a referred book series dedicated to the study of all topics, individuals, and cultural productions that fall under what we might consider that larger umbrella of all things Italian and Italian/American.

The following volumes are forthcoming:

Paolo A. Giordano, editor
The Hyphenate Writer and The Legacy of Exile

Dennis Barone
America / Trattabili.

Fred L. Gardaphè
The Art of Reading Italian Americana

Anthony Julian Tamburri
Re-viewing Italian Americana: Generalities and Specifities on Cinema

Sheryl Lynn Postman
An Italian Writer's Journey through American Realities: Giose Rimanelli's English Novels. "The most tormented decade of America: the 60s"

David Barone and Peter Covino, editors
Essays on Italian American Literature and Culture

Peter Carravetta
After Identity: Critical Challenges in Italian American Poetics and Culture

www.ingramcontent.com/pod-product-compliance
Lightning Source LLC
Chambersburg PA
CBHW062203080426
42734CB00010B/1774